ASPECTS OF
SUCCESS

A playbook
to get more
out of life

RUSS KAMIS
B.S. Engr., M.Mgt, Ph.D. Psych.

Give Life Its Due Publishing
New York
2015

Aspects of Success
www.aspectsofsuccess.com

Edited by Nancy Jo Eckerson
Jacket and artwork by Rachel Grunert-Meyer
Layout by Linda Gates

Give Life Its Due Publishing
New York, U.S.A.
ISBN 978-0-9862163-0-5

May 2015
First Edition

Bulk copies of this book may be purchased for education, business, or promotional use. For information please send email inquiry to info@aspectsofsuccess.com

Back cover quotes John 10:10 & John 15:11 from NLT Bible.

Dedication

For Elena, Emilia, and Henry—may the wonder of life's possibility always shine upon you.

For everyone who wants to become their best or anyone who has lost their spark, feels stuck, or thinks something is missing in life—a life of fulfillment, happiness, and success lies before you.

Note that profits from this book will be tithed to improve the lives of others.

Disclaimer

This book is designed to provide insight and techniques to help people live more successfully. While all the stories and anecdotes described in this book are based on true experiences, most of the names and some of the situations have been changed slightly to protect privacy and for educational purposes. This book is sold with the understanding that the Author is not engaged in providing personal, psychological, business, coaching, or other professional services of any kind by publishing this book. As each individual situation is unique, any and all decisions made by the readers are understood to be the sole responsibility of the reader. Should expert advice or counseling be needed, the services of a competent professional practitioner should be sought. The Author specifically disclaims any liability, loss, or risk which is incurred as a consequence, whether direct or indirect, of the use and application of any of the contents of this work.

CONTENTS

Disclaimer ii

INTRODUCTION 1

ASPECTS OF SUCCESS 6

    Satisfaction with Life Scale 7

ASPECT I: THE WISE KING 14

    Behavior 1: Understanding your Role 17

        Thought Expander 1.1: Core Beliefs 20

        Thought Expander 1.2: Alternative Beliefs 24

    Behavior 2: Taking Responsibility 27

        Thought Expander 2.1: Personal Problems 28

        Thought Expander 2.2: Recurring Issues 30

    Behavior 3: Focusing Attention 36

        Thought Expander 3.1: Your Life Story 40

        Thought Expander 3.2: A Better Story 42

        Thought Expander 3.3: Best Possible Self 45

    Behavior 4: Becoming More Aware 47

        Thought Expander 4.1: Subconscious Commitments 52

        Thought Expander 4.2: Commitment Tradeoffs 53

        Thought Expander 4.3: Commitment Payoff 56

    Behavior 5: Making Good Choices 60

        Thought Expander 5.1: Sense of Control 62

        Thought Expander 5.2: Shifting Perspective 65

        Thought Expander 5.3: Emotion Drivers 69

    Summary: The King 72

iv

ASPECT II: THE INSPIRED WIZARD 74

Behavior 6: Following Your Spirit 77
   Thought Expander 6.1: Interests & Talents 79
   Thought Expander 6.2: Additional Abilities 80
   Thought Expander 6.3: Golden Shadows 82
   Thought Expander 6.4: Matching Interests to Ability 84

Behavior 7: Looking Far Ahead 90
   Thought Expander 7.1: Current Direction 92
   Thought Expander 7.2: Preferred Course 93

Behavior 8: Dreaming Bigger 98
   Thought Expander 8.1: Life Desires 102
   Thought Expander 8.2: Life's Wish 106

Behavior 9: Creating a Plan 108
   Thought Expander 9.1: Life Plan 113
   Thought Expander 9.2: Action Opportunities 114

Behavior 10: Envisioning Success 120
   Thought Expander 10.1: Success Story 122
   Thought Expander 10.2: Personal Affirmation 126
   Thought Expander 10.3: Opportunities Captured 127

Summary: The Wizard 130

ASPECT III: THE STRONG WARRIOR 132

Behavior 11: Taking Action 135
   Thought Expander 11.1: Action Plan 138
   Thought Expander 11.2: Action Drivers 143

Behavior 12: Embracing Work 145
   Thought Expander 12.1: Work Benefits 146
   Thought Expander 12.2: Effort Options 155

Behavior 13: Managing Time 157
   Thought Expander 13.1: Time Optimization 159
   Thought Expander 13.2: Activity Alignment 164

Behavior 14: Focusing Efforts 169
   Thought Expander 14.1: Top Priorities 171
   Thought Expander 14.2: Multitasking 175
   Thought Expander 14.3: Focus Assessment 176

Behavior 15: Doing the Next Best Thing.................. 180
    Thought Expander 15.1: Valuable Action 185
    Thought Expander 15.2: What One Thing.......... 187
Summary: The Warrior... 190

ASPECT IV: THE CONTENTED MONK 192
Behavior 16: Renewing Yourself.............................. 195
    Thought Expander 16.1: Self-Actualization Scale 197
    Thought Expander 16.2: Development Opportunities.......... 202
    Thought Expander 16.3: Intrinsic Growth............ 205
Behavior 17: Serving Others 208
    Thought Expander 17.1: Ways to Serve................. 211
    Thought Expander 17.2: Selfless Pursuits............. 212
Behavior 18: Expecting Good Things 219
    Thought Expander 18.1: Positive Shifts 223
    Thought Expander 18.2: Appreciative Shifts 223
    Thought Expander 18.3: Better Expectations........ 226
Behavior 19: Having Faith 231
    Thought Expander 19.1: Rationalizing Fear.......... 233
    Thought Expander 19.2: Desired Outcomes.......... 235
    Thought Expander 19.3: Getting in Faith 240
Behavior 20: Enjoying the Journey 244
    Thought Expander 20.1: Appreciation 247
    Thought Expander 20.2: The Good Life 253
    Thought Expander 20.3: My Great Life 253
Summary: The Monk.. 257

CONCLUSION 260
    Reflection: My Best Opportunity 262

Appendix A: Bible Translation Key...................... 268

Appendix B: Theory References............................. 269

Appendix C: Research References 272

About the Author 290

INTRODUCTION

Success is broad concept. There are many paths to an accomplished life. However, all success, no matter how diverse, is achieved through several consistent ways of approaching the world, or aspects of success, as I refer to them. As a result of my advisory work with thousands of executives, leaders, and other highly accomplished people, it has become evident that a well-lived, fulfilling life is almost assured if you become developed, mature, and balanced in all four of these aspects of success.

This book is a summary of what I have come to understand. It is my life's work. All told, I've spent forty years acquiring and assembling the ideas presented herein. They are derived from the writings of philosophers, scientific research on the mind, and the world's holy books. These ideas are validated in the accomplishments of the world's great leaders, innovators, scientists, and change agents who have used them to achieve great success. *Aspects of Success* explores the fundamental truths behind living well. Every truly successful person has used some mixture of these ideas.

The four aspects of success, and the five success behaviors that underlie each, are powerful. Throughout the ages, they have proven their value by allowing those who practice them to achieve real success. Collectively, these aspects of success, and their supporting behaviors, encompass the best approaches you can take to become fully accomplished and realize a life well lived.

Most importantly, these success behaviors work—not just in theory, but in practice. They produce results not only for the renaissance men and woman who we revere today for their successes, but for everyone who desires to live a more complete life. Through my advisory practice which includes personal development retreats, executive coaching sessions, and motivational speeches, I have seen the positive impact they can have. In fact, this book was written in response to the many requests for a tangible way to study and use this material. Even after decades of use, I continue to rely on these success behaviors, putting them to work for myself whenever I get knocked down, stuck, or discouraged. They act to refocus my efforts, improve my motivation, and increase my happiness all while delivering to me what I have set out to achieve.

Aspects of Success is designed to help you do the same. Each aspect of success is presented in a way to help clarify where your increased effort may benefit you the most. The supporting behaviors are then meant to be immediately useful. The suggested behaviors behind each aspect of success are presented through an active framework of thought exercises. Each Thought Expander invites you to directly participate in your own situational analysis, helping you craft a way forward, customized to your needs and wants. A playbook approach is taken to encourage you to adopt a playful attitude, find the lighter side, and experience joy while achieving your dreams.

The goal of sharing these powerful ideas through personal exercises is to increase the likelihood that you will directly incorporate these behaviors into your thinking and your life. The good news is that achieving success can be creative and pleasurable. While some effort is required to become your best self, the rewards come quickly and benefits are life-changing.

I encourage you to get out a highlighter or pen and have fun with this book. Mark it up, take notes, and do the exercises. Make it yours. There are lined pages at the end for your thoughts, impressions, and key learnings.

Consider picking one aspect of success and studying one behavior at a time. Reading the book all in one sitting may make you feel like you are drinking from a fire hose. Instead, spend time getting to know the content until you really understand it and have taken steps to integrate the behaviors into your life. Each of us is in a different place at different stages in our lives. Therefore, to maximize value, focus on sections that most resonate with you now. Chances are they represent your best opportunities. Study these, take action surrounding them, and stick with an idea until change is seen.

While the four aspects of success are covered sequentially in this book it should not be construed to mean they must be employed in any particular order. Real-life situations may demand you focus on one over another to best address an issue or capture an opportunity at hand. Moreover, as you grow, your situation will change such that the aspect of success that delivered your latest accomplishment may need to evolve in order to yield your next one. The opportunity for your best life comes when you continually focus on maturing, developing, and growing in the aspects that will most benefit you based on the situation at hand. Over the months and years that follow, therefore, it will be helpful to revisit this material. Completely different areas will ring true to you as you advance through the natural stages of life. The comprehensive scope of this material means that twenty years from now you will still find new insights herein that will help you live better. *Aspects of Success* is to the mind what a shower is to the body—both are recommended on a regular basis.

A fully-accomplished life is my wish for you. I want you to be successful in every sense of the word. I want you to avoid living in the grey shadow of mediocrity. You have the potential to seize life and wring from it the very essence of whatever it is that you want. You can get from where you are to where you want to be, achieving whatever it is your spirit longs for. *Aspects of Success* will show you how to live better, achieve more, and feel happier.

THE WISE

KING

THE INSPIRED

WIZARD

THE STRONG

WARRIOR

THE CONTENTED

MONK

ASPECTS OF SUCCESS

A re you as successful as you would like to be? Too many people are stuck, spinning their wheels, and making scant progress in life. They are dissatisfied and unhappy, living in silent angst, and they don't know what to do about it. What they have tried hasn't worked. Exasperated and tired, many seek escapes and diversions while others quit altogether. Numb, some put on a satisfied face and continue on, even though they have an uncomfortable sense that there simply must be more. There is.

Thriving is what *Aspects of Success* is all about. This book is a guide to getting more out of life, a map to reach your goals. It provides direction that is useful in any place, situation, age, and stage. *Aspects of Success* will help you continually identify the next best opportunity for success, while providing a pathway to achieve it. Our children see this clearly. Ask any adolescent if they want to grow up and be like the adults they know, and most will balk in response. Truth is, children aren't always inspired by what they see. Although they can't put their finger on it, they know something has gone awry. Something is missing in the lives of their elders. That is because at the moment these adolescents are living more fully and feeling more alive than many of their parents. Yet, if they follow the path most trod, they, too, are headed for the same mediocrity.

To help them, and the world at large, you must first help yourself. Success is a habit. Learning to be more successful not only stands to improve your life but it will also raise the collective consciousness—making the world a better place. To thrive, you must be willing to be different, go a step beyond, and become the person you want others to be. You must actively take steps to avoid a so-so life. The Bible is clear on this truth; "Do not conform to the pattern of this world, but be transformed by the renewing of your mind" (Romans 12:2; NIV).

So, where do you stand? Are you satisfied? The <u>Satisfaction with Life Scale</u> provides a well-validated and accurate way to measure your overall contentment with life. The Introductory Reflection, <u>Satisfaction with Life</u>, has five statements with which you may agree or disagree. Using the 1 – 7 scale included in the header, indicate your agreement with each statement by placing the appropriate number, ranging one to seven, on the line after that item. Then add up the scores and enter the total in the bottom box.

Satisfaction with Life Scale

Strongly Disagree 1	Disagree 2	Slightly Disagree 3	Neither Agree or Disagree 4	Slightly Agree 5	Agree 6	Strongly Agree 7	Score
1. In most ways, my life is close to ideal.							
2. The conditions of my life are excellent.							
3. I am satisfied with my life.							
4. So far, I have gotten the important things I want in life.							
5. If I could live my life over, I would change almost nothing.							
						Grand Total =	

"The Satisfaction with Life Scale" by E. Diener, R. A. Emmons, R. J. Larsen, and S. Griffin, 1985, *Journal of Personality Assessment, 49*(1), 71-75. doi:10.1207/s15327752jpa4901_13. Scale in public domain.

The highest possible score is 35 and the lowest 5. Researchers have found that the average person scores 24 out of a possible of 35, equating to answering a five out of the seven on each question.[1] This metric has been used around the world, and it consistently indicates that people are generally satisfied with life.[2] The fact that people are more positive than they are negative has been called the positivity offset (Diener & Diener, 1996). It indicates that most moments in life are at least mildly good unless one is mentally ill.[3] Consistently feeling bad, it appears, is relatively rare, as is feeling really, really good.

The results appear encouraging, until the question is expanded to delineate not just how satisfied they are with life, but the degree to which they are flourishing. Flourishing is defined as a state of optimal living. It is a way of becoming all one can become, a pathway to personal growth, individual accomplishment, and psychological health. Such self-actualized people are fully developed and highly productive. They are also profoundly fulfilled and happy. Flourishing is the highest level of being one can attain. It is a superior measure of well-being. To flourish is to be successful, in the fullest sense of the word.

However, researchers have found that only one in five American's are actually flourishing.[4] Most people, 70% it turns out, consider themselves happy, and yet they are not really, truly successful. Instead, they are just getting by. As Henry David Thoreau proffered, "Most men lead lives of quiet desperation and go to the grave with the song still in them."

> **People unintentionally choose acceptable lives when great ones are available for the taking.**

The opportunity gap this represents is astounding. The vast majority, more than four out of five people, are languishing to some degree. They are living lesser lives, not realizing there is more. People unintentionally choose acceptable lives when great ones are available for the taking.

It doesn't have to be this way. An answer exists within the pages of this book. I challenge you to study this playbook and find your own answer. The payoff is yours if you want it. The aspects of success presented here are provocative and motivating. They will broaden your perspective, rekindle your spark, and if you let them, they will change your life and help you succeed.

My research has identified four primary dimensions of self that are consistently well-developed and strong in highly successful people. First, they think well and make good decisions. Second, they allow themselves a creative outlet where they craft their dreams. Third, they are unafraid to take well-considered action, even when risky. Fourth, they don't force life, but rather allow, appreciate, and enjoy it. Collectively, their success is achieved through developing a strong mind, being creative, taking action, and embracing an appreciative and compassionate spirit. These behaviors can be thought of as four distinct dimensions of self—the King, Wizard, Warrior, and Monk representing the mind, spirit, heart, and soul respectively. Each aspect represents an essential power that resides in every one of us.

Adapted from the archetypes developed by psychologist Carl Jung (1959) and loosely on the later framework advanced by Moore and Gillette (1990), these dimensions of success are an abstract reflection of the human psyche. These and other authors, researchers, and practitioners have traditionally focused on interpretations that theoretically conceptualize the unconscious self—or shadow—as an attempt to portray how each archetype serves or sabotages.[5, 6, 7] While these approaches build an awareness for how people think, they don't provide clear methods for improvement. Too often they leave people uncertain what to do, unclear how to overcome the negative feelings and counterproductive behaviors that stand in the way of real success.

> **Master each aspect and success will be inevitable.**

A more pragmatic and valuable approach is to assess the degree to which each dimension of success is developed in each of us, and to provide specific techniques to address any gaps and offset imbalances. Here the King, Wizard, Warrior, and Monk archetypes are treated as fully accessible parts of ourselves whose power can be actively managed and developed. Combined, these four dimensions comprise the core components of a lifetime of success. They are the aspects of success.

Let's briefly explore each in turn. The King is the part of you that is in charge. Your inner King analyzes, considers, and decides. This aspect of success deals with your thinking and decision-making processes. It manages your belief system, determines what is true, integrates new information, and makes choices in your life. Knowledge and wisdom reside here. For God tells us, "My people are destroyed from lack of knowledge" (Hosea 4:5, NIV). A wise King is fundamental to success.

Complementary to the King is the Wizard. The Wizard is the creative reflection of your psyche. Your inner Wizard is the part of you that imagines, dreams, plans, and ideates. This aspect of success deals with visualizing change and creating possibility. Invention and innovation evolve from your Wizard. It provides insight into what is desirable in your life. Like a wise King, an inspired Wizard is pivotal in achieving success.

Combined, the King and Wizard are engaged in a dance of knowing and creating, of what is and what might be. These two aspects of success contrast one's beliefs against what could be possible. To be useful, however, they need an outlet—a way to play out in the world. That is the role of the remaining two aspects of success—the Warrior and the Monk.

The Warrior is the part of you that takes action. Your inner Warrior performs, executes, and gets things done. This aspect of success dislikes standing still. It prefers motion and is willing to practice, train, and work hard to become more efficient and effective. It is the part of you that is incessantly driven toward accomplishing goals. A strong Warrior is critical to accomplishment and success.

Complementary to the Warrior is the Monk. The Monk is the reflective aspect of your psyche. Your inner Monk is the part of you that believes, enjoys, appreciates, serves, and loves. It is positive and optimistic. It is the spiritual component where your faith, peace, and joy reside. Like a strong Warrior, a contented Monk is also essential element in achieving true success. Combined, the Warrior and Monk are the active aspects of success—constantly engaged in a dance between doing and being, between striving and appreciating.

It should be noted that while these aspects of success may appear male in gender, that was not the intention. Rather, each was constrained by the limitations of language where conveying a point accurately was favored. A feminine version of these, the Queen, Witch, Amazon, and Nun for example, provide challenges in interpretation due to underlying connotations and limitations. Other words acted only to further dilute.

Clearly men and women alike share each aspect of success, irrespective of label. While the King, Wizard, Warrior, and Monk terminology symbolically capture the core essence intended, there are many other ways each could be effectively represented. In the workplace, they might be the Executive, Strategist, Worker, and Coach; at home the Parent, Planner, Provider, and Teacher; in a relationship, the Partner, Suitor, Giver, and Lover; in your spiritual life the Elder, Prophet, Disciple, and Servant.

Beyond their specific designation, these four energies exist in every one of us. However, successful people have learned how to get theirs to work together as a team, each reinforcing, backing up, and supporting the other. They have created a success cycle in their lives. You can, too. That is what this book is about. It provides a tool kit of thoughts, exercises, and approaches to live more successfully.

Success requires all four aspects of success—the King, Wizard, Warrior, and Monk—to be engaged, healthy, and productive. Your King, Wizard, Warrior, and Monk must all be mature, each able to act independently and work synergistically with the other. When an aspect is immature or weak, it solicits overcompensation from the other aspects. Conversely, when an aspect is inflated or over-relied upon, it detracts from effectively engaging with the other aspects. A lack of development within any one aspect or an imbalance between them is what stands in the way of achievement.

Here is an example, to clarify. I love my Wizard. I spend a lot of time thinking, planning, and brainstorming. I visualize, ideate, and dream. But think what would happen if that was all I did. If my King was feeble, I would not be able to smartly choose from the many plans my Wizard creates. If my Warrior was weak, I would never get around to implementing my plans. Even if my King and Warrior were strong, if my Monk was shallow, I would not be able to enjoy the process—negating the ability to call any outcome a real success. Each aspect of success is essential.

Anyone can be successful. Victory is a result of developing the fours aspects of success. Together, a wise King, an inspired Wizard, a strong Warrior, and a contented Monk will help you achieve your goals and accomplish your dreams. Master each aspect and success will be inevitable.

This process starts with your thinking. What you know and believe matters. Therefore, success starts with your King...

King [kiNG]. A supreme ruler, one who possesses ultimate power. Sovereign; self-governing or autonomous. One with charge over a realm or dominion.

ASPECT I: THE WISE KING

The King is the part of us that realizes and understands. It can be thought of as an internal compass residing within each person's psyche. Your King knows, analyzes, considers, and decides. An accumulator and processor of knowledge, it determines what is right for you and what is not. When mature, the King possesses a deep and timeless wisdom that makes successful living possible. Intelligent, this part of you allows all other aspects of yourself to function well.

The King's knowledge and wisdom guides the creative possibility of the Wizard. The former understands what is; the latter imagines what could be. The King provides good judgment to the Warrior and powerful insight to the Monk. Taking into account the ideas of the Wizard, the abilities of the Warrior, and the blessings of the Monk, your King rules over your life. From a seemingly infinite number of possibilities, this aspect is full of discretion, adept at setting boundaries, and helps make good choices.

If this aspect is passive, weak, or immature, success will be stilted. When you frequently feel unworthy, doubt yourself, make poor decisions, need external validation, or are over-accommodating, it is an indication that your King is underdeveloped. In this state, your King is not able to properly represent you or make decisions that are in your best interest. Conversely, when you are regularly self-centered, overconfident, unsupportive, or demanding, it is an indication that your King has become aggressive. In this state, your King over-represents you and, as a result, stifles valuable wisdom available from your Wizard, Warrior, and Monk.

To see where your King stands, do the following exercise. Check up to ten items from any of the three boxes below that best describe emotions you most commonly experience. Consider not only what you think, but also what others close to you say about you as well.

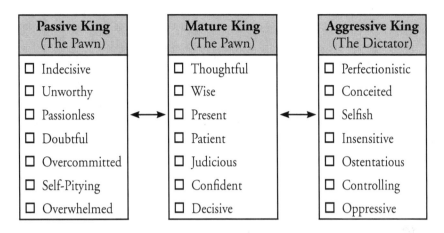

Passive King (The Pawn)		Mature King (The Pawn)		Aggressive King (The Dictator)
☐ Indecisive		☐ Thoughtful		☐ Perfectionistic
☐ Unworthy		☐ Wise		☐ Conceited
☐ Passionless	⟷	☐ Present	⟷	☐ Selfish
☐ Doubtful		☐ Patient		☐ Insensitive
☐ Overcommitted		☐ Judicious		☐ Ostentatious
☐ Self-Pitying		☐ Confident		☐ Controlling
☐ Overwhelmed		☐ Decisive		☐ Oppressive

Now look at where most of your marks reside. If there are more checked items on the left-hand side of the graphic, then your King is probably underdeveloped. A passive King, or Pawn, tends to be weak and immature. Fully considered, this section of the book will help you develop a masterful King.

Alternatively, if most of the circled items tend toward the right-hand side of the graphic, your King is probably heavily relied upon to the point where it is counterproductive. An aggressive King, or Dictator, exemplifies an effort to compensate for unaddressed weaknesses in your Wizard, Warrior, or Monk. While this section will most certainly be of value, it is important that you also identify which other aspects(s) might be suboptimal. Focusing and strengthening these aspects will level and restore balance thereby reducing the need and tendency toward overreliance on your King in ways that do not fully serve you. It is common for an overactive aspect to occur as a compensatory device to cover up another weaker aspect.

To be successful in life, your inner King must be wise and mature. As such, your King can readily tease out the inferior and select the superior. A judicious King can weigh the pros and cons of any situation, consider a wide range of nuances and contingencies, and make astute decisions. Your King can think in ways that are healthy and protective, providing for you while benefiting others and the world at large. A wise King astutely understands life, sees the bigger picture, and allows you to function adeptly in any situation. Developing a wise King is essential to achieving success in life.

There are five critical behaviors attributed to a wise King. Your mature King knows how to: (1) understand your role, (2) take responsibility, (3) focus attention, (4) become more aware, and (5) make good choices. We will explore these five behaviors, in turn, throughout the pages of this section.

BEHAVIOR 1: UNDERSTANDING YOUR ROLE

"One's first step in wisdom is to question everything." — *G. Lichtenberg*

Every belief is self-constructed. All the ideas you hold, and all the certainties of the world believed to be true by you, were created by you. This belief creation process occurs as follows: First, you get an idea. The idea can come from many sources. While it can be self-originated, more often it comes from outside the self such as our families and friends, our schools, workplaces, and churches, as well as television, the media, and other societal influences.

For example, let's say you get the notion that the world is a scary place. Next, you test the validity of this idea. You look for evidence that it is true. As you go about your life, you seek feedback from the environment as to the soundness and validity of your proposition. Since there are examples in everyone's life that the

Everyone is engaged in a lifelong process of finding what they are looking for.

world can be a scary place, you no doubt find supporting evidence. Finding what you are looking for acts to reinforce your idea. Eventually, you find more and more evidence that your idea is true, and you become increasingly certain that it is. Finally, you create a new belief—you become convinced that the world is, indeed, a bad, frightening place. You are certain this is true. You know that the world is a scary place. You then use this belief as a guidepost for all your future life decisions.

As a result, you create your beliefs. All your deeply held convictions are selected, developed, and decided upon by you in this way, and even though they are of your own making, you believe them to be accurate and infallible. As a result of the belief creation process, every belief, therefore, is make-believe to some degree. Each and every belief was fashioned by your thinking and judged to be valid by you.

Everyone uses a process like this to understand the world in which they live. The problem with this approach is that we think we are unbiased observers running objective tests on a linear world. We are not. Everyone is engaged in a lifelong process of finding what they are looking for. Any idea that you propose to the universe has the potential to become a self-generated belief. Ideas become beliefs. In this way, the possibilities of life become fixed over time and, eventually, they act to limit our future. This occurs irrespective of the nature of the idea. To understand this better, let's take an opposing point of view on our query.

Suppose your original idea was very different. What if someone of influence in your life, a religious uncle, a successful father, an optimistic grandmother, caused you to ask a different question? What if you wondered if the world was a good, kind place? You would then look for evidence to support this idea. Do you think you would find it? Of course, you would.

So which is it? Is the world a bad scary place or a good, kind one? It is both. In a world of infinite possibilities, every eventuality can be experienced. Therefore, you will find whatever it is you are looking for. Psychologists call this confirmation bias (Wason, 1960), and it reflects the tendency to search for information that supports our ideas.

It is far easier to observe something we are familiar with because we have developed a way to process and understand it. As a result, we tend to observe what it is we want to see, finding whatever it is we are looking for. In asking the question above, we put forward an expectation to which the cosmos responds in kind. "The universe works to mirror your beliefs; it will prove you right every time" (Peggy McColl).

Such beliefs have a dramatic impact on how we experience life. In seeking to validate the possibility that the world is a good place, one might be more apt to notice benevolent meaning in the acts of others. Examples include: another person waving you into the close parking space ahead of them at the crowded mall, a person letting you go ahead of them in line or giving you an extra coupon at checkout, or the friend who calls you when you are struggling with a personal issue. Likewise, one is less likely to pay as much attention to the guy who cut you off earlier, the person with a full cart in the express lane, or the friends that didn't call during a challenging time. In spite of these potentially negative events, due to observational bias, one is able to overlook them, maintaining that the world is indeed a good place. Interestingly, a person with an opposing view might have concluded exactly the opposite after exposure to the same series of events.

One outlook is not more valid than the other. The world is indeed both a good and bad place depending on one's perspective. Neither view is inherently right or wrong; there are advantages to each. However, one outlook often works better than the other depending on what you are trying to accomplish.

Your mature King understands that you play a role in every belief. Expectations act to condition our thinking in ways that end up shaping our beliefs. Such beliefs act to influence our preferences, tastes, values, and even the approaches we use to face life's challenges. Each of us has trained ourselves to think

> # The crucial question is what viewpoint is most helpful?

and act in certain ways stemming from what we know is right. This occurs across the swath of important perspectives that results from answers to questions such as: "Am I a good person or a bad person?" "Am I worthy or unworthy?" "Am I smart, capable, talented, or good looking or am I the opposite?"

Beliefs also include decisions about others and the world as a whole. Answers to the following questions provide insights into such thinking: "Are people helpful, generous, and kind?" "Am I well liked, appreciated?" "Do I need to protect what I have or can I live in a state of openness to life's possibilities?" "Is the world full of opportunity or problems?" "Do I have something to offer?" "Can I make a difference?" There are an infinite number of questions one can ask the universe. Likewise, there are an infinite number of beliefs that can result. The crucial question is what viewpoint is most helpful?

Thinking the world is a good place can give the peace and confidence that enhance personal efforts. However, it could also lull one into complacency. Thinking the world is against you can motivate you to prove the world wrong. It can also create hopelessness and helplessness. The most helpful beliefs are those that help you accomplish your goals.

Too many people let current circumstances or their past experiences shape their thinking. Perhaps this is the reason solution-focused therapy is effective in psychological treatment.[8] Solution-focused therapy works by asking a person to consider what could be accomplished in the future. Only productive resources and successes from the past can be included when answering the question. As a result, the technique focuses on possibility not limitation. The same approach is useful when considering the beliefs you hold.

Let's explore your viewpoints. Take a moment and write down a few of the key beliefs you hold about yourself, others, and the world at large in the left-hand column, Thought Expander 1.1, <u>Core Beliefs</u>. In the right-hand column, explore how your thinking impacts you. For example, you might believe the future is uncertain so there is no reason to prepare or plan for it. That might impact you by discouraging drive-based actions such as education, advancement, savings, and goal setting. Alternatively, you might believe the future is full of possibility, and it is within your ability to influence it. This would impact you because you would more readily take action to make your future what you wish.

Thought Expander 1.1: Core Beliefs

Subject	What I believe:	How it impacts me?
Myself		
Family		
Friends		
Work/ School		
Economy		
The Future		
Other (write in)		
Other (write in)		

Now review each response and ask the following questions. Is this belief helping or hurting me? Which ideas about myself, others, or the world might be holding me back? What beliefs are getting in the way of me accomplishing what I want to accomplish? Then consider changing those beliefs that don't work and adding beliefs that will help you become more successful. It is better to seek out beliefs that provide possibility instead of limitation, honing in on those that allow you to believe in "I can" versus "I can't." The wisdom of this can be seen in the following recommendation: "Set aside all the reasons why you're not getting what you want and start to focus on all the reasons you can get what you want" (Ray Stanford, adapted).

Beliefs provide a set of rules that guide your perceptions, feelings, and behaviors. They limit or expand what you think you can accomplish, the goals you set, and the progress you make in life. As such, your beliefs determine your reality. They frame life's possibilities. Researchers in psychology have found that performance is more likely to be adversely impacted by negative beliefs than limited ability.[9] Beliefs create perceptions which go on to affect every area of life. However, each of these limitations is self-fabricated. We don't see the world as it is, we see it as we think it is.

To achieve success throughout life, it is essential, therefore, that you evolve your thinking and your underlying beliefs. People grow and situations change. Over time, it is almost certain that beliefs you now hold will stop being productive, or worse yet, get in the way of future success. You can create many unhealthy beliefs over a lifetime—each limiting the ability to think clearly and to make good decisions. Beliefs are simply mental habits. As such, they often provide effective, short-cut ways of taking experience and applying it to decision making. When these short-cuts stop being effective, negative results can show up quickly. Outgrown beliefs result in suboptimal choices and yield undesirable outcomes. They get us stuck. Desirable results wane, progress slows, and frustration increases. For "A man is a slave to whatever has mastered him" (2 Peter 2:19, NIV; see appendix for Bible translation key).

The impact of ineffective beliefs can show up suddenly after serving us for many years, and occur in every stage of life. It is a normal part of the maturation process. For example, as a child it may be helpful to believe the world is a scary place, this could provide protection in adverse environments. However, as a young adult, the very same belief can stilt adventurousness and limit possibility.

You created every belief you hold—each being a reflection of your curiosity looking back at you. They are self-derived conclusions reinforced through self-selected exposure. Many are formed early in life and maintained by you ever since. The good news is that because your beliefs are of your own making, you can change them. As such, beliefs become tools of success that can be interchanged and shaped to serve you.

If you want to change any facet of your life, a bad habit, or a persistent, unwelcome outcome, start by examining what you believe. Yes, raw effort and determination can be used, but often a brute-force approach is difficult to maintain long-term, rendering it temporary and ineffective. When enough time passes or stress appears, the undesired behavior resurfaces. Real change is accomplished not, by force, but through understanding.

If you want to change any facet of your life, start by examining what you believe.

For example, I used to believe people were always reliable. This was a problem because, given enough time, every relationship ended with the other person letting me down at one time or another. Maybe it was exposure to too many movies with happy-endings, but I went through life expecting that people were consistently reliable. Not surprisingly, that belief didn't work out very well as no one was able to achieve this standard.

As a result of my belief, I didn't give people the benefit of the doubt; I didn't forgive, expecting too much. I let relationships with these "violators" lay fallow—walking away from friendship and support in the process. I spent a lot of time alone. My belief acted as a form of protection that kept me separate, and safe—possibly a left-over approach invoked during my tumultuous, formative years. While it never worked well, as I aged, this belief became ever more problematic. It kept me isolated, slowing my personal and professional growth. It held me back and pushed me down.

Although it took some time to come to this conclusion, I eventually realized that I was expecting people to be perfect. While it sounds ridiculous, I was holding everyone to an impossible standard which ignored the inherent foibles and proclivities of people.

Ironically, it was only when I accepted the idea that everyone is inherently flawed that my relationships flourished, and a series of new opportunities presented themselves. In allowing people to be human, I started to better accept, appreciate, and love them. In this shift, compassion blossomed. Today, my new belief provides a more healthy perspective that allows me to function better in the world.

We all carry beliefs that stand in the gap between where we are and what we want to accomplish. What are yours? Leveraging your list from Thought Expander 1.1, <u>Core Beliefs</u>, reflect on your life and identify a few areas in your life that are not working as you would like. Write them in the left-hand column of Thought Expander 1.2, <u>Alternative Beliefs</u>. Then in the middle column, identify what underlying beliefs you might be holding that create or sustain them. Next, in the right-hand column, consider what you could believe instead. For each alternative belief, identify the potential impact the new conviction would have on your life today, and write it in the area entitled Ideal Outcome. For example, you might find yourself frequently taking others comments as hurtful. The underlying belief you hold might be that you are a bad person. Alternatively, you could believe that their comments might not be specific to you, but may, instead, be a generic reflection of their own inner problems, inadequacies, and worries. The ideal outcome, therefore, might be that you empathize with them, feeling a sense of compassion and shifting to a place where you can improve the relationship.

> We all carry beliefs that stand in the gap between where we are and what we want to accomplish.

Thought Expander 1.2: Alternative Beliefs

What is not working in my life today	Underlying belief	Alternate Belief (What I could believe instead)
Item #1		
		Ideal outcome:
Item #2		
		Ideal outcome:
Item #3		
		Ideal outcome:

This exercise helps identify opportunities to improve your life by changing your beliefs. But how do you go about replacing an ineffective belief for one that serves you better? It is easier to do than you might think. As you go through life, look to see if your alternate belief is true. See if you can't find evidence to support this new perspective. You will most certainly find evidence that whatever it is you are looking to justify is indeed true. Given enough time, this approach will help change how you look at the world.

How can you tell if your new belief is working? Look at the results. You will know your new belief is taking root when your thoughts, feelings, and actions start to change. This will create a momentum shift in your life resulting in better, more productive outcomes. Things will start working again in areas previously constrained.

Every success in life, like every failure, is driven by your beliefs.

Every success in life, like every failure, is driven by your beliefs. Beliefs are habitual, self-validated thoughts. Thoughts generate feelings and shape subsequent actions, and these actions drive the outcomes that result. Roman Leader Marcus Aurelius understood this when he noted that, "The happiness of your life depends upon the quality of your thoughts."

One of the most successful and widely used techniques employed by psychologists today is cognitive behavioral therapy (Beck, 1979). As a practice, cognitive behavioral therapy is the process of modifying a person's thinking to drive changes in what they perceive, how they feel, and what they do. Here, maladaptive beliefs and ineffective thinking processes are addressed directly. The approach works by identifying errors, or suboptimal processes, of thought. These could take place due to excessive generalizing, over focusing on negatives and under focusing on positives, or holding unrealistic assumptions. In this form of therapy, each thought pattern is challenged and, when appropriate, replaced with a more realistic and effective perception. The goal of the psychologist in using this technique is to reduce distress and generate more effective life outcomes.

Everything you do is based on what you believe. Modifying the thoughts you hold, therefore, acts to alter the underlying beliefs. The results you can achieve in life can be profound. So much so that the Bible cautions you to continually pay attention to and manage your thoughts. "Be careful what you think, because your thoughts run your life" (Proverbs 4:23; NCV).

Your thoughts and beliefs matter immensely. Childhood is sprinkled with ideas you don't fully understand or appreciate. Added to this, your expectations further cloud the truth from adolescence through adulthood. Wisdom comes when you see your role in this process clearly, and take steps to sift out what works from what doesn't. "Great minds discuss ideas, average minds discuss events, small minds discuss people" (Eleanor Roosevelt).

To succeed you must optimize the way you think.

To succeed you must optimize the way you think. Your wise King recognizes that you create your beliefs. Now you know to challenge every viewpoint, assumption, and value that doesn't serve you. Consider discarding beliefs that limit possibility, accept lack, or demean what you could become. "Make your ear attentive to wisdom, incline your heart to understanding, then you will discover a fear of (respect for) the Lord and discover the knowledge of God" (Proverbs 2:2-5; NAS).

Embrace your role in the belief process. Don't take your current ideas as being universally correct and true, leaving them untested. For better or for worse, ideas have a way of becoming beliefs that ultimately determine the outcome of your life. Take charge of your life by taking charge of your beliefs. In doing so, you will open the door for more of what you want in life. Success is determined by the thoughts you hold.

BEHAVIOR 2: TAKING RESPONSIBILITY

"A man sooner or later discovers that he is the master-gardener of his soul, the director of his life." — *James Allen*

Be accountable for your life. If something is not working in your life, if you are not getting what you want, if you are unhappy, realize that you are responsible for that experience. The same holds true if you are blissfully happy and fully content. In both cases, the beliefs you choose drive the thoughts you have, which sway the subsequent actions you take, which ultimately influence the outcomes you get.

Your life is a net result of your thinking. To become more successful, you must shift your thinking. Better thoughts can lead to greater freedom and clear the way for immense achievement.

Take marriage for example. During my retreats, CEOs often bring up various issues they are experiencing with their marriages. These are usually directed at the shortcomings of their spouses such as, "She does this thing," or "She doesn't do that thing," or "He won't change this," or "He won't become that." To assist them in shifting their perspective, I will often ask what percentage of their spousal relationships they consider to be their responsibility. The answer is typically 50% or so, in-line with how one might split workload, food, or pay between two people. However, successful relationships require a different approach.

> **People who are willing to take responsibility, quickly shift from helpless victims to active achievers.**

Next, I ask them to consider the possibility that relationships are different, and for a relationship to flourish, each person is required to be 100%

committed, each fully responsible for the relationship's health. You can almost see the lights go on when they realize the truth in this perspective. The impact is often immediate and profound. This shift often causes people to see that they play an immensely important role in their relationships and, by logical extension, in each and every problem that exists. Realizing this allows movement from a place of blaming toward a position of owning.

People, who are willing to take responsibility, quickly shift from helpless victims to active achievers. Looking at the situation from this angle allows the partner to form a broader range of options. It heightens the impetus to invest in the relationship in order to rectify the situation. Improvements follow almost immediately when full accountability is embraced.

Taking responsibility is an approach that works not only in relationships but also in every aspect of life. To see this for yourself, identify three long-standing issues in your life and write them in the left-hand column of Thought Expander 2.1, Personal Problems. For each item, ask yourself if the problem would remain if you did not exist. For example, you may have a disabling fear of bees which originated as a child, or may have developed a disdain for authority in your teens. In both cases, the problem could not exist without you as you are an essential component, defined in the problem itself.

Thought Expander 2.1: Personal Problems

Issue	Does it exist without me? (circle one)
Problem #1	Yes / No
Problem #2	Yes / No
Problem #3	Yes / No

Notice anything? Except for significant social issues or general geo-political problems, the vast majority of your problems require your direct involvement. As such, they disappear when you remove yourself from the equation. Logically, therefore, you must play an important role in their existence. If a problem can't exist without you, then you are, by definition, part of the problem.

While you would not intention-ally create a problem, in every case you unwittingly allowed it to start and have, since, acted in ways that keep it alive. Take the simplistic example of a person afraid of bees. An instinctive, protective mechanism may be playing a role, but it was the inner King which ultimately allowed the fear to rule over the person's thoughts and reactions. Immature at the time of possible abdi-cation, the person's inner King always holds sovereign right and has the abil-

> **Every issue that keeps you from achieving your goals you have unknowingly initiated, supported, or contributed to in some way.**

ity to take reign over the fear. The same is true with more complex prob-lems such as failed relationships, social anxiety, systemic laziness, damag-ing levels of procrastination, a disdain for others, poor drive, failed goals, unhappiness, and hopelessness. Every issue that keeps you from achieving your goals you have unknowingly initiated, supported, or contributed to in some way.

There is an old story about two monks making a pilgrimage. During their journey they came to a deep river. At the edge, a beautiful young woman sat weeping, too afraid to cross the river without help. Upon seeing the Brother, she asked if they might carry her across the river. The younger Brother was offended and turned his back in disgust because their order was forbidden to touch a woman. But the older Brother didn't hesitate, and without a word, he picked up the woman and carried her across the river. She thanked him and went on her way, while the monks resumed their journey.

As they walked, the younger monk brooded and became distracted to the point where he could no longer keep silent. "Brother," he exclaimed, "you have broken your vows. You not only touched a woman but carried her on your shoulders." For many miles, he continued to scold and berate the older Brother. Finally, at the end of the day the older monk turned to the younger one and said, "I set her down on the other side of the river hours ago, but you are still carrying her."

Another way to think about this idea is to identify problems that seem to recur in life. Have you ever noticed that almost everyone has a problem type that seems to follow them around wherever they go? For example, someone you know might have been fired three times in a row; another may have been in multiple failed marriages where they were treated similarly in each; a third may find it difficult to pay the bills no matter how much money they earn. To bring this concept home, take a moment to think of undesirable situations that keep repeating in your life. This could include issues, circumstances, or situations where you seem to have more than your fair share of tribulations. Add them to Thought Expander 2.2, Recurring Issues.

Thought Expander 2.2: Recurring Issues

Repeating Situation or Problem
Undesirable #1
Undesirable #2
Undesirable #3

If the same challenges keep showing up in your life or you are consistently getting unwanted results, what is the constant? Ineffective patterns continuously shape how you see the world and influence what you do. Around the problems in the above Thought Expander, these patterns are generating suboptimal outcomes. While much of this happens subconsciously and unintentionally, each of us plays a leading role in causing our problems. "Our attitude toward life determines life's attitude towards us" (Earl Nightingale).

This is true in every aspect of life. As an engineer, I have inadvertently become the point person for late night technical emergencies in my neighborhood. Not long ago, I got a phone call at 1 a.m. from a frantic couple who were battling a flooding basement. They indicated their sump pump was not working, and water was rising quickly. Wading through ankle deep water, I asked what had happened, and what they had tried so far. The power had been off for a short period earlier, but had been restored, and yet water levels continued to rise. They told me that when the power was out they heard water rushing, so they turned off a nearby valve to silence it. What they didn't know was that the sound came from a backup pump driven by municipal water pressure. In addition, the primary electric pump had a stuck float and had not turned on. I freed the float and turned the water back on to the backup pump. The basement was water-free in a half hour.

> ## To solve any problem, the most important step is to own it.

In shutting off the backup pump, my neighbors had done what many people do—they created their own problem. Turning the wrong valve, they flooded their own basement. Life is like this. You have a hand in your troubles. While you don't sabotage yourself deliberately, you play a part in your outcomes, both good and bad. This can occur directly through actions you do or do not take, or indirectly by what you allow yourself to be exposed to or believe. The good news is, since you've had a hand in creating your problems, you are also in an excellent position to fix them.

To solve any problem, your inner King knows the most important step is to own it. For "Even if I have truly erred, my error lodges with me" (Job 19:4; NAS). People have a tendency to look beyond themselves when they have a problem. They blame, accuse, or judge others. They indict groups, governments, cultures, and races. In divesting themselves of the issue, they only wind up making it much more difficult, if not impossible, to solve. In addition, shifting responsibility to forces beyond the self, hands over our control and power.

Reconsider relationships, for example. Have you ever tried to get someone else to change? Ask someone who has been married for any meaningful period of time how successful they have been at changing their spouse. They will openly laugh at you indicating the foolhardy, ridiculous nature of the question. They know the futility of that approach; changing others simply doesn't work. It is almost impossible to alter other people to be who you want them to be and do what you want them to do. There is a much better option. It is much more productive to change yourself. "Seek not to change the world, but choose to change your mind about the world. What you see reflects your thinking. And your thinking but reflects your choice of what you want to see" (Helen Schucman). If you have a problem or some change you want to see in your life, the place to start is with you.

Emotions are the result of beliefs bumping up against reality.

To understand what most needs to change; the best place to look is at your emotions. Emotions are excellent indicators of what is working and not working in your belief system. Emotions are the result of beliefs bumping up against reality. Beliefs drive attitudes influencing your perceptions, which then impact how you feel. These emotions then drive your responses which, in turn, determine the end result you achieve. The final outcome then acts to reinforce or reshape the beliefs in a never-ending, iterative process. It is in this process that our feelings prove to be excellent gauges, since they are readily apparent and most obvious. Specifically, negative feelings indicate that some part of our thinking process is ineffective and not serving us properly, while good feelings show that our thoughts are serving us well.

Evolutionary psychologists suggest that emotions convey a wide range of information regarding our lives.[10] Positive feelings motivate us to move toward others and spend time in situations so as to create social capital for future benefit.[11] Meanwhile, negative feelings do the opposite, driving us to move away from others in order to protect and preserve. For example, a belief that people are being critical could lead to oversensitivity resulting in one isolating oneself and, subsequently, experiencing the feeling of alienation and loneliness. These negative feelings indicate that a better approach is available, such as learning to effectively relate to others by, for example, recognizing that critical people are really unhappy with themselves.

As a result, monitoring your feelings is an excellent way to identify any beliefs that are not working for you. Awareness is a tool of the wise. This includes sometimes bringing to the surface beliefs you hold subconsciously of which you are not aware. But the good news is: techniques that facilitate the identification of subconscious beliefs exist. Meditation, prayer, mindfulness, and other awareness practices, covered later in this book, will lead your wise King to establish a deeper connection with your inner self and lead you to a world of self-discovery.

In addition to ineffective beliefs, people also harbor many conflicting beliefs. In my seminars, I often ask people to raise their hands if they believe in heaven. Many do. Then I ask them to keep their hands up if they are afraid of death. Most hands stay up. How is this possible that they are afraid of the journey to a wonderful afterlife? Unless they think they are going to hell, the reality is that the heaven-bound hold two, unresolved conflicting ideas. Conflicts like this occur across every facet of life and become particularly important when they impede your progress.

> **Negative feelings indicate that some part of our thinking process is ineffective and not serving us properly.**

In general, people become uncomfortable when they hold two beliefs that are in conflict. Mental conflicts are unconscious struggles resulting from contending needs, desires, and impulses. Everyone has internal conflicts of one sort or another. Incongruous perceptions that remain unreconciled result in inner discomfort known as cognitive dissonance (Festinger, 1956). When such conflicts interfere with achievement or impede living well, they need to be dealt with or they will stand in the way of your success. There are four general approaches to handle conflicting beliefs.

The first of the four approaches to dealing with a problem is to ignore part of it. If you love ice cream and desire to lose weight, one way to deal with it is to put the weight issue out of your mind whenever the desire for ice cream arises. Similarly, if you love the thrill of falling in love but also value a stable relationship, you would merely avoid thinking about one when involved in the other. Not surprisingly, this approach can prove unhelpful long-term, allowing problems to grow into crises. This book is about taking charge of your life, so ignoring a problem is not recommended.

The remaining approaches are more proactive and useful. The second approach, creating a new belief, was covered in Thought Expander 1.2 Alternate Beliefs, where I mentioned that I expected people to be reliable, but in accepting their inherent flaws, I was able to have more meaningful and longer-lasting relationships.

The third approach to handling conflicting beliefs is to increase the importance of one belief over another. It is common for people to chastise themselves for not taking steps to address problems in their lives sooner. They often beat themselves up over "knowing better" and still not taking action to address long-standing issues. This approach is counterproductive and progress is more readily made by shifting from believing that you may in some way be inferior because you waited, to a new belief that holds if you could have made the change, they would have done so. Holding beliefs that more readily allow for progress, shift your momentum toward success. In considering the possibility that you were not ready for change, you move from self-judgment to empathy, understanding that, when you are ready for change, you can and will make it. Taking a compassionate and progressive view serves to better facilitate progress.

> Every adversity is an opportunity or an issue, depending on how you see it and what you do with it.

The fourth approach to addressing conflicting beliefs is to allow them to coexist in paradox. Paradox is the state that occurs when two or more beliefs seem contradictory or absurd, but are instead transcended. For example, the executives and leaders I work with often struggle between the beliefs that they need to provide for their families and that they need to be an active part of their family's lives. By entering paradox around these propositions, they accept that they must expend significant efforts to succeed and provide for their families even though this creates an imbalance of the desired time spent with those they love. Often, they succeed by striking a healthy balance between them, knowing neither desire will be completely satisfied. Holding these two conflicting desires together and allowing them to both be important, provides a sense of acceptance, allowing you to migrate away from feelings of angst and move toward peace while living well.

To keep conflicting beliefs from impeding your progress in life, the solution is to consciously allow both beliefs to coexist. It is an act of wisdom to recognize both as being valuable while also being incompatible. While reconciliation between them may come, that day has not yet arrived. As a result, value is captured by permitting both beliefs to be merged into a third, more complete and higher synthesis—one that maximizes possibility in lieu of a more rigorous resolution. Paradox is a superior state where dichotomies are fused and resolved from a higher, more holistic plain. It enhances your ability to understand, address, and improve your life.

Holding beliefs in paradox is also an act of compassion. Embracing logical irony makes it okay for each of us to be imperfectly human. For example, accepting ourselves, for who we are, with all our deficiencies and inconsistencies, is essential to living well. Paradox provides a place for things that don't make sense. Instead of being confused, frustrated, or unclear regarding what is right, both beliefs are accepted as being true and allowed to coexist in the moment. In summary, if you are unhappy and are not getting what you want in life, seek to understand your beliefs, either upgrading to those that better serve you or accepting those you currently hold. "As water reflects the face, so one's life reflects the heart" (Proverbs 27:19, NIV).

To be truly successful, you must take responsibility for everything that happens in life. The vast majority go through their days believing that forces beyond their control are the cause of their problems. Millions practice this "no fault" thinking by shifting their responsibility to other people and events beyond themselves so that, no matter what happens, it isn't their fault. The good news is that your mature King understands that you play an important part in every problem you experience. You need not be a victim to anything, but can choose to be the victor.

> By taking charge of your beliefs, you clear a path for success and happiness to flow into your life.

Every adversity is an opportunity or an issue, depending on how you see it and what you do with it. Instead of using feelings as gateways to blame and judge others, your wise King uses emotions as markers to identify opportunities for personal growth. Over time, through practice and self-reflection, better beliefs take hold yielding faster results and better outcomes.

Your mature King understands which views stand in your way and which help you accomplish your dreams. When your mature King is established and strong, you can create better ways to look at, interpret, and react to events in your life. It is within your power to choose beliefs that support, build up, and provide possibility. By taking charge of your beliefs, you clear a path for success and happiness to flow into your life.

BEHAVIOR 3: FOCUSING ATTENTION

"Whatever you focus on expands." — *Christopher M. Knight*

Center your efforts. One of the most powerful abilities we have as human beings is our ability to focus our attention. The control to direct attention provides a commanding influence on what takes place in our lives. This process occurs both directly and indirectly through both conscious and subconscious channels.

Take a common situation. Let's say you have decided to buy, or have just purchased, a specific new car—a yellow jeep for example. Immediately afterwards, you notice that there are yellow jeeps everywhere. Turn down the street, get on the freeway, or pull into the shopping mall, a banana–colored, four-wheeler lurks. It seems everyone owns one.

In psychology, this attention-based phenomenon is called attenuation (Treisman, 1960). Attenuation theory proposes that for humans, relevant stimuli are more likely to be processed while irrelevant stimuli are more likely to go unnoticed or be ignored. Therefore, a recently purchased Rolex Watch, Coach Handbag, or Porsche Sports Car will have you seeing them all around. The difference in observation occurs because these newly purchased items have undergone significant increases in relevance to you. As newly invigorated points of interest, they are more readily noticed.

Attenuation is an unintentional cognitive reflex that takes place without awareness. However, such observational relevance can also be influenced consciously. Take the popular game "slug bug" (known by other names in various parts of the country such as "punch buggy"), for example. The first person to notice a Volkswagen Beetle car punches the other person in the arm and earns points. The player with the most points wins. As my kids became teenagers, this game became a staple to pass drive time.

I had never really noticed how many Beetles were on the roads before. Now, I seem to see an awful lot of them. My right shoulder seems to hurt more often, too, and I'm not sure it's due to old age. Choosing to play the game has shifted my entire family's focus and our behaviors. When a VW Beetle comes into view, it causes me to tense up or to prepare for a punch—even when I'm driving alone. It is obvious; our attention alters what we see and influences how we feel and what we do.

Consider also the popular internet video of the moon-walking bear.[12] Millions have seen the video with a web link provided in the reference section of this playbook. (Spoiler alert, if you want the full effect, take the test before reading further or skip to the next paragraph.) In the video, you are asked to count how many times the team in white passes the basketball. It is somewhat challenging to count the passes because another team, dressed in black, is passing another basketball among themselves. When the sequence is finished, the correct number of passes turns out to be 13.

You go where you are looking and you see what you expect.

In doing this at various events, most people get the pass count correct. However, when asked if they saw the moon-walking bear, they respond with a mixture of curiosity and surprise. A quick replay of the video makes the answer clear. With their newly-established focal point, there, front and center in the middle of the clip, as obvious as the nose on your face, is a person dressed up as a bear, moon–walking across the frame. The video closes with a statement, "It's easy to miss something you are not looking for." While the promotional ad is to caution drivers about bicycle riders, the point it makes is highly relevant to life.

Focus determines success. Each of us perceives our lives through our current center of attention. The frame of reference we use dictates what we notice and what we ignore. Herein, lays the key to developing your wise King—focused attention drives success. In general, you go where you are looking and you see what you expect. To achieve our goals, we must become more aware.

The tendency to miss what we are not looking for narrows our experience and leaves opportunity unidentified and uncaptured. "Most of the mistakes in thinking are inadequacies of perception rather than mistakes of logic" (Edward de Bono). Nowhere is the problem possibly more endemic than in corporate America.

As CEO, I was continually frustrated by the fact that I could never seem to make progress and get ahead. Yes, we had many great successes, but the problems never went away. When addressed, they were readily replaced with other problems. The job was like squeezing a water balloon. Push in here and another lump pops out over there. My job was to find problems and fix issues, and there seemed to be a never-ending stream of them. It was depressing and discouraging. No wonder the average tenure of American CEOs is so short. The work can become drudgery.

Now, take a look at this idea from its angle of perception. If you look for problems to fix, when are you going to stop finding them? The answer is never. Likewise, the reverse is also true. If you look for opportunities, when will you stop finding them? Again, you will never run out of possibilities. It is exactly this thinking that is the idea behind the leadership development theory of appreciative inquiry (Cooperrider & Srivastva, 1987). Researchers at Case Western Reserve University's business school, considered a provocative alternative. They suggested that if leaders were to shift their focus from problems and issues to seeking out what works well in the workplace, such as strengths and opportunities, that their companies might be better able to achieve positive change. They found that shifting the focus from limitation to possibility made a difference, in both atmosphere and outcome, with a positive focus yielding better results.

> By shining a spotlight on what is good, right, and valuable, success is more readily achieved.

Psychology researchers have come to a similar conclusion. Although many of the early pioneers explored ways to improve well-being prior to World War II, it was the introduction of positive psychology (Gillham & Seligman, 1999) that formalized this effort. Prior to its introduction, psychology had become fixated on addressing what was broken in people lives and not functioning in their minds. Traditional psychology attended to issues such as dysfunctional thinking, abnormal behavior, and serious mental illness. Its goal was to fix what was broken and make people functional—a commendable and important task. Positive psychology however, shifted this focus. It sought to better understand the science behind helping people to flourish. It set the objective of optimizing already functional people to become better, happier, and more successful—taking people from good to great.

Both appreciative inquiry, the model for making more effective change created at Case Western Reserve University, and positive psychology take advantage of the power that resides through a shift in focused attention. In doing so, they provide an important life lesson. By shining a spotlight on what is good, right, and valuable, success is more readily achieved. Focusing on what can be expands possibility, whereas focusing on what stands in the way diminishes it. "Argue for your limitations, and sure enough, they're yours" (Richard Bach).

Another place this is readily evident is with the stories we tell ourselves. Consider the following stories of my life. Read both life stories and decide which is true.

Story A: Growing up, I experienced significant psychological distress. Harsh physical discipline was the norm. My parents fought regularly, divorcing when I was ten years old. Between the remarriages and divorces, dating and separations, I moved to four different homes and attended four different schools in four years gaining and losing step siblings in the process. I was small for my age and new on the scene. I regularly got beat up by other kids. With my mother's loss of alimony and only her hair dresser income, we had very little money. We were the epitome of the working poor, relying on the generosity of others and the courts to provide survivable levels of child support. The oldest child, at age 13, I became the man of the house responsible for its maintenance and upkeep. As a result, I have spent my life trying to create the security I lacked as a child. I have difficulty forming relationships, a fear of groups, and I am not certain how to be a good father. I have also been prone to depression.

Story B: I grew up in a beautiful, bucolic setting. As a child, I had an extraordinary amount of freedom and autonomy to explore the world. I learned early on to rely on myself. I also realized that I could accomplish anything I set my mind to. I became independent, confident, and strong. At age eleven, I decided I would take the responsibility to make my life a success. I learned to study and get good grades. I attended some of the best schools in the country earning engineering, business, and psychology degrees while achieving the highest education level possible. In my professional career, I advanced rapidly at a series of Fortune 500 companies culminating in the position of CEO in my mid-thirties. Financially independent before age 40, I have been able to do what I want with my life.

That includes helping people live better and more successfully.

So, which of these stories is true? Both are! It depends on perspective. But which story do you think has been more helpful in my life? Which has better enabled me to accomplish my personal objectives and achieve my goals? The second story has been much more productive. Why? You get from life what you see in it.

You get from life what you see in it.

Whether you look for limitation or possibility, you will never stop finding them. If you focus on something you want, like abundance, you will get more of it. If you focus on something you don't want you will get more of it. It doesn't matter whether you allow or resist, whatever you focus on will persist. Had I fixated on Story A, like so many people do, I could have gotten mired in a fog of worry and self-doubt, believing that a lousy life was my destiny or a reflection of my worth. Clearly, that would not have served me well. Yet, that is the state of many.

Let's see what your life story says about your focus. Take a few minutes, and without much contemplation, complete Thought Expander 3.1, Your Life Story. In the top row, write out a negative version of your life story. In the bottom row, draft a positive version. There are no wrong answers, so write down the first impressions that come to mind in any format that works for you. Feel free to use additional pieces of paper, as necessary. Invest time into this exercise, for the seeds of success lie within.

Thought Expander 3.1: Your Life Story

Negative Version

Positive Version

Do you notice anything when drafting these? How does each of them feel? Does one feel better, inspire you, or create a feeling of possibility? Which do you think will best help you accomplish what you want out of life?

Your wise King understands that what you focus on matters. It starts with the stories you tell yourself about yourself. There are three elements of a personal story that have been found to be important in creating a personal narrative identity that results in well-being.[13] First, people who create life stories that emphasize personal growth and becoming all they can be tend to experience more well-being. Second, people who have stories that frame adverse experiences as transformative, where suffering led to new self-insights, tend to experience more well-being. Third, people who have stories that reflect success toward redemption (e.g., liberation, acceptance, recovery, reconciliation, etc.) also tend to experience more well-being. Ideal stories include achieving personal growth, making needed change, and deliverance from major challenges. People who include these dimensions in their stories of self tend to be more successful and happier.

Fortunately, you are the sole author of your story; it is yours to edit as you like. Look back on the stories you drafted in Thought Expander 3.1, Your Life Story. Note that one is not necessarily more correct than the other. Rather they are impressions or ideas of your experiences. As such, your stories can be thought of as beautiful pictures painted on top of pencil tracings of truth both faded and stained with the passing years.

> **It doesn't matter whether you allow or resist, whatever you focus on will persist.**

There is a joke about three buddies who die in a car crash. They go to heaven and at orientation are asked, "When you are in your casket and friends and family are mourning you, what would you like to hear them say about you? The first guy says, "I would like to hear them say that I was a great doctor of my time, and a great family man." The second guy says, "I would like to hear that I was a wonderful husband and school teacher who made a huge difference in our children of tomorrow." The last guy replies, "I would like to hear them say, 'Look! He's moving!'"

So what is your story going to look like? Which story will benefit you the most? It is up to you. Your story is the substance of life. It sets the stage for what you are willing to go after and what you will ultimately achieve. Well-being and success are tied directly to the stories you tell yourself. Toward that end, rewrite the positive story you created in Thought Expander 3.1, Your Life Story in Thought Expander 3.2, A Better Story. Be sure to include aspects of personal growth, overcoming adversity, and past successes. Spend some time on it. It is the foundation for your future successes.

Thought Expander 3.2: A Better Story

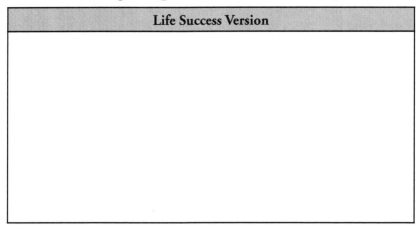

Life Success Version

Your inner King knows that people find evidence which supports what they expect to see. Ultimately, human's seek substantiation to what they believe is true. The story of your life acts as a foundation upon which your future is built. That is why you should "Consistently focus upon your great life story, and visualize with emotion those things you want to manifest" (Natalie Ledwell). The story you hold regarding your life is vital. It is all too easy to miss important opportunities due to preoccupation with limitations. Some miss relationships while building security. Others miss breaks because they are focusing on problems. Many don't have joy because they are caught up in worry. For "No one can serve two masters" (Matthew 6:24, ESV).

> You are the sole author of your story; it is yours to edit as you like.

Whatever you focus on expands. The power of stories lies in their ability to shift your attention toward what you want and away from what you do not want. They can be applied to every issue, circumstance, and situation. There are an unlimited number of ways to look at your experiences and an infinite number of perspectives from which a meaningful narrative can be constructed. "Our life is what our thoughts make it. A man will find that as he alters his thoughts toward things and other people, things and other people will alter towards him" (James Allen). The meaning you have assigned to what you remember about your past is only one possible interpretation.

Every tomorrow is lived from today's story of yesterday.

Let me demonstrate. When I was a young child, my Mother spent what seemed to me to be a considerable amount of time on the phone. I found this frustrating and, as it progressed, I took this to mean that I was unimportant. I constantly heard, "Not now." "Can't you be quiet?" "It will have to wait," and my personal favorite "Can't you see I'm on the phone?" Of course, I could. From these responses, I gathered meaning that would go on to impact my life regarding my worthiness, how relationships operate, and what love is.

But was my perception accurate? For each and every life experience, there are a great many accurate ways to portray it. Not until I was an adult, did I become aware of what else was going on at that time in my mother's life which caused me to rewrite my story. It is highly possible that my Mother may have been finding solace in friends and securing necessary resources to support her exit from a dysfunctional marriage. Reframing

Your thinking directs your life.

the story allowed for the creation of a completely new and equally valid perspective. In moving beyond considering only me, a memory of angst with my mother was transformed into one of courage, initiative, dedication, and love.

Your mature King recognizes there are an endless number of ways to look at any situation. A shift in perspective can change the past. Not literally, of course, but you can certainly change what it means and, therefore, what you can do with it. Your past is just that, it's yours. Do with it as you like. You get to choose. You are the one who gives import to certain events while ignoring others. You assign each and every meaning to the perspectives you hold. By reinterpreting your past, you influence it to your advantage. By changing it you alter your future. The story you create influences both who you are and what you can do. Every tomorrow is lived from today's story of yesterday.

It is this influence on your thinking that you must guard with your life. For, in a very real sense, your thinking directs your life. Therefore, what you expose yourself to becomes important, as it can easily become a part of your story, altering the outcomes of your life. As such, your environment also acts as a fundamental component to what you can achieve and what you will become.

The Bible talks about this. "As iron sharpens iron, so a man sharpens the countenance of his friend" (Proverbs 27:17; KJV). If you spend time with kind people who inspire you and challenge you to become the best you can be, you will grow to meet the expectation. If you hang out with unhappy people who are stuck in life, you, too, will flounder. Exposure to achievement breeds success; regular contact with dysfunction encourages apathy and decay. For "He who walks with wise men will be wise, but the companion of fools will be destroyed" (Proverbs 13:20; KJV).

> **Tomorrow is shaped by choosing who you are today.**

Be careful who you spend time with for you will become like them. "You must constantly ask yourself these questions: Who is around me? What are they doing to me? What have they got me reading? What have they got me saying? Where do they have me going? What do they have me thinking? And most important, what do they have me becoming? Then ask yourself the big question: Is that okay?" (Jim Rohn). Subtly, imperceptibly, the people you spent time with shape your perspective. For better or worse they mold your story. Each of us is a composite of the people we spend the most time with. Other's concerns, preferences, ambitions, and preoccupations influence us. Pay attention as these viewpoints will influence you. The question, therefore, is who will benefit you most?

Consider the top five people you spend time with. Ask yourself, "Are they who I want to become more like?" If so, great; if not, it is time to set some boundaries. The goal is to find people who support, inspire, and strengthen you, and spend more time with them. Often, the ideal associate looks a lot like the person we wish to become.

So who do you want to be? Tomorrow is shaped by choosing who you are today. One way to do this is to craft your best possible self. This is a visualization exercise where you imagine who you could become in a way that is both interesting and pleasing. The best possible self often includes goals that allow you to reach your full potential in some way. It might include exhibiting traits of character, honor, leadership, hard work, perseverance, accomplishment, self-discipline, or morality in range of motivating, supportive, and positive ways. It is your ideal story of self—the one you want to be teaching your grandkids, or telling your retirement buddies about, someday.

Through focused attention, dreams come to be.

Take a few minutes to craft your best possible self in Thought Expander 3.3, Best Possible Self. If you don't have enough space, feel free to expand on a separate page or use the note pages in the back of the book. The goal is to arrive at a fairly clear and specific image about who you wish to become.

Thought Expander 3.3: Best Possible Self

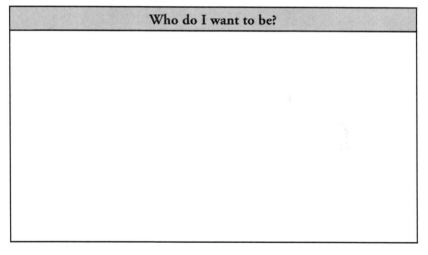

Who do I want to be?

Most people find this exercise inspiring and invigorating. Regularly thinking about who we could become has been found to raise positive moods and increase optimism.[14,15] Further, it provides a foundation for establishing a meaningful life direction that will be explored in later chapters. Therefore, it is recommended that you come back to this exercise and repeat it from time to time. You may also wish to print your story and place it somewhere that will cause you to think about it regularly.

To be truly successful in life, you must master your thinking. Your wise King understands that you get what you think, and what you focus on becomes reality. It is in changing your focus that you change your experience. If your King is weak, believing life is hard, unfair, and strewn with limited opportunity and privation, success will be hard to come by. If your King is strong, trusting that life is good, peppered with abundance, and containing challenges that can be overcome, the floodgates of success will open to you. Focused attention leads to a powerful and productive way of being.

Are you focusing on possibility or limitation, progress or stagnation, blessing or curse? You now know that you get more of whatever it is you are attentive to. A shift in attention can profoundly alter the meaning you assign to life's events and, ultimately, their impact on you. There is no lack of opportunities and no shortage of problems; it only depends on the stories you hold and the expectations they emanate. The key is to dwell on desire over doubt and possibility ahead of limitation. When it comes to where you are going, it matters which direction you look. Through focused attention, dreams come to be.

BEHAVIOR 4: BECOMING MORE AWARE

"Thinking is the hardest work there is, which is probably the reason why so few engage in it." — Henry Ford

Wake up. Almost everyone in the world is asleep. Most of the people you see, know, and love reside in a state of mental slumber. Only a rare few are fully awake, and they live in a state of deep wisdom and continuous amazement at the wonder of life. Religious leaders, scientists, philosophers, and leaders have been counted among their ranks. These revolutionaries are more aware of themselves and the world around them then the average man, and, as a result, live more vibrant and flourishing lives. You, too, can become more fully alive.

Your inner King wants you to wholly embrace the potentiality of life. To do this, you must become more aware. You are in charge of your thinking. In fact, your thoughts are the only thing in your life you are solely, 100% in control of. Consider it. Is there any other aspect of life where you have complete and ultimate say in what occurs? Any place or relationship where you decide everything that can and will happen? Certainly this is not true of any external aspect since environmental and situational forces always contain elements beyond your control.

Your thoughts are the only thing you have complete control over.

Your thoughts are the only thing you have complete control over. Yet few people understand, let alone, take advantage of this unique fact. Many do not preside over their thoughts. Unintentionally, they give up their birthright to a full, well-live life by letting their thoughts run them. Walking away from their inheritance, they leave vast fields of personal power fallow and reservoirs of potential untapped. Most people live like a cork in the sea, bobbing here and there, blown by the wind and moved by water currents.

I was no different. Growing up, my mother was always telling me to, "Think before you speak!" I had a common childhood affliction—a race-car mouth and a jalopy mind. Add this to the bevy of incomplete and inaccurate ideas a child holds about the world, and you have the recipe for many amusing and embarrassing situations. Like asking within earshot why Grandpa has "wires" sticking out of his nose and ears. Fortunately, the majority of people manage to outgrow this malady at least to some degree. I am still working on it, spot me another 50 years, and I'll have it down pat.

You can only achieve what you can perceive.

People live lives of habit. Habits develop when we repeat what has worked for us so many times that it becomes an unconscious reaction. Using this built-in autopilot mechanism, we go day-to-day doing what we have always done. We do this for good reason—it is efficient. When situations come our way, habit allows us to respond quickly and with minimal effort. Habits are generally good as they allow us to get additional things accomplished more quickly. They make us more efficient by freeing up the energy-intensive mental processing required in complex decision making.[16] Hence, habits are a powerful evolutionary adaptation except, of course, when they stop serving us.[17] Habits can also strip us of our awareness of the wonder of life.

"We first make our habits, and then our habits make us" (John Dryden). The challenge is that people don't recognize when their patterns of thought no longer serve them. Due to an ever-evolving environment and differing stages of life, thought patterns which generated successful results for decades can start acting as governors that keep us from getting what we want in life. Old, counterproductive habits can all too easily leak into the months and years ahead, standing in the way of success. Indicators that your thinking habits need to change include being dissatisfied, experiencing angst, encountering systemic problems, and not achieving desires, among others. Ineffective thinking yields suboptimal results.

Your King knows that success lies in your awareness. You can only achieve what you can perceive. Fortunately, awareness can be improved. You are able take control of perception patterns, and their underlying thoughts, to serve you better. It is exactly these shifts in thinking that stand behind some of the greatest people and events in history. Choice of perspective often makes the entire difference, and this is possible only by becoming astutely aware.

Take Victor Frankl's life as an example. During World War II, Frankl survived three years interned at various German Nazi concentration camps, including six months at Auschwitz. Only one in thirty of those who entered the camps survived the ordeal. Frankl lived through the horrific experience and went on after the war to explain how he stayed alive. A student of human behavior, Frankl noticed that the outcome of the camp experience was not random. Those that survived tended to have one stark similarity. Each was careful to manage their thinking through an intentional shift in focus.

It is not that they didn't see the suffering as it was pervasive and poignant. However, survivors consciously shifted their point of focus. They found purpose in what was, by every definition, a dire and hopeless situation. Many lived to serve others, comforting and sacrificing what meager valuables they had. In general, survivors focused on controlling the only thing they had left—their ability to choose their own attitude.

Like Frankl, survivors found something to live for—if not others to serve, then a loved one to be reunited with, a new theory to share with the world, or a goal to achieve. In doing so, they chose possibility over hopelessness. As such, they were more likely to reap life then death.

Frankl understood the importance of choosing one's own perspective stating, "Sufficient proof that everything can be taken from a man but one thing: the last of the human freedoms—to choose one's attitude in any given set of circumstances, to choose one's own way."

Your thinking is solely your own. Thousands of stimuli come at you every moment, but you notice only a select few. To see how narrow your focus becomes, stop and take a moment to be still. Simply sit and do nothing. Feel yourself breathing, listen to the sounds in the room, and notice the temperature of the air around you, feel it on your skin. These stimuli and many others are always present but you have expanded your awareness and consciously shifted your attention. Habitual thought practices have you tuning out these and other, "more relevant," stimuli. Over time, these engrained patterns of thinking and responding can come at a cost. A person numb to the world around them could miss a fire smoldering, a tornado warning, or an intruder. Unproductive habits can limit our ways of seeing, thinking, and behaving.

Your mature King knows that every person's experience of the world depends on their awareness. Suboptimal, habitual thinking produces limitations, while active, conscious thinking creates potential. You have what you have and you are who you are, based on what you suppose. Therefore, to generate more success in life, you need to wrestle back control and become more aware.

How does one go about doing that? A helpful approach is to realize that you are not your thoughts. This can be accomplished by taking steps to intentionally expand your awareness.

One technique to do this is to stand back and watch your thoughts as if you were an unbiased, third-party or uninvolved observer. From this vantage, you let your thoughts pass by and allow them to just be. When practicing self-awareness, you are open to what is going on, cognizant of underlying meanings, and receptive to thinking in new and different ways.

Realize that you are not your thoughts.

Self-awareness practices and mindfulness meditation, where one learns to think in the present moment, have both been found effective in reducing mental noise while improving awareness of habitual thought patterns.[18]

Another technique to gaining control over patterned thoughts is to identify your subconscious commitments. To gain a better perspective, look at what you frequently complain about. Before I became a self-proclaimed, "recovering CEO," I often complained that I felt a lack of passion for my work. The job was, not surprisingly, hard and rather isolating. After realizing this was the eleventh position in my sixth career, I had become subconsciously committed to the idea that I would never find work I was passionate about. It was from this belief that that I created other issues in my life. With this idea in place, I avoided pursuing opportunities from the heart, and I gave up believing there was more. Unknowingly, to keep my belief in place, I was not willing to take any action which would make my belief untrue. To hold on to this perspective, I needed to remain stuck where I was—helpless to change, identifying only with my complaint. I went from a passionate young, enthusiastic go-getter to a miserable and passive complainer, all without realizing it.

We all have subconscious commitments. What counterproductive beliefs are you holding onto? To find out, write a few of your "favorite" complaints in the left-hand column of Thought Expander 4.1, Subconscious

<u>Commitments</u>. Take your major life grumbles and place them in the left-hand column. Everyone has complaints about themselves or their lives. Consider complaints about yourself that get in your way, situations that no longer work, or behaviors you don't like. Preferably, select issues that have been systemic and long-standing over which you have some control. (Note this exercise is not intended to address illness or trauma where professional help is recommended.)

There are always hidden advantages to maintaining suboptimal situations.

Now comes the fun part, next to each complaint, in the middle column, create a short lesson to teach others to achieve the same problems in their lives. Explain how they too could "be dysfunctional just like you." Feel free to poke fun at yourself, and be sarcastic. For example, in teaching another how to avoid passion in their work, I might encourage them to: "Take any job as long as it pays well," "Stay with boring work you don't like," "Believe no one likes what they do," "What you have is good enough," "Don't bother taking time to find what you love," or "The quickest way to ruin a hobby is to try to make a living at it," etc. We have all heard supposed pearls of wisdom like these. But such faux pearls have a hazy luster that will distract you from the best life has to offer.

Finally, in the right-hand column, make a frank assessment of what you might be subconsciously committed to. This might take some thought and reflection. I encourage you to spend some time here and dig deep. Often first impressions are valuable. Continuing my previous example, I might be committed to "Striving and never arriving," "Not worthy of enjoying the rewards of success," or "Using my work as an escape from dealing with important relationships." What are you committed to? Take your time, and think it through. Consider a diverse range of possibilities as you uncover the framework supporting your subconscious commitment.

Thought Expander 4.1: Subconscious Commitments

Complaints	Teach Others to Get Same Outcome	Subconscious Commitment
Complaint #1	Lesson #1	Commitment #1
Complaint #2	Lesson #2	Commitment #2
Complaint #3	Lesson #3	Commitment #3

The exercise might seem a bit silly. It is anything but. In some way, each of us is invested in the problems we experience. We derive some, albeit twisted, value from them. Therefore, understanding our involvement is critical. The purpose of this exercise is to make you aware of a few of your hidden mental habits and to provide you with a tool to pull those weeds. Doing so makes room for more healthy thought processes and an extra bountiful harvest in life.

But how do these counterproductive thoughts create value? To see this, take one of the subconscious commitments from Thought Expander 4.1, Subconscious Commitments, and write it again in the top header row of Thought Expander 4.2, Commitment Tradeoffs. Next, in the left-hand column identify at least three risks, or costs of keeping your current commitment. Next, in the right-hand column, identify at least three benefits or payoffs to keeping your current commitment.

Do you avoid exercise, because it more pleasurable to eat junk food and watch television? Do you spend too much time at work because you can control that situation better than you can your spouse or family? Do you avoid making needed changes in life because it seems easy? Be open, blunt, and honest when completing this exercise.

From my prior example, I was committed to the belief that I would never find work that I was passionate about. Assessing the risks and costs of this commitment is relatively straightforward. For me, they included being unhappy, experiencing depression, having limited outlets for personal growth and creativity. So why did I stay in this situation for years after I should have left? I stayed because there were significant benefits and payoffs. These included significant income, an impressive title, and the social prestige of the job. Benefits also included avoiding the fear of going out on my own and becoming an entrepreneur, of making hard decisions, and of being clear with myself. I put up with the negatives, because I wasn't ready and willing to give up the substantive positives.

Thought Expander 4.2: Commitment Tradeoffs

Subconscious Commitment:	
Risk/Cost to Keeping the Commitment	**Payoff/Benefit to Keeping the Commitment**
1)	1)
2)	2)
3)	3)
4)	4)
5)	5)

The cost-benefit exercise is valuable in shedding light on what is driving the outcomes we experience. People are extraordinarily good at identifying problems, but they are not so adept at seeing the personal benefits they are deriving by keeping these undesirable situations in place. This creates a perception imbalance studied in the field of evolutionary psychology. Evolutionary psychologists suggest that a preference to noticing threats is a leftover adaptation of the human psyche (Buss, 2000). These scientists propose that a constant attentive state tuned toward the possibility of negative outcomes allowed humans to survive a danger-ridden existence on the savanna and beyond. Unfortunately, this cognitive tendency continues even though we are now seldom exposed to life-threatening situations. As a result, people still tend to over-focus on negatives and under-emphasize positives. It is in deriving clarity around how our current situation benefits us that the seeds for both change, and our future success, can be found.

The risk of change often seems too big, instead of focusing on the risks, compare the benefits of staying the same versus the benefits of making change.

What did you realize when you focused on the pay-offs? If you give it some thought, you will notice there are always hidden advantages to maintaining suboptimal situations. If this were not the case, you wouldn't allow them to continue.

Your current commitment clearly benefits you, albeit in a dysfunctional way. Now that you are aware of your subconscious commitment—it has become a conscious choice. As such, it can no longer lurk behind the scenes doing damage without your permission. You can look at it and gain important clarity as to why this issue perpetuates. You have now set the stage for getting your subconscious commitment behind you and making a new, better one.

There are always benefits to avoiding change. It has been said that people are afraid of change. They aren't, they are afraid of the unknown. Specifically, they are afraid of loss. Researchers have shown that people are much more likely to work harder to avoid a loss then they are to achieve a gain. The behavior is known by economists as loss aversion (Kahneman &

Tversky, 1984). Unfortunately, this tendency creates an intellectual inertia of sorts that acts to keep people trapped in counterproductive habits. The risk of change often seems too big, especially when the benefits are unclear. Therefore, we tend to look at the risks of staying the same versus making change, forcing ourselves to choose between the devil we know and the one we don't. No wonder so many people are stuck in situations they don't like. Instead of focusing on the risks, compare the benefits of staying the same versus the benefits of making change.

> To make successful change, focus on the upside.

For example, if you don't exercise, you are, no doubt, well-aware that there are risks involved. These might include additional weight-gain, poor body tone, feeling lousy, and dying younger. But if you consider the alternative, you could note that exercising is a challenge. It might require that you get up earlier, reduce your free time, cost you money (e.g., membership or equipment), and possibly be hard, challenging, or even embarrassing. Here loss aversion encourages you to focus on the negatives of making a new commitment—not the benefits. It snuffs out needed change. Staying where you are seems safer and less risky when you compare the negatives of your options. As a result, change seems too hard or just not worth it.

To make successful change (i.e., a better thought process, belief, or behavior), it is more powerful to focus on the upside. Instead of looking only at the negatives, change is more readily accomplished by shifting toward a comparison of the positives. In comparing benefits, better decisions are made and motivation is piqued.

> The best approach to making change is to consciously realize the underlying reasons you do what you do.

To gain clarity, another exercise might prove helpful. In Thought Expander 4.3, Commitment Payoff, rewrite the subconscious commitment from the header of Thought Expander 4.2, Commitment Tradeoffs. Next, copy over the benefits and payoff items in the right-hand column of Thought Expander 4.2, Commitment Cost Benefit, to the left-hand column in Thought Expander 4.3, Commitment Payoff. Once complete, come up with a better commitment than the one you currently hold. For me, a better commitment would be that I could find work that I am passionate about and create a life I find engaging. Alternatively, if you see exercise as embarrassing, you could choose to believe instead that people will be impressed that you are making an effort. Finally, identify a few payoff/benefits of your new commitment and place them in the right-hand column. For me, payoffs included the joy of pursuing something of strong personal interest, experiencing increased energy, being excited to get up and go to work every day, and the promise of becoming all I can be. Take your time here, it is worth it.

Thought Expander 4.3: Commitment Payoff

Subconscious Commitment:	New Commitment:
Benefit/Payoff	**Benefit/Payoff**
1)	1)
2)	2)
3)	3)
4)	4)
5)	5)

It was, in fact, this comparison of positives that became a watershed event for me. When I lined up, side-by-side, the benefits of both commitments, my previous subconscious commitment held only fear-based items that required protecting and maintaining. Meanwhile, my new commitment held deeply meaningful benefits that were opportunity-based and focused on personal exploration and growth. This shift in perspective helped me change my commitment and, in so doing, my life.

So, how does this approach work to achieve better outcomes? First, by making your unproductive commitments conscious and considering how they benefit you, you can see, possibly for the first time, why you are dedicated to them. You start to understand and gain an appreciation for why you do what you do and the subsequent results that are showing up in your life. Second, by clearly assessing the benefits of a new, potential commitment you provide an apple-to-apple comparison detailing what you have to gain. Combined, this two-step process facilitates awareness and sets the stage for change.

Your mature King realizes that effective change starts with understanding. Most self-help methods to alter habits suggest that we simply stop doing one thing and start doing another. It is not that simple. Their approach to change

Change enlightened through understanding is more likely to happen.

requires significant, vigilant effort and the advantages remain unclear. It is often not readily obvious how the costs of change stack up against the benefits. While we may start off strong with good intentions, when stressors surface or enough time passes, it is often difficult to maintain the effort needed to engrain a new habit using these methods. It is much more likely we will fall back on old, comfortable ways, even when they are not in our best interest. Too often this approach to tackling change doesn't work, leaving us with a bad taste in our mouths and despair regarding future progress.

A better solution, initially, is to not pursue change, but to simply observe. That's right; I don't want you to do anything different right now. The best approach to making change is to first understand it. In consciously realizing the underlying reasons behind why you do what you do, you set the stage to permanently stop making suboptimal choices. So, don't change for now, simply see. Consider the benefits of better options that lie before you. In fully understanding the potential upsides, and the current downsides, the seeds for successful change are planted.

Change is better accomplished by putting thinking ahead of action, recognition ahead of force. Embracing possibility, you consciously recognize that you have a choice—you either have opportunities to capture or problems to overcome. No longer is a sacrifice required, but, rather, there is something better to be gained. Recognizing this, action toward a new, better way of being will become desired. This seed, once planted, will eventually experience the right conditions for it to grow. Change enlightened through understanding is more likely to happen even though it may take longer to realize than the brute force method.

> **Awareness is the child of consciousness and the father of every success.**

Everyone has habits of thought that no longer serve them. However, habits operate in the subconscious leaving you unaware when they go awry. You no longer consciously realize that you are acting in ways that don't serve you. Especially in challenging times, you think you are choosing all the important elements of your destiny when, in fact, you are not. The only result is a bevy of bad feelings that come from the disappointment of not achieving your desires.

The opportunity before you, and countless others, is to gain understanding and awaken. "Stay awake at all times" (Luke 21:36, ESV) and work on becoming the master of your thoughts by growing in self-awareness. Awareness is the child of consciousness and the father of every success.

Consider the example of two waiters working at a restaurant together. One waiter goes to work challenging himself to see how many people's days he can brighten. Meanwhile, the other waiter dreads the obnoxious people he will have to serve that day. They carry very different thought processes regarding their work. Even though they have the same job, the first is rewarded and the second punished. Each makes a choice. The only challenge is that neither of them likely realizes it. In both cases, each waiter generates his own experience. While, it is the second waiter who will suffer from his thinking, it is his very pain that acts as a sign post toward the path of needed change.

The habitual mind acts on what happens; the awakened mind asks what it can do differently. "It isn't what you have, or who you are, or where you are, or what you are doing that makes you happy or unhappy. It is what you think about" (Dale Carnegie). Success is the result of focusing on possibility not constraint, strength instead of weakness, what could be rather than what is.

Your mature King knows that to be truly successful you must become more aware. Everything works toward success when you awaken to the possibilities which permeate life. Our thoughts can be powerful allies when actively managed. Every alert moment is an opportunity to allow your wise King to reign more effectively.

Fortunately, what you think is up to you. Whether you think intentionally or reflexively is a choice. Thought is a powerful precursor to getting the good things out of life. Success is achieved when you take back your mental power--comprehending why you do what you do—and choosing ways of thinking that provide greater benefits and payoffs. Life is an amazing adventure when lived fully awake and aware.

BEHAVIOR 5: MAKING GOOD CHOICES

"If you think you can do a thing or think you can't, you are right."
— *Henry Ford*

Everything is a choice. How you will live, what you will accomplish, and who you will become are entirely up to you. Ultimately, you choose your life. Even if you avoid the decision, you've still made a choice. The question is are you living life or is life living you?

Life is lived one of two ways. At the extremes, people either see themselves as being in control and fully capable of securing what they want, or they feel that life is a process of accepting and dealing with whatever comes their way. For those in control, their thoughts and actions have a more direct impact than those who believe otherwise. The former are set for success, the latter, not so much.

The view you hold determines what you achieve in life.

Perspective is of fundamental import. The view you hold determines what you achieve in life. Fortunately, it is something you choose. What you believe, how you feel, and the way you think are entirely up to you. You decide many things about life including how much control you have. Significant personal power resides in this choice. Success is a function of where you focus. "Whatever is true, whatever is honorable, whatever is just, whatever is pure, whatever is lovely, whatever is commendable, if there is any excellence, if there is anything worthy of praise, think about these things" (Philippians 4:8; ESV).

Take your environment for example. It can be thought of as the aggregate atmosphere of all the external factors and constraints in which you operate. While you can't always choose the specific circumstances surrounding you, you do get to decide what they mean, how you respond to them, and how you live in light of them. That choice is a form of control. Certainly, the settings where you find yourself act on and influence you. Likewise, you too act on your environment, shaping and influencing it. It is the balance maintained between these two opposing forces that affect the success you achieve in life.

Psychologists denote this sense of feeling in charge—the capability to influence one's own environment—as perceived control (Thompson, 1981). Perceived control is an important idea with wide ranging implications. People who see themselves as being in control have different life outcomes. For example, they

Control your thinking and the world is yours.

tend to experience greater levels of health, happiness, and personal well-being.[19,20] Such people have been found to perform better and achieve greater results.[21] Intuitively, this makes sense. A person who believes their efforts can influence outcomes would be more likely to apply effort and, therefore, be more likely to alter the outcome. Via this mechanism, higher levels of perceived control translate into more accomplishments in life.

So how much control do you feel over your own life? The following Sense of Control Scale might provide some insight. In Thought Expander 5.1, Sense of Control, circle one number for each statement that indicates the extent to which you agree or disagree. Here, the answers range from strongly disagree at a score of one to strongly agree at a score of four. Remember, there is no right or wrong answer. After answering the ten questions, sum up each column and then total the four columns for a grand total.

Thought Expander 5.1: Sense of Control

Adapted Scale	Strongly Disagree	Disagree	Agree	Strongly Agree
1) I feel that I have little influence over the events in my life.	1	2	3	4
2) Worrying is a waste of time as what will be, will be.	1	2	3	4
3) Dealing with people successfully seems to be more the result of their own predilections rather than my actions.	1	2	3	4
4) It is a challenge for regular people to influence the actions of our country's leadership.	1	2	3	4
5) Success is primarily the result of getting good breaks.	1	2	3	4
6) Planning is unwise as things turn out to be a matter of luck.	1	2	3	4
7) Often I feel that I would be just as well off making decisions randomly.	1	2	3	4
8) When good or bad things happen, they are often due to chance.	1	2	3	4
9) Having life turn out well is a matter of good fortune—the result of being in the right place at the right time.	1	2	3	4
10) What happens in my life is going to occur irrespective of my actions.	1	2	3	4
Grand Total = ← Totals				

(Note these scales are for general insight only and have not been scientifically validated.)[22]

The average grand total score is 25, with a minimum of 10 and a maximum of 40. Where did you come out? People with scores over 25 likely have an external sense of control. They perceive life as something that happens to them and feel a diminished sense of influence over various outcomes. Conversely, people with scores under 25 tend to have an internal sense of control. They see their actions helping to drive the results they achieve in life. Internal sense-of-control people have higher levels of perceived control.

Fortunately, your mature King recognizes that you choose your sense of control. Understanding that you have direct influence over your life's outcomes predicates the success you achieve. Control your thinking and the world is yours.

Let me explain. During my final years as CEO, I was frustrated, stuck, and miserable. Unfortunately for my friends and family, I pretty much let everyone, except my bosses, know about it. I complained about the decisions being made, or not made, at the corporate level. I whined about the responsibility changes, product decisions, integration plans, backstabbing, and the general incompatibility of company cultures. This occurred so often and with such regularity that even I, eventually, got tired of listening to myself complain. However, quietly suffering and stuffing the issue down inside also didn't make the problem go away. I am embarrassed to say, this complain and stuff-it process went on for years.

Choice is your birthright; good choices are your responsibility.

Then one day while driving home from work, I had an epiphany. It was so vivid that I remember exactly where I was, under the I400 viaduct on Transit Road, headed south, in West Seneca, New York. It was there that I realized that I was choosing my situation. That's all I did—and it changed my world.

In that moment, I recognized that every morning I was making a choice to go back to work. I was getting up, and with my own free will engaging in a non-tenable career, doing a job I dreaded. Prior to this new realization, I had attributed my every problem to the people I worked with, our parent company, the industry we served, and/or the terrible post 9/11 economy. I blamed, judged, and accused. I subsisted on a diet of anger, frustration, and disappointment. I believed that I was the victim and, as such, saw my life as out of my control. My great epiphany was the realization that I was not a victim of my situation, but that I was an active contributor—one who permitted, engaged, and allowed it, by not choosing to leave.

From that point forward, I was no longer angry or frustrated. How could I be? I was causing the problem. Every morning from that point forward, I was relieved. When I went to work, I did so knowing I was selecting it over other options. I was choosing the security of a paycheck versus the risk of starting my own business; I was choosing being comfortable versus following my heart; I was choosing wealth over personal growth.

My new realization was a stroke of genius. In that minor shift of perspective, I regained my power. Since the situation was my doing and therefore my responsibility, I now had complete control over it. So, for the first time in a long time, I grabbed the steering wheel with both hands. A floodgate of vigor seemed to open fueled by years of pent-up energy. It wasn't a week later I had framed out an exit plan. I figured out how much money I needed to save to accomplish the plan, then I identified eight potential next step careers I wanted to try, and I even set dates for these goals, including my deadline to exit.

Taking back my power made all the difference. Change flowed almost effortlessly as a result of recognizing that I had a choice. "Again and again, the impossible problem is solved when we see that the problem is only a tough decision waiting to be made" (Robert Schuller). My life was mine to give away or to manage. The decision was up to me—it always was.

Everyone has challenges in life that stand in their way. The secret to overcoming them is to understand where you have a choice and to wrestle back that sense of control. Choice is your birthright; good choices are your responsibility.

People with high levels of perceived control succeed because they are more willing to try.

To gain clarity, think about a long-standing situation in your life where you feel like a victim. It could be that someone in your life bullies you or treats you poorly; it could be that you have been stuck in a dead-end or low paying job. Write that situation in the header of Thought Expander 5.2, Shifting Perspective. In the left-hand column entitled Limiting Factors, expound on this limitation by identifying up to five reasons it gets in the way of you living the life you want. Now shift into a state of control, this is the fun part. In the right-hand column, assume you are choosing the constraint—fully complicitous and willing to have it in your life (hint, you are). Next, list at least five ways can you could potentially use the current situation to get more of what you want out of life. Consider a wide-range of options and benefits. For example, being bullied can build character and also teach you to stand up for yourself, setting more healthy boundaries. Alternatively, your current situation could be an incentive to set new goals, a step toward making needed change, or motivation for securing a better future. Every positive perspective is available to you. The field is replete with four leaf clovers.

Thought Expander 5.2: Shifting Perspective

Situation:	
Limiting Factors	**Choose Instead**
1)	1)
2)	2)
3)	3)
4)	4)
5)	5)

Repeat this exercise with any life constraint you feel manages you. Choose to take your power back. The cost of avoiding responsibility is the loss of future potential. Choice is power. Don't squander yours by believing any part of your life is beyond your control.

You have the ability to influence and improve every situation. Each constraint is simply an opportunity, depending on the perspective you hold. Success is up to you.

A major reason people with high levels of perceived control tend to be more successful is that they are more willing to try. Effort acts in ways to influence the potential outcomes, making people who feel in control more likely to succeed.[23] As we will explore in the Warrior section, better outcomes result from those who try harder, longer, and more often. Accomplishment is seldom the by-product of luck. "Luck is what happens when preparation meets opportunity" (Lucius Annaeus Seneca).

Adversity is not the problem, the beliefs you choose about it are.

Another reason people with greater perceived control are more successful is that they believe their efforts will help them succeed. They create a self-fulfilling prophecy surrounding their lives which then causes them to act in ways, both consciously and subconsciously, that make the foretold come true. Accepting their ability to control, they establish their power to do something, and then act in ways that confirm their beliefs.

Your mature King realizes that control matters. Psychological researchers have validated the importance of control in numerous ways. Their study on dogs in the mid 1970s, for instance, showed that some dogs stopped trying to avoid electrical shocks even when an escape was possible.[24] These dogs laid down, whimpered, and gave in to the periodic shocks. They no longer made any effort to escape the unpleasant situation. Scientists believe this occurred because some of the dogs had given up and become helpless. They no longer saw options to escape the shock even after the situation was altered, and the dogs could have easily avoided further discomfort. In humans, feeling a diminished sense of control is related to greater instances of hypertension even when corrected for other diseases and poor living habits.[25]

Not being able to influence one's environment is problematic for both animals and humans. A telling experiment on rats provides an insight into this dynamic.[26] Three groups of rats were injected with cancer cells which typically had resulted in the rats developing cancer approximately half the time. One of these groups was a baseline group and, as expected, 54% got cancer. The second and third groups, also injected with cancer cells, received electrical shocks. However, in the second group the rats had no way to stop the shock, while the in the third group the rats could stop the electrical current through various manipulations.

What do you think happened? Not surprisingly, the second group of rats got even more tumors with 73% going on to develop cancer, almost 20% more than the baseline. A lack of control over their environments and the stress associated with it was clearly not healthy. But what about the third group that could influence the electrical shock? Since they were experiencing stress and discomfort, shouldn't they also show some increase levels of cancer? No. Surprisingly, only 37% got cancer, more than 10% below the baseline. Both differences are statistically significant—and profoundly meaningful. Having perceived control during adversity appears to actually improve health. Therefore, the adversity is not the problem, the beliefs you choose about it are.

Consider the mindset brought to changing a habit. You are more likely to beat a habit if you refer to it as something "I don't do," rather than as something "I can't do."[27] The language used indicates the perspective held. The "I don't do" statement is more powerful because it indicates that you perceive yourself as in control therefore, change is more readily accomplished. The "I can't do" statement indicates that you see your habit as controlling as and more powerful than you. From this vantage point, change will require forceful effort and, as a victim, you will be less likely to overcome the habit.

People who procrastinate inadvertently give away their personal power.

A sense of control matters beyond simply knowing how to go about changing habits. Someone who experiences serious trauma or adversity has a choice as well. They can extract from their trauma a sense of destiny, or they can become a victim. Those who do well are those who wrestle with the adversity and manage to manipulate it to their advantage. Examples include the crippled person who partakes in athletic competition, the terminal patient who inspires others, and the philanthropist who uses their assets to change the wrongs they themselves experienced. In overcoming, each takes control of what remains and leverages their experience to flourish and prosper. They do not let their experience get the upper hand, and they won't lie down whimpering and quit.

Your King understands that control matters. Gaining control is the answer to achieving your objectives, whatever they are. A sense of power not only expands what you can achieve, but it is life affirming. Control has a profound influence on well-being and life satisfaction.

Having taught business strategy at the university level, I was regularly faced with students who ceded their personal control. One area where this was readily evident was through procrastination. While this approach was arguably motivating for some, my experience was that it consistently led to lower quality work and less learning in the classroom. People who procrastinated accomplished less at school, work, and life. Why?

Events are neither positive nor negative until you attribute meaning to them.

People who procrastinate inadvertently give away their personal power and control. By waiting until the last minute to complete their work, they sacrifice their ability to influence and manage the situation. They shift from a position of proactive management to one of reactive responding. As such, procrastinators give their personal power over to the vagaries of their environment. Using deadlines and panic to motivate, comes at a price. Procrastinators, in all walks of life, are less likely to succeed. To live life regularly waiting until last minute to do what needs to be done, is a choice—a poor one.

Now consider those who choose proactivity in life. When I ask these "schedulers," among students and CEOs alike, what they do, they are go-getters, deciding when and where to act in all areas of life, constantly shaping their worlds to their advantage. To a lesser degree than the rats studied earlier, schedulers also feel the pressure of deadlines and the stress to achieve, but they control it. In so doing, they get a deep sense of satisfaction and accomplishment when finishing a project with plenty of time remaining to reflect on it, modify, or polish it as need be. Schedulers choose to keep their power and it pays off.

Every person has two choices. You can be proactive and motivate yourself, or you can be reactive and allow your environment to motivate you. Which do you think serves you better and ultimately allows you to become more successful?

Another way to cede control in life is with your feelings. Many people rely on their emotions to tell them how they feel. It is normal for such feelings such as sadness, anger, or worry to happen, but problematic when they don't go. What you might not realize is that your feelings can be consciously influenced. There is no condition, circumstance, event, or situation that has the power to make you feel one way or another. By choosing how you perceive any situation, you take control of how you feel.

Your wise King appreciates that events are neither positive nor negative until you attribute meaning to them. Ultimately, you choose what every comment, situation, and experience means to you. Every event is neutral and the reaction to it a separate happening. It is through choice that we create or constrain possibility, that we maximize or limit potential. For "nothing is either good or bad, but thinking makes it so" (Shakespeare).

> It is within your ability to control how you feel.

To better understand this concept, think of a negative feeling that you regularly experience, say anxiety, for example, and write it in Thought Expander 5.3, <u>Emotion Drivers</u>. Next think about what you believe that might be contributing to that feeling. With anxiety, you might be thinking that you will fail in some way. Detail that in the second row. Then, in the third row, consider what you could believe instead. What if you considered every challenge common to all and each as an opportunity for growth? In this way, adverse feelings can lead you to living in better ways.

Thought Expander 5.3: Emotion Drivers

Negative Feeling	
Belief feeling comes from	
What you could believe instead	

We all have the opportunity to decide the level of influence our experiences, thoughts and feelings have over us. Most people allow their feelings to run their lives. We have all been surprised by people who are set off by, or overreact to, the littlest thing. Living reactive to our feelings is volatile and unstable. Ultimately, we each choose to be subject to our feelings or to rule over them.

Success comes from taking charge of your life.

I am not proposing that you stuff or ignore your emotions, or that it is possible not to have any feelings at all. Clearly, that wouldn't be healthy or reasonable. Suppressing emotions only causes them to linger longer and acts to reduce well-being.[28] I am suggesting that you recognize your emotions, and then manage them in a way that is most productive. Sometimes productive means accepting the emotion, as with the death of a loved one, and experiencing the grieving process. Sometimes, productive means changing the beliefs behind an emotion. Other times, productive means taking charge of your emotions and choosing to see the situation in a way that results in a more productive self.

Are you in charge or are your emotions? Emotions run more of our lives than most of us would be happy to admit. Unfortunately, if you let your feelings run your life, you become subject to every minor perturbation, blown about like a leaf in the wind. Negative feelings color your viewpoints and distort your decisions. Emotion-driven people can be erratic, unpredictable, and miserable. But master your emotions and the world is your oyster. Smith Wigglesworth, the British evangelist, was onto something when he famously quipped, "I never ask Smith Wigglesworth how he feels; I tell him how he feels!"

Your inner King knows that it is within your ability to control how you feel. While a significant portion of every person's psyche is relatively fixed, researchers in positive psychology have found that each of us has a tremendous influence over our well-being, of which emotions are a major component.[29] Studies on identical twins indicate that approximately half of your dispositional well-being is genetic and another 10% due to defining life experiences. That means a full 40% of your disposition is changeable through effortful action and developed awareness.[30] The success of cognitive behavior therapy (CBT) in psychological therapy supports the idea that you can choose. By looking at situations differently, by choosing to reframe perspective, CBT has provided substantial improvement in the lives of millions.

If you are not in charge of your feelings, they will run you ragged. Emotions not under your rule will weaken your King. This is especially true with powerful emotions such as fear, anger, doubt, and desire. To be more accomplished, you must learn to avoid following your feelings around, and reacting to your life. Instead, your mature King wants to understand, control, and preside over them. Outside events cannot make you feel one way or another. Feelings require consent. "We get to choose how we're going to live - what level of energy, what level of vibrancy, what level of excitement" (Brendon Burchard). We are in control, unless we choose not to be.

People achieve more success when they take charge of life. Life is a free-will offering. You decide what you believe, how you think, and what you will feel. The particular behaviors and actions that result drive outcomes that correlate with these decisions. Ultimately, you decide your course. "Life and prosperity, death and destruction...blessings and curses" (Deuteronomy 30:15-19; NIV). Options lay before you; you choose. If you are consistently getting bad results, it is in your power to change them. You can change how you see them, what they mean to you, and what you can do about them.

Success comes from taking charge of your life. Your inner King knows that everything is a choice. Most people take what life gives them, instead of living life on purpose. You know better. You now understand that success is a result of your perceived relationship with the world. You get to choose. Choose better. Decide in favor of yourself. As the mature sovereign of your kingdom, take full responsibility. Preside over your life, rule it, and make it what you want it to be. You fully control your destiny. Health, happiness, and success are yours—if you so choose.

THE KING

Your King recognizes that success comes from understanding your role, taking responsibility, focusing attention, becoming more aware, and making good decisions. Developing a wise King is essential to productive thinking and good choices. While focused awareness and a deeper understanding of yourself are key components of success, wisdom is impaired without the ability to innovate and create new knowledge. New challenges and fresh ideas are crucial to thriving. As such, your King will stagnate without its companion aspect…

ASPECT II: THE INSPIRED WIZARD

Wiz·ard [wiz-erd]. A person with special powers; one who is wonderful or excellent. To conjure or call to mind; to create, invent, or ideate.

ASPECT II: THE INSPIRED WIZARD

The Wizard, the King's partner, is the part of us that envisions and ideates. It is the creative aspect present within each person's psyche. Your Wizard imagines, dreams, invents, and plans. It identifies innovative ways to live and exciting things to achieve. Your inner Wizard sees new options and deciphers ways to manifest them. This part of you explores and exploits potential.

Spectral opposites, the King and Wizard represent the "know" and "create" aspects of life, respectively. The King understands what is, while the Wizard seeks to invent what could be. Success is achieved when they both exist in harmony, reinforcing and supporting each other in a state of balance. You must have knowledge in order to achieve, but you also must capture possibility in order to live successfully.

The Wizard's creativity advances your King understanding. It takes what is and strives to create what can be. Taking into account the knowledge of the King, the ability of the Warrior, and the passion of the Monk, the Wizard crafts your life's course. From a potentially infinite number of possibilities, your Wizard divines your purpose and strives explore the unknown.

If this aspect of success is passive, deflated, or immature, your success will be stifled. When you see few options, can't plan, are stuck, or are making scant progress, it is an indication that your Wizard is underdeveloped. In this state, your Wizard is not able to properly help you identify and plan for a future that is in your best interest. Conversely, when you are frequently distrustful, take advantage of others, or find yourself rationalizing your actions, it is an indication that your Wizard has become aggressive and that you are over relying on it and sacrificing valuable wisdom from other, more appropriate aspects such as your King, Warrior, or Monk.

To see where your Wizard stands, do the following exercise. Check up to ten items from any of the three boxes below that best describe emotions you most commonly experience or one's that you find most challenging and problematic. When answering, consider not only what you think, but what others say about you as well.

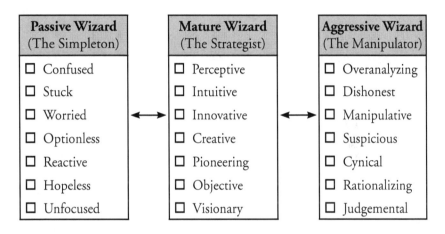

Passive Wizard (The Simpleton)	Mature Wizard (The Strategist)	Aggressive Wizard (The Manipulator)
☐ Confused	☐ Perceptive	☐ Overanalyzing
☐ Stuck	☐ Intuitive	☐ Dishonest
☐ Worried	☐ Innovative	☐ Manipulative
☐ Optionless	☐ Creative	☐ Suspicious
☐ Reactive	☐ Pioneering	☐ Cynical
☐ Hopeless	☐ Objective	☐ Rationalizing
☐ Unfocused	☐ Visionary	☐ Judgemental

Now look at where most of your marks reside. If there are more items checked on the left-hand side of the graphic, then your Wizard is likely underdeveloped. This section of the book will help you develop an inspired Wizard.

Alternatively, if most of the circled items tend toward the right-hand side of the graphic, your Wizard is probably used to the point where it can be counterproductive. An aggressive Wizard, or Manipulator, tends to compensate for unaddressed weakness in the King, Warrior, or Monk. While this section will most certainly be of value, it is important that you also identify which other aspects(s) might be suboptimal. Focusing and strengthening these aspects will level and restore balance thereby reducing the need and tendency toward overreliance on your Wizard in ways that do not fully serve you.

To be successful in life, your inner Wizard must be both mature and inspired. As such, your Wizard can help you achieve your dreams. A mature Wizard knows how to develop a path that is right for you. It can weigh personal strengths, interests, and aspirations to generate a range of innovative and challenging opportunities. An inspired Wizard is a master of possibility—one essential to achieving success in your life. Envisioning potentiality, the Wizard plans and sets goals. It creates and brings into being what is not.

Like the King, there are five major behaviors that strengthen an inspired and savvy Wizard. Your mature Wizard knows how to (6) follow your spirit, (7) look far ahead, (8) dream bigger, (9) create a plan, and (10) envision success. We will explore these five success behaviors, in turn, throughout the pages of this section.

BEHAVIOR 6: FOLLOWING YOUR SPIRIT

"Doing what you love is the cornerstone of having abundance in your life."
— *Dr. Wayne Dyer*

The meaningful life requires a purposeful goal. Your Wizard under-stands that to be successful, you must listen to your heart and pursue your interests, desires, and dreams. The good life is a result of honoring your spirit.

Do you live an unfulfilled exis-tence? Are you trapped in a career you don't like or stuck in a situation you barely find tolerable? Maybe you are no longer pursuing your desires and dreams, going through life in neutral, coasting and settling for the status quo.

People who follow their spirits are the wealthiest among us.

Experiencing an ache of dissatisfaction that cannot be directly attributed to anything in particular, you may have a nagging sense something is wrong. You just don't know what it is or what to do about it. Unfortunately, the underlying angst often won't subside with time instead, it will get worse. Curious if others feel this way, you wonder if something is missing.

Perhaps you have stopped listening to your heart.

To endure an average life of mediocre satisfaction is uncomfortable, un-acceptable, and unnecessary. I can think of nothing worse than to get to the end of life only to realize you never really lived. It would have been better if you had sailed off for your treasure and were dashed on the rocks or starved on a deserted island. At least, your dream would have been given a chance.

People who follow their spirits are the wealthiest among us. If you aren't following your spirit, now is the time to do something about it. But how do you go about it? While some people can readily articulate what their heart calls them to do, the rest of us have to figure it out. We have to rekindle our spirit, awaken our hearts, and find our genius.

It is surprisingly easy to delineate. As many high school students trying to select careers are shown, the trick is to identify your interests and passions and compare them against your strengths and talents—your success lies at the intersection.

Interests and passions are things you love doing. They are intriguing and energizing, and you find them enjoyable and rewarding. Frequently, they are things you dream about doing or activities you may already work into your life outside of work. Often, you pursue them simply for the joy of it. How you spend your time and money are often indicators of your interests and passions.

Identify your interests and passions and compare them against your strengths and talents—your success lies at the intersection.

Complementary to interests and passions are your strengths and talents. Strengths and talents are the natural skills or aptitudes you possess. They represent areas where you excel. I became a chemical engineer because I was good at problem solving and liked both physics and chemistry. To figure out in what areas you may flourish, consider what things you do unusually well, relative to other people.

Your inner Wizard realizes that personal genius lies where strengths meet interests and talents interact with passions. Often, it is in this very place we forget ourselves by becoming fully-engaged. This psychological experience is known as "flow" (Nakamura & Csikszentmihalyi, 2002). Flow is a unique juxtaposition where one's skills match well the task at hand. Here, the edge of a person's ability meets the activity's challenge in a positive, synergistic way. Time passes quickly, almost unnoticed, as one fully connects in this place. Living in a state of flow is indicative of a heart at play.

To exemplify your best vocational options, take a moment to complete Thought Expander 6.1, Interests & Talents. In the left-hand column entitled Interests & Passions identify a few interests or passions you hold. These often answer the questions "I am inspired by…" or "I am excited about…" Next, in the right-hand column entitled Strengths & Talents, list your strengths and talents. These are the things you are good at or that come easily to you. As you complete the Thought Expander, consider that there are two rows for you to fill-in from three different periods in your life—when you were a child, a young adult, as well as yourself today. These three stages are included because deep personal interests can get lost as we grow.

Thought Expander 6.1: Interests & Talents

Interests & Passions	Strengths & Talents
1. (child):	1. (child):
2. (child):	2. (child):
3. (adolescent):	3. (adolescent):
4. (adolescent):	4. (adolescent):
5. (today):	5. (today):
6. (today):	6. (today):

Now, sit back and look at the list. Notice any patterns? Often, our interests and passions align well with our strengths and talents. This is not at all surprising. People like to spend time doing things they are good at. It is this lack of alignment between interests and what is often required in a job that is responsible for millions of miserable people. Are you engaging these dimensions in your life today? Is there a strong interest you are not honoring?

Unfortunately, subjective reviews like this can be distorted. Psychologists have long recognized that self-generated assessments can be systematically flawed and differ substantially from reality. Strengths and talents, in particular, are one area where people tend to mislead themselves. In a large study of students, it was found that 70% of them believed they had above average leadership skills while only 2% felt they were below average.[31] Similarly in another study, 60% of the students rated themselves in the top 10% of their class and 25% rated themselves in the top 1%.[32] As ridiculous as this statement is, it appears human's harbor strong self-image biases.

To reduce that myopia, there are two steps you can take to improve accuracy of the assessment. First, you can take into account the input of others. Throughout life, people have been giving you information about yourself. You may have discounted these comments as the very things that impress others often don't seem like a big deal to us. That is because our strengths and talents often come easily. Yet, the input of others can be an important indicator regarding where we can head to reawaken our hearts. As you solicit the feedback of those whom you know well and trust, listen carefully for new insights and possibilities. In Thought Expander 6.2, Additional Abilities identify additional strong points and abilities that others have consistently said you are good at.

Thought Expander 6.2: Additional Abilities

Strengths	Talents
1. (child):	1. (child):
2. (adolescent):	2. (adolescent):
3. (today):	3. (today):

Second, consider your golden shadows. The shadow is psychologist Carl Jung's (1960) description of the parts of ourselves that we suppress and deny. This occurs in response to our upbringing, socialization, and life experiences. These are typically dark forces that act to sabotage life. However, there is another type of shadow. The golden shadow is a reflection of the constructive talents or abilities we have, that, for one reason or another, we have not valued or developed. You golden shadows offer important clues to your hidden genius.

> Living in a state of flow is indicative of a heart at play.

To identify your golden shadows, you need to identify what it is about others that most impresses and inspires you. Often these are the things that amaze, captivate, and astonish you. They are abilities you wholeheartedly appreciate and admire. Ones you wish you had.

For example, in college I was always very impressed by one of my fraternity brothers who lived life his own way. He found unique ways to get by and pay his bills. One year he worked at the food court simply because he could eat for free. Later, he climbed the sales ranks and started his own company. He knew how to negotiate, was self-confident, and unafraid to live life on his own terms. His approach to life resonates with me even after all these years. However, I took the safe route, punching the corporate time clock and paying my dues while always feeling I was missing out on something. I reflected on this during a retreat some two decades later and realized this was exactly who I wanted to be. This way of life was my golden shadow—and today it is my life.

What you probably don't realize is that what most impresses you about others is a golden shadow that exists in you. You have interests, talents, and abilities in these areas you are not utilizing. Each admiration indicates a hidden, underdeveloped talent; a strength or ability lying dormant, in wait for your discovery. Your golden shadows reflect aspects of the self that have not been fully recognized, appreciated, and honored. Each is a possible new direction of spirit, a potential gateway to the heart.

What is it that really impresses you about others? Think about different people in your life who amaze you in some way. In Thought Expander 6.3, Golden Shadows, detail what impresses you and the associated strengths and talents they characterize.

Thought Expander 6.3: Golden Shadows

Person's Name	What Impresses Me	Abilities

Each of these people's strengths and talents, likely reside in you, as well. Albeit ignored, malnourished, and underdeveloped, each golden shadow represents a vein of untapped potential, ready to be mined. Do any of your golden shadows inspire you to do something different or become someone new?

Combined, the three prior Thought Expanders provide a roadmap to rekindling your spirit and awakening your heart. Your mature Wizard knows that to be fulfilled, you must find a life that engages you. This often occurs where your interests leverage your abilities and your passions synergize with your talents. By taking advantage of this unique juxtaposition, you are better able to grow in alignment with your nature. Doing so greatly increases your ability to be successful in life. Not only can you better achieve your potential, but you will be happier in the process.

But where, specifically, can you put these potencies to work? Is there a life you wish to live, a career or vocation you have in mind? If not, use the prior exercises to complete the left-hand column in Thought Expander 6.4, <u>Matching Interests to Ability</u>. List two of the talents you identified by yourself, two garnered from the input of others, and two from the golden shadow exercise. Then for each item, brainstorm possible lives that would fit your strengths and talents and be of interest to you. Enter those in the right-hand column. When answering, consider times in life when you were most fulfilled, satisfied, and happy. Look to your childhood, early adolescence, college years, or young adult life for ideas. Also be sure to consider options that will invoke the interests and passions you outlined in Thought Expander 6.1, <u>Interests & Talents</u>, in identifying your options.

> **In selecting a life that is right for you, it is essential that your passion be stirred.**

Finally, ask yourself, the following: "If I could do anything with my life, and was guaranteed I would not fail, what would it be?" "What have I always wanted, but never gotten?" Focus on what energizes and fascinates you. Consider what brings you joy or satisfaction, and write that in the bottom row. "Let your deepest desires direct your aim. Set your sights far above the 'reasonable' target. The power of purpose is profound only if you have a desire that stirs the heart" (Price Pritchett).

Thought Expander 6.4: Matching Interests to Ability

Strengths & Talents	Potential Future Life
1. (self):	
2. (self):	
3. (others):	
4. (others):	
5. (shadow):	
6. (shadow):	
What would you do if you couldn't fail?	

Congratulations, you are one of the blessed ones to ever go through this process and invest the necessary time to purposefully choose meaningful direction for their lives. University placement officials say that students often spend more time researching a car they want purchase than they spend researching their career. In another example, a major clothing retailer surveyed almost 2,500 women, ages 16 to 60, and found they spend

14 to 16 minutes per day, an average of one year of their lives, deciding what to wear.[33] Discovering how to align your life with your spirit is time well spent.

Similarly, people often make decisions based on non-relevant factors. Researchers have found that people tend to select careers based on the similarity between names, with more feminine sounding names avoiding math and more masculine sounding names gravitating toward it.[34] Similarly, people are more likely to live in cities that sound similar in name (Louis and Louise more commonly reside in St. Louis) and take jobs that are related (Dennis and Denise are more likely to be dentists).[35]

I wonder how many careers are picked because, "It sounds good," "My friends are," or "It is available." I suspect such unstructured decision-making processes are the plight of many and a recipe for discontent. This might be the reason why the average American changes jobs approximately once every three years.[36]

The end result is that too many people do not put in the effort required to make high-quality life decisions. They don't do the necessary due diligence by taking reasonable steps in analyzing a decision before committing to it. In my merger-and-acquisition years, we bought dozens of companies. In every instance, we did a very thorough review of the business to ensure we were investing wisely. How much more valuable are our lives? Do your homework thoroughly so you can choose wisely.

In selecting a life that is right for you, it is essential that your passion be stirred. Before taking a leap, research is needed. Read about various vocations, find people who do it for a living, assess what you might like or not like about the work. Become familiar. After that, find people who excel in that field and talk with them. People are often thrilled to talk about themselves and their vocations. Such steps will build a strong foundation for informed decision making.

To get a better read, it is also invaluable to sample various options. Much can be learned by trying something related to an area of interest. This approach may require some creativity and flexibility but also generates valuable insights. For example, consider working for no pay or doing something that provides relevant experience, even if it is not exactly what you seek. Pursue your interests through charity involvement, part-time work, hobbies, and affiliated groups. Such experiences will help ensure your passions are given a fertile environment where they can grow into achievements, accomplishments, and success.

When I left my CEO position, I had a range of interests I wanted to explore. For two decades, I gazed longingly at the green grass on the other side of the proverbial fence. During that time, I made a list that included teaching, writing, speaking, training, strategic consulting, CEO advising, retreat facilitation, and graduate school among others. From this, I formulated a meaningful way to test out each opportunity. I started a monthly newsletter, created and gave a few inspirational speeches, joined a global training organization, took a couple of strategic consulting jobs, became a certified, life coach, facilitated dozens of corporate and group retreats, taught college courses, and took classes in philosophy and psychology. It was a valuable exploratory process through which I learned a great deal about myself.

Surprises lurked everywhere. I came to realize that some careers were much better fits with my interests than others. As an illustration, I got a part-time adjunct professorship position at New York State University teaching business strategy. Teaching sounded really cool. I would get to spend time with bright young minds brimming with energy. We would discuss the latest innovative, business theories, and I would inspire them to succeed while enjoying the romantic campus experience. The experience wasn't anything like that. I found the material was dry and boring, since it was well-established and familiar to me. Worse, many of the kids didn't want to be there, were tired, and often were distracted by the electronic devices of the day. The class was a means to an end. I found this frustrating. Worse, adjunct pay was abysmal and, as an outsider, there was little or no camaraderie with other professors. Needless to say, teaching was a poor fit.

So what would have happened if I hadn't tried teaching first? There is a distinct possibility I could have walked into a worse career than the one I was leaving. What if the job required a special degree? I may have invested years of my life before realizing the direction was wrong. I could have easily uprooted my family, passed on other good opportunities, and spent years aligning my life to capture the teaching dream, only to have secured a job that was wrong, unfulfilling, or a mistake. What a waste of time and energy that would have been—and yet, this is the path trod by many.

Another common career selection technique is to do something because it pays well. Income is a particularly sticky trap. It is easy to put your head before your heart when it comes to income. Clearly, if you are subject to abject poverty, then earning a dollar any way possible makes sense. However, for most of us, choosing a job simply because it pays well is not a good idea. How great would it be if everyone found work that was engaging, meaningful, and fulfilling? Life is far too short. There are simply too many creative ways to make a living to tolerate being miserable. Sacrificing your happiness is not worth it. Consider someone you know who has been unhappy in their work for a long period of time. What has it done to them? Do they inspire you or terrify you? Is that what you want?

The biggest challenge with money is that it appears enduring, but money is actually temporal and can move on quickly. A primary motivator behind the success of a large number of self-made millionaires is that they suffered deep privation early in life. To keep this from ever happening again, they work very hard in order to create wealth. On my pre-retreat surveys, worries about money are frequently noted. The vast majority of CEOs agree readily with the statement: "I have achieved financial independence, and I am afraid of losing it." Conversations reveal that they see wealth as a form a security. It protects them. However, wealth is a mirage. Security can never be adequately achieved through physical means. Peace of mind can't be purchased. That is one reason why no amount of money ever seems like enough.

> **Money is a useful servant, but it is an evil master and a pitiful god.**

Research supports this idea. Regardless of how much wealth people have, if you ask them to indicate how much is "enough" they will tell you it is 25-75% more than they have now. This means that if you have $50,000, then a $100,000 should be adequate; while those with $500,000 need a cool $1 million. But does it end at some point? Can we eventually get enough?

Many CEOs, especially those who experienced deprivation, find this question particularly challenging. Regardless of their current net worth, they often push for more—just to be safe. So it shouldn't be a surprise that one client indicated that the $20 million he amassed wasn't enough after all, as he reset his sights on achieving $50 million. Taken to a natural conclusion, it becomes obvious that enough is a slippery concept. There can't ever be enough. Peace and security require faith—neither of which can be purchased.

Money is a useful servant, but it is an evil master and a pitiful god. Using money as a proxy to acquire security or peace of mind is a recipe for disappointment and unhappiness. I know, setting out to be a millionaire, and accomplishing it early in life, let me see clearly the void such a goal creates. No meaning, purpose, or passion resulted no matter how much wealth I accumulated. My barn was full but my soul barren.

When solicited, wealthy CEOs conceded that money can be fleeting. When asked "How much would you spend to get better if you, or a loved one, were terminally ill?" "All of it" is the usual answer. In fact, researchers have found that medical problems are the leading cause of bankruptcies in the United States resulting in 62% of the economic collapse experienced by families.[37] This brings up an interesting point. Money engages the mind and, in so doing, distracts us from matters of the heart, all too often causing us to sacrifice our essence. For, "What do you benefit if you gain the whole world but lose your own soul?" (Matthew 16:26, NLT). For those who love money, the problem is that it can't love you back.

To live fully, pursue what interests and excites you.

Early on as CEO, I realized the job wasn't a good fit for me. Not surprisingly, while I didn't like the job, the money was excellent. I decided that I would work the job for a couple years, save some money, and then pursue something that fit better with my skills and interests, something I was passionate about. One year became three, and then three became five. Over-focused on the security I thought money brought, I took seven long years to break away. As fate would have it, I left my CEO position in mid-2008. Just a few months later, the stock market crashed, and I lost half my net worth. Ironically, my financial losses were exactly equal to the money I saved during my time as a CEO. This was an eye-opening experience and a valuable life lesson.

After the Great Recession started, I had nothing to show for the seven years I spent working a job that made me miserable. Had I done something I was passionate about, something that interested me, or something with meaning, no economic condition could have taken the years of joy away. Essentially, I sacrificed my life for the protection I thought wealth would provide, and I paid the price. Are you doing something similar?

Pursuing riches for riches sake clouds your ability to follow your heart. Wealth can also delay the realization that we are going down the wrong life path. In making life easier, money placates natural drives. Filling life with pleasantries and distractions—it can create a psychic slumber. Wealth, with its shiny bobbles and its noisemaking toys, begs to be doted on, making it hard to hear the heart.

Money is transient and fickle. It comes and goes. There is nothing wrong with wealth, per se. It is "The love of money (that) is the root of all evil" (Timothy, 6:10, KJV). Acquired as the by-product of creating value for others and managed wisely, wealth is an excellent tool to help us live well.

Success requires discipline—a regular willingness to see and use money as a tool that enables, not a goal or destination. Used well, wealth provides unique access to a life fully-lived in concordance with the spirit.

As a general rule of thumb, to achieve victory in life, avoid working for money alone. To live fully, pursue what interests and excites you. Pursue your passion, and the money will follow.

People who do what they love have a huge advantage. Because they more readily engage themselves, they do many things that actually enhance their likelihood of success. Driven by passion, they tend work harder and are more enthusiastic and focused. They tend make added progress, outperforming the more talented and outlasting the

Live life on purpose.

less committed. The results show up in the pay of the top performers across every field. These people are fulfilled and earning well-above-average incomes.

Confucius once said, "Wherever you go, go with all your heart." The truth is that people who get to do what they love are the lucky ones. If you are not sure what that is, explore your options. Consider selecting opportunities that help you find your passion in smart ways that don't put your well-being at risk. Pursue goals or a life you want to live with an eye open to areas that interest and engage you. For people who live in integrity honoring whom they really are, tend to experience greater levels of well-being and are happier than those who do not.[38]

Your inspired Wizard recognizes that success is the result of being intentional. So what are you waiting for? You deserve a life where you jump enthusiastically out of bed every morning. Even if you are in the twilight of your working career, following your heart is an essential component of a healthy life. It is never too late to seek a meaningful existence. Live life on purpose. Your success depends on it.

BEHAVIOR 7: LOOKING FAR AHEAD

"Only he who keeps his eye fixed on the far horizon will find the right road."
— *Dag Hammarskjold*

Take the long view. Where we go in life is a direct result of where we are looking. Great lives are achieved by gazing far ahead and then maximizing the potential of today. For the direction you head makes all the difference. Success is a result of a course fully-charted; mediocrity, the outcome of chasing vague whims.

So where are you headed? If you are like most people, you probably aren't sure. To craft a meaningful life, each of us must chart a course. Then we must hold fast to the direction we set. To accomplish this, many decisions will need to be made along the way. How we make those decisions is of particular importance as our success is a culmination of these choices.

The direction you head makes all the difference.

Choosing a path in life can be challenging. How does one go about it? There are different techniques used to make decisions. In considering their options, some people throw a dart, roll the dice, or flip a coin. This approach is risky, leaving life up to chance. Many more choose not to decide, taking what life gives them. This approach is the approach of the masses.

A smaller, select group seeks out options. They research an idea, talk with others, sample some choices, and analyze their selections thoroughly. Left-brained engineering types, like me, make pro-con lists and score or rank their options, while right-brained artistic types often do what feels right, preferring to follow their instincts. Some people assess the worst that could happen and, if they can live with the downside, go ahead, and do it.

Living life without a vision is like sightseeing while blindfolded—rather pointless.

Great decisions are made by taking a long-term view. To do this you will need to involve your Wizard. Your Wizard is a master planner, the part of you that can envision alternatives and play out scenarios. Great decisions are made with the end in mind. To awaken and engage your Wizard, consider doing the Rocking Chair Exercise.

> **Great decisions are made by taking a long-term view.**

To do this, imagine yourself as an old man or woman nearing the end of your life. You are sitting in a rocking chair on your porch looking out over your favorite place. It could be the ocean, a mountain range, rolling hills, a lake, forest, the beach, or even your back yard. As you sit in your chair and rock on your porch, soaking in this idyllic setting, you reflect back on your life contemplating your past, seeing your life as if it has already happened. From your rocking chair, you then consider the options before you today, in the present time. "Don't ask if it is going to be easy. Ask if it's going to be worth it" (Michael Josephson).

To gain clarity on any major decisions before you, it is important to consider where you are and where you could be. To get a sense of this, complete the following two Thought Expanders. From your rocking chair, look back at your life to this current time period and assess the direction you are currently headed in Thought Expander 7.1, <u>Current Direction</u>.

Thought Expander 7.1: Current Direction

Statement	Current Situation
Describe the degree to which your activities/ direction will be meaningful and important at the end of your life.	
Elaborate on how continuing your actions/direction may make you proud or ashamed.	
Assess the degree to which you are maximizing your potential to have a positive impact.	

Now that you know where you are currently headed, again sit in your rocking chair and consider where you could go. What sets your sense of passion on fire? What direction will best serve you or others? Which options will make you feel most alive, allowing you to live fully satisfied, without regret? To create a more intentional course, complete Thought Expander 7.2, Preferred Course. Explore opportunities to clarify, expand, or alter your direction. Be willing to consider options that will maximize the value of your life, let you live fully, and leave you regret-free.

Thought Expander 7.2: Preferred Course

Question	Direction Indicator
What new choices would most improve your life?	
What direction would have the most meaning at the end of your life?	
What accomplishment(s) would please you the most?	
What changes would this course entail or require?	

Success requires a good heading. There are many roads to travel. Each is unique with its own twists, turns, rises, and pitch. Hundreds of small adjustments of the car wheel are needed to compensate for the unevenness of the road, so as to avoid the ditches. At every intersection, there is a choice to be made, a new route to consider. To select well, you need a clear idea of where you want to go. Good decisions keep the journey productive and focused on the destination of choice. "Forgetting what lies behind and straining forward to what lies ahead...let those of us who are mature think this way" (Philippians 3:13-15; ESV).

Enlisting your Wizard, you can get a more clear idea how your current actions might play out. You may find that a better course is needed, one more in line with your aspirations and dreams. Your inspired Wizard is ready and able to help you identify high quality options that will make you feel more inspired and alive. Yet, how do you measure your sense of enthusiasm and satisfaction toward life?

Psychologists use two terms to represent a positive sense of well-being and aliveness: hedonia and eudaimonia. Hedonia represents a feel-good life characterized by the experience of pleasure and the avoidance pain.[39] It is composed of positive emotions as a result of something enjoyable in the moment. Often these are external, extrinsic factors. Eudaimonia, on the other hand, represents a life of purpose, meaning, and virtue.[40] It, too, is distinguished by positive emotions; however these are gained through the internal, intrinsic process of living virtuously and intentionally.[41] Psychological well-being theory (Ryan, Huta, & Deci, 2008) puts forward the idea that living eudaimonically is fundamental to experiencing a deep sense of satisfaction and well-being in life.[42]

> **Well-being from internally-oriented, value-based activities is more satisfying and less fickle.**

Of the two types of well-being, hedonic pleasures tend to be more fleeting. People quickly adapt to external gratifications causing exterior things to lose their ability to generate happiness. Think back on how quickly feelings from a recent crush, first paycheck, new car, or promotion faded. People readily adapt to emotions from extrinsic events, rapidly recategorizing them from novelty to normalcy.[43] This diminishes the extrinsic event's ability to create a sustainable feeling of aliveness. Over time, greater and greater doses of pleasure or stimulation are needed. As a result, life-long satisfaction through hedonic activities alone is difficult to maintain.

Eudaimonic satisfaction is different. It is based on more tenacious and less fleeting motivations. These include positive feelings that come from behaving in self-directed ways, pursuing valued principles, taking mindful action, and acting in ways to develop personal competence.[44] Such intrinsic goals are derived from ancient philosophy in the Aristotelian tradition where living in virtuous, self-actualizing ways was considered pivotal to living the good life. Eudaimonic activities are an underappreciated, but fundamentally important, source of aliveness. This is because well-being from internally-oriented, value-based activities, while requiring more effort and being harder earned, is more satisfying and less fickle.

Neither form of well-being is inherently better than the other. Both hedonic and eudaimonic well-being are important in living well. In fact, they are thought to be interrelated constructs. In growing to maximize your potential (eudaimonia), you experience a sense of happiness (hedonia) which then motivates you to strive for more personal accomplishment, making you feel good again. Such patterns work together in a self-reinforcing upward spiral of aliveness and success. The trick is to find the right blend between them.[45]

> ## Achievement comes from opportunity pursued.

Unfortunately, many people tend to over-focus on hedonic activities and under-focus on eudaimonic ones. As such, people are more interested in what they can get now rather than investing for an even better future. Known by economists as hyperbolic discounting (Chung & Herrnstein, 1967), this behavior reflects the human tendency to value the present more than is appropriate and the future less than is fitting. In general, people over-discount the future, seeing far-off events as less important and valuable than events right in front of them.

Your inspired Wizard understands that excessively discounting the future is problematic to success. To secure the desires of tomorrow, you must take steps to overcome the disincentive of taking appropriate action today. To accomplish this, you need to make plans that avoid a preoccupation with the pleasurable and the distraction of the mundane.

Pleasure overdone is the foundation for imbalance and addiction. It is a fleeting gain, a disloyal mistress. "I can think of nothing less pleasurable than a life devoted to pleasure" (John D. Rockefeller). Seeking pleasure excessively can derail success.

Likewise, the mundane is a sink hole to life's potential. It is a voracious consumer of time and energy. "In absence of clearly-defined goals, we become strangely loyal to performing daily trivia, until we ultimately become enslaved by it" (Robert Heinlein). Minutia unmanaged can consume success.

While there is nothing fundamentally wrong with feel-good activities, success is the result of establishing and maintaining productive direction— where purpose and virtue reside. Hyperbolic discounting tendencies encourage people to spend more time on distractions than spending time with their kids, on watching television than on reaching their full potential, on having fun rather than finding meaning and purpose, on fantasizing instead of following their dreams. "The two most important days in your life are the day you are born…and the day you find out why" (Samuel Clemens).

Achievement comes from opportunity pursued. Your inspired Wizard realizes that years are going to pass either way. The question is, "How are you going to wring the most life from them?" For "Where there is no vision, the people parish" (Proverbs 29:18; KJV).

A few years back, I was sitting in my metaphorical rocking chair and spending time at the end of my life, reflecting. I realized that I had always wanted to continue in my education. As an undergraduate in engineering school at Case Western Reserve University, I fell in love with physics. I enjoyed the problem solving so much that I dreamt of pursuing a doctoral degree. I even wrote down getting a Ph.D. as a personal goal. Unfortunately, jobs for advanced degrees in physics were not plentiful at the time, and I couldn't afford to stay in school beyond the first four years. So, like millions before me, I went off to work. Some twenty years later, as a recovering-CEO, I found myself still wanting the academic brass ring of a Ph.D. degree. Working for myself, I realized that I was now being presented a unique opportunity. Although my interests had shifted toward the science of the mind, the top educational achievement still felt right. I wanted, no needed, to learn more about myself and others. It was where I wanted to go, both personally and professionally.

My friends thought I was nuts. Sure they were careful to not say as much directly, but the questions they posed and the looks on their faces made it clear. Evidently, 44-year-olds are not supposed to want to go back to school, especially for heady, advanced degrees like this. During this time, I got the distinct impression that people assume that dreams are only for the young. As you have probably realized by this book, I don't subscribe to such narrow thinking. A dream is a dream; it is just as good today as it was thirty years ago. Dreams don't expire. They have no "use by" date.

Not surprisingly, everyone wanted to know "Why?" Yes, it was a judgment question—one where I was pressed to validate my desire. The best response turned out to be, "Why not?" I told them that the years were going to pass anyway, whether I pursued a Ph.D. or not, and I wanted to have something to show for my time. I was right. The years did pass—and quickly. There is something about age and time—as the first gets longer, the second goes faster. Before I knew it, I was defending my dissertation and fulfilling a lifelong dream.

Yes, time is unstoppable. Your success lies in how you use it. The present is a deep reservoir of opportunity if you use it wisely. Your mature Wizard recognizes that many times "no" is a superior option. You don't need a reason to not do something. "No" should be your default answer to anything that takes time away from the direction you wish to go. Saying "no" may make you uncomfortable for a short while, but saying "yes" to the wrong things can hound you for years, even a lifetime. To achieve success you must keep the path clear and avoid putting things in your own way.

> By looking far ahead and pursuing what makes you feel most alive, you craft your future and cast a net to catch your dreams.

A better way to make decisions is to require a solid rationale before offering a "yes." A good reason is needed to justify the expenditure of your life energy. Agree to spend your time on things that create the most value. These should be directly in line with your long-term goals. Did you get up today and start that project you've always wanted to do, or did you waste time on marginally important e-mails or surfing for news? Did you research that education you have always wanted to achieve or did you watch television instead?

What option will matter more five, ten, or even fifty years from now? Don't let good things get in the way of the great things in life. Each of us knows this intellectually, but we don't embrace it practically. Time is life, and life is finite. As Ben Franklin cautioned, "Do not squander time, for that is the stuff life is made of." We need to embrace the inevitable end if we are going to really live. The successful life is seized, every last drop of potentiality wrung out.

The Wizard in you knows that to be truly accomplished, a long-term view must be taken. You must not look at your life as it is, instead you must create a vision for what you want it to be. The future is the end result of decisions taken in the current day. For "It's never too late to be who you might have been" (George Elliot). Every goal is accomplished by holding the end in mind. By looking far ahead and pursuing what makes you feel most alive, you craft your future and cast a net to catch your dreams.

BEHAVIOR 8: DREAMING BIGGER

"The greater danger for most of us is not that our aim is too high and we miss it, but that it is too low and we reach it." — Michelangelo Buonarroti

Life's possibilities are infinite. When it comes to what you want to accomplish, most likely you're thinking too small. Life can be much more than you probably think it can, imagination being your only limitation. The bigger your wish, the more that can be accomplished; the clearer your vision, the faster it can be realized. In life, anything is possible; so dream bigger.

Everything is possible, both science and religion agree on this point. Take physics for example. During my college engineering courses we studied Schrödinger's equation. This formula postulates that a wave-function best predicts the probability of an event or outcome. The novelty of this approach is that, in it, Schrödinger allows for all outcomes—the formula makes every eventuality a real possibility. One college professor of mine extended this idea to life itself, arguing that no matter how remote, the possibility that we may move instantaneously to another point in space and time, while unlikely, exists.

The bigger your wish, the more that can be accomplished; the clearer your vision, the faster it can be realized.

Recent advances in quantum mechanics, suggests other similar, surprising, and bizarre outcomes.

Similarly, the Bible reinforces the idea that you can, indeed, accomplish anything. Jesus tells us, "If you have faith and don't doubt, you can do things like this (wither the fig tree) and much more. You can even say to this mountain, 'May you be lifted up and thrown into the sea,' and it will happen" (Matthew 21:21; NLT). That is some powerful imagery, and it provides an important insight to living successfully. If there are no limits, you need to be dreaming bigger. You need to look past your front yard to adventures in the mountains, forests, fields, and oceans beyond.

All limitations are self-imposed, including restrictions about who you are, what you can do, and what your life can become. Ironically, this explains a counterintuitive finding often observed in creative settings. Relatively new engineers frequently come up with solutions to long-standing problems or create innovations that ruffle traditionally held ideas and approaches.

Creativity is the bloom of unrestrained thinking.

When I was a research engineer, I worked on several projects where I was told, "You're wasting your time" and "It can't be done." Young people don't always listen—thank goodness. Today, I have several adhesive chemistry patents because I wasn't "smart" enough to listen. Today's young computer and internet billionaires make this readily evident. In the last few decades, the best known of these young innovators include Bill Gates, Steve Jobs, and Mark Zuckerberg. These founders of Microsoft, Apple, and Facebook didn't assume limits, so they went out and did what others could not envision. Genius is often born out of unwillingness to accept limitation.

Thought boundaries become self-fulfilling. Young people are often highly successful because they aren't willing to accept what "can't be done." Creativity is the bloom of unrestrained thinking. Anything is possible. Matthew 14:25-29 (NIV) notes: "During the fourth watch of the night Jesus went out to them, walking on the lake. When the disciples saw him walking on the lake, they were terrified. 'It's a ghost,' they said, and cried out in fear.

But Jesus immediately said to them: 'Take courage! It is I. Don't be afraid.'

'Lord, if it's you,' Peter replied, 'Tell me to come to you on the water.'

'Come,' Jesus said. Then Peter got down out of the boat, walked on the water, and came toward Jesus."

Self-generated thinking that limits your reach, building a box around you, is the only thing that actually stands in your way. Invariably, during my seminars on this, someone challenges this proposition. They argue that,

logically, it doesn't make sense. An overweight, fifty-year-old man recently said, "Explain how anything is possible! Say I want to be an Olympic
sprinter—that is not going to happen." A middle-aged woman stated "I
want to be 27 years old again. How can I do that?" Clearly, neither of these
things is going to happen. But if you can achieve anything, what is the
disconnect?

Know it is definitely within your power to accomplish your dreams.
However, every wish needs room to flourish. Each of you must allow space
for life (or God, the universe, fate etc.) to fill in
the particulars. Accomplishment is a result of
possibility expanded.

Pursue the spirit of your goals.

Yes, it is highly unlikely the fifty-year-
old, overweight man who posed this question
will ever run in the Olympics. Likewise, the
middle-aged woman will never again be 27 years old. But in no way does
that mean they both can't achieve their dreams. They can. Each can fully
embrace and achieve these and even more spectacular wishes. To do so,
however, they can't dictate the particulars. Instead, they must identify and
follow the desire underlying the request. Let me explain.

You can accomplish anything you want. However, your dreams will
seldom play out exactly how you envision them. Particulars such as getting
a specific job, marrying a distinct person, or achieving a goal in a certain
way on an exact date are unlikely. The universe, fate, and/or God must have
room to play. To be successful, you must pursue the spirit of your goals.

The answer <u>to</u> getting what you want lies in understanding the drivers
behind the aspiration itself. To do this you to need ask, "Why?" So let's say
your dream is to become a world-famous athlete. To achieve the spirit of
this request and generate a go-forward life plan, it is important that you
know why. Perhaps it is because you want to be recognized, appreciated,
and valued. Maybe love of self or love from others is lacking. Perhaps it is
because you want the money that goes with fame so you can have more
control over your schedule and life. Possibly you want to become a world-
famous athlete so you are more able to support a special cause or in some
other way use your fame to help others. Each of these desires sheds light on
very real and important needs. Reframed, each can be crafted into a fully
achievable goal sans the particulars and restraints of the original wish.

Likewise, the woman who wanted to be young again has similar opportunities. What is it she really wants to accomplish? Does she believe an

improved body shape will make her feel better about who she is, or help her recapture a feeling of being desired? Does she yearn for a new start, a chance to do things left undone, a sense of excitement and adventure? Each of these goals lies squarely within her reach. It isn't the younger age that is really important to her—it's what it provides. Like the world famous athlete in the prior example, what matters is the desire behind your wish. The man and the woman are both trying to replace something lacking in their lives. Opportunity resides in clarifying what is missing, and then plotting a path to get it.

There are many routes you can take to capture your dreams even if they first manifest as some bizarre, fantastical, out-of-reach option. The trick is to understand the desire behind the wish, and use it to craft more relevant goals. Your inner Wizard understands that you mine life's gold by sequentially asking, "Why?" you want what you want. You do this until the underlying basis of your yearning, the vein of precious desires, is exposed. Then, go to work!

When I was a child, my dream was to become an actor. Looking behind the wish, however, provides insight into my desires. I wanted to feel excitement, be a part of something bigger, give of

> What matters is the desire behind your wish.

myself, and be loved. While I never became an actor, I have fully accomplished the spirit of my wish. Today, I have crafted an exciting life that lets me be on stage, inspire, teach, and motivate people.

My work also satisfies a much needed personal desire to be engaged in a continuous process of learning and growing. Further, it provides an opportunity to give of myself while helping others and simultaneously participating in raising the collective consciousness of mankind. I have achieved my dream.

Do you want to walk on the moon, become president, win the World Series, or have a billion dollars? Great, go for it. However, your mature Wizard understands that each of these choices include specifics that could actually work to limit life's ability to provide other, better, and more fulfilling possibilities. Possibilities that better fit with your core desires, wants, and needs. Overly-specific goals make life's gateway narrow and passage less likely, while spirit-based goals blast the road canyon-wide.

Therefore, it is helpful to understand the desires behind our dreams.

For example, I know that if I really wanted to be an actor, I still could be. But I am not certain that it would be the best way to honor what my spirit desires. In asking, "Why?" it is readily apparent that many other important personal interests would be sacrificed. There is not enough meaning in traditional acting for me—so I am pleased to pursue the underlying wish through teaching and speaking.

What is your wildest dream? Write it in the top row of Thought Expander 8.1, Life Desires. Fulfillment resides in understanding what drives your wish. To gain insight on your underlying desires, take a few minutes and complete the rest of the Thought Expander.

Thought Expander 8.1: Life Desires

My "impossible" dream is:
Why do I want that?
If I had that what would it get me?
My spirit's wish is:

Nothing is impossible. You can do, be, or have anything you want. You can be wonderfully accomplished curing disease, solving world problems, and winning notable events. You can be a pioneer in deed or thought, change the world, and accomplish great things. Anything is possible for you when you pursue the spirit of your desire.

Success is achieved by invoking our inner Wizard. It is through the imaginative and ingenious dimensions of our inspired Wizard that possibility is born. Dreaming big, you set the stage for a full and accomplished life. "Empty pockets never held anyone back. Only empty heads and empty hearts can do that" (Norman Vincent Peale). Your mature Wizard appreciates that the best dreams require you to become more. They call you to fulfill your potential and live completely.

> Overly-specific goals make life's gateway narrow and passage less likely, while spirit-based goals blast the road canyon-wide.

Now that you have a wish, how do you achieve it? An excellent way to accomplish something big is to start planning small. Meaningful objectives appear insurmountable when you consider them as a whole. Each wish is accomplished through a large number of seemingly inconsequential steps.

Regular, consistent investments of time and manageable chucks of attention can have dramatic long-term impacts. Small things become big as the result of regular compounding. Mountains and Redwood trees grow only a few inches a year and yet rise to the highest points and become the tallest living things on the planet. Likewise, progress is the result of many well-planned activities linked together and actively implemented. The secret is to realize the imminent power in the current day. A seed planted today is the fruit of tomorrow.

Unfortunately, progress against large goals is frequently subtle and hard to observe. Psychological researchers note that people tend to prefer smaller actions with more readily apparent outcomes over larger actions with less certain outcomes.[46] As such, progress toward a goal can feel like watching the hour hand of a clock move. It doesn't seem like it is going anywhere.

Combined with the push for immediate gratification of today's society, people generally believe that big things should be accomplishable today, tomorrow, or at latest month's end, otherwise they have failed. Most people seek instantaneous satisfaction. Look at what American's eat, how we exercise, the money we save, the goals we set, and the relationships we pursue. Fads in fashion, various get-rich-quick schemes, and activities such as gambling and the lottery, play to wishes for immediate gratification. We want it now or we don't want it at all. As a result, frustration can readily arise, causing hopes to sag and efforts to flag in the face of reasonable time requirements and readily predictable obstacles. Unfortunately, people often believe the movies they watch—appreciably overestimating what is doable in a day.

People tend to overestimate what can be done in a day, but grossly underestimate what can be done in a month, year, or lifetime.

Simultaneously, people grossly underestimate what can be done in a month, year, or lifetime. When you persist in continuously applying incremental efforts, you can generate progress that builds on itself, compounding over time. Persisting is like investing a penny which, if doubled every day, would result in a million dollars after only a month. Daily efforts over long periods compile to create and accomplish great, if not impossible, things.

Great plans take both dynamics into account. Achievers use the given day to pursue steps that will most likely contribute to their goals. Feeling satisfied and grateful by the current progress, they continue, day by day, such that in a year these achievers can accomplish extraordinary things that originally appeared challenging and questionable.

Tied to the issues of the current day, people are not particularly good at envisioning who they can become or proficient at forecasting how they will change and grow. Humans tend to suffer from the "end of history" illusion where they expect much less change going forward then they have experienced in the past (Quoidbach, Gilbert, & Wilson, 2013). It is as if recent history has come to a complete stop, ending with the current point in time. As a result, people perceive themselves today as being in their final form when, in reality, they might not even recognize their future selves if they met them. Not surprisingly, it is easier to conceive what has happened to us than it is to prognosticate what can happen. It is in this weakness where opportunity lies.

In setting direction, you must be careful not to make choices that depend exclusively on who you are today. For example, you may not choose to pursue your dream of becoming a world famous author, because the travel required would conflict with your desire to spend time at home with your family. Your kids will grow up, eventually, and right now might be the best time to start writing that book. You need to take care when making decisions based on preferences that are less likely to remain stable than you might expect. Instead, it is more powerful to reflect on the potentiality of who you can become; to set goals that stretch, shape, and allow you to be something better, new, and more. A magnificence of possibility lies before you.

> **Don't settle for what is readily achievable.**

Your inspired Wizard recognizes the need to pick a life course that takes into account the possibility for substantial personal growth. It can help select a destination that allows you to become fully yourself. Your mature Wizard is a master of considering accomplishments and purposes that are both unseen and beyond the self. These might include being a catalyst for making a difference in others lives or changing the world for the better. Successful people, when confronted with the prospect "If you could do anything you wanted, what would it be?" Don't settle for what is readily achievable. Instead, accomplished people ask for what they really want, avoiding the safe and predictable that neither includes imagination nor challenges possibility.

Clearly, such an approach is life-limiting. If you aim too low, and set your sights on what is pedestrian, that is exactly what you will get. Albert Einstein noted that, "Your imagination is your preview of life's coming attractions." Superior goals are achieved by dreaming bigger. To help you broaden your imagination, complete Thought Expander 8.2, Life's Wish. It is a brainstorming exercise meant to expand your thinking and broaden your consideration. To complete it, find a quiet place when you are in a positive mood and reflect on the following question. "If I found a magic lantern, rubbed it, and awakened a genie who could grant me as many wishes as I wanted, what life would I ask for?" Work through the exercise until you find something you can commit your life to—a purpose. You will know you are onto something when the goal simultaneously inspires and intimidates.

Thought Expander 8.2: Life's Wish

Magic Lantern: List three desires	1.
	2.
	3.

After those got old, what might I do next?

When I got tired of that, how might I spend my time?

What goal would challenge and fulfill me long-term?

The goal of this exercise is to move you beyond pleasures and things to meaning and purpose. To check the quality of your choice, consider the following. If your picture of the future isn't too big for the frame of reference you hold, then it isn't large enough. It should be large, a little frightening, and at first blush, a tad outrageous. If your vision is something you can see readily through to completion, then you are not dreaming big enough. Avoid fixation on the cards you were dealt in life and choose something superior.

Your inspired Wizard wants you to reach beyond what is obviously possible, and choose a life of success and satisfaction. It strives for an existence marbled with meaning, purpose, and adventure. Most people seek what they think they can achieve and end up living opaque, grey, nominal lives.

Truly successful people have challenging, audacious ambitions. They don't allow their past experiences to define what they can do or who they can become. They prefer goals that push, stretch, and challenge. While the exact method of accomplishment often resides beyond their current faculties to discern, they pursue it anyway. Their objectives represent worthwhile endeavors that leverage their skills and capabilities while honoring their interests and aspirations. Innovators, leaders, and visionaries all seek after goals that require them to become more.

> **Innovators, leaders, and visionaries all seek goals that require them to become more.**

Dream big; anything is possible. There are infinite powers within you seeking expression. You can accomplish whatever it is you desire. The solution lies in understanding the spirit behind your request and setting ambitious goals to satisfy it. Not one to watch pitches go by; your inspired Wizard is a firm believer in swinging for the fence.

Go ahead imagine, dream, and make your wish—for it plants the seeds of your future harvest. Set your sights higher, look further ahead, and strive for more. Dreams set the stage for where you will go and what you will accomplish. Find the path that lets you live in the light of who you really are. Wonderful things await you.

BEHAVIOR 9: CREATING A PLAN

"If you don't know where you are going, any path will take you there."
— *Sioux Proverb*

Goal setting is life sculpting. Setting a course for your life is one of the most powerful activities you can undertake. A plan is but an about-to-be-captured dream. After envisioning the life you want, plans are the route by which your wish is achieved. Life plans include the goals of what we want to accomplish and the details of how we will get there. Without clearly defined plans, it is all too easy to wander, follow another's dream, or allow the superfluous and inconsequential undue access.

Yet, life plans are rare. As a result, countless people aren't pursuing their dreams. Instead, they are going through the motions, experiencing tiresome days and wasting valuable time. Successful people avoid such drudgery. With plans in place, they don't feel the need to stir up drama or create problems simply to feel alive. Accomplished people avoid a hijacked existence by actively creating the lives they want. For "Life can be pulled by goals just as surely as it can be pushed by drives" (Viktor Frankl). But, such big picture visionaries are few and far between.

A plan is but an about-to-be-captured dream.

Of the hundreds of CEOs I have worked with over the years, the vast majority are thoughtful and cautious. They are wise and prudent business people. As such, these leaders will seldom invest a dollar of their hard-earned money without a clear understanding of several issues. First, they will insist on a detailed plan outlining how the investment will be brought to fruition. They will require a market analysis and sales forecast along with detailed vendor quotes, not only for the required capital, but also for installation and ongoing operational costs.

Second, they call for an assessment of the project's likelihood of success, its return on investment, and some clarity regarding the worst case outcome should things not go as planned. Collectively, such information makes sense, as it helps make solid business decisions. The process reflects the active conversion process from a company's goals into specific plans that can be implemented and managed. It is good decision making. While it doesn't always guarantee a positive outcome, the process greatly ensures the likelihood of success.

Business experts such as Michael Porter (1980) have known this for decades. Porter makes an art out of using various analyses to select appropriate goals and developing supporting plans as part of the corporate strategic planning process. Personal development experts such as Steven Covey (1989) and Napoleon Hill (1937) espouse similar actions when working to improve people's chances for success, using techniques such as purpose identification, personal goal setting, and life planning. Across the spectrum, planning improves the possibility of achieving a goal and, ultimately, generates better results.

> **Dreams have the flip of a coin probability of succeeding, but write them down, share them, and hold yourself accountable to them, and their chance of materializing skyrockets.**

However, while most CEOs go to great lengths to ensure their money is invested wisely, their efforts are anemic when it comes to managing their greatest resource—the energy of their lives. These able individuals will invest enormous effort to ensure even small business decisions are made well; yet, they will frequently live their entire lives without a clear goal or purpose.

It has been suggested that the vast majority of people, approximately 84% do not have any goals at all.[47] Another 13% have goals but they are not written down. Only 3% have written goals. Anecdotally, my seminars directionally support these findings with 2 to 5% of participants indicating they have written life goals. The low percentages are an indicator that people don't realize the benefits of planning. As Thomas Carlyle aptly noted, "The most unhappy of all men is the man who cannot tell what he is going to do, who has got no cut-out for him in the world."

Researchers have found that people with goals are, indeed, more likely to accomplish them. One reason, according to goal setting theory (Locke, 1968), is that clearly defined goals provide a source of motivation. Such benefits are evident as formulating goals resulted in more than half of one study's participants achieving their objectives. The form in which the goals are created is also important. People with goals, in one study, achieved them 54%, 76%, and 95% of the time if they are held in their mind,

Plans are harbingers of dreams realized.

written on paper, and reviewed with others regularly.[48] Dreams have the flip of a coin probability of succeeding, but write them down, share them, and hold yourself accountable to them, and their chance of materializing skyrockets.

As an investor, if you were to earn 2% more over your working career you would have twice the nest egg. Imagine what happens if your yields are 20 to 40 percentage points better because they are written and shared/ reviewed, respectively. Although extraordinarily difficult to study, qualitative estimates suggest that planners could easily earn substantially more over a lifetime. You are practically assured success in life if you make a habit of planning by writing your goals down, working at them regularly, making them known, and having others hold you accountable. Successful people hold clear, comprehensive, and synergistic ideas of what they want to accomplish. "People with goals succeed because they know where they're going" (Earl Nightingale).

Goals work because they shift one's focus and every subsequent behavior in subtle but powerful ways. Think of goals as stars in the sky. Knowing where you are going, you need only look up every evening, find the right celestial marker, and follow it. No matter what else is going on, simply do your best and follow that star. Eventually you will get where you want to go.

In addition to being direction indicators, goals also work to cause an objective to come to pass. Take relationship-oriented goals for example. Such goals often contribute to increased interpersonal responsiveness which then acts to help make the objective self-fulfilling. Merely by creating a relationship-based goal, you become more focused on the quality of the relationship, thereby increasing the likelihood that your interconnection will improve.[49] If you decide that you want to be worth a million dollars you will act in ways that help that goal come to pass such as working harder, pursuing higher paying jobs, saving more and/or investing more wisely. A note was found in the desk of the baron industrialist, Andrew Carnegie, reading "I will spend the first half of my life earning a fortune and the second half of my life giving it all away." He did both.

Intention reframes attention; formal goals sharpen our focus, allowing our aims to be more readily achieved. The impact can be positive both near-term and long-term. Researchers in one study found that growth-oriented goals predicted greater personal development and enhanced well-being for at least three years.[50]

It is the benefit of goal setting and strategic planning that explain its wide spread popularity in corporate America today. Written plans clarify the direction a business will take, while providing both a review and a feedback mechanism. Formal plans act to align internal efforts, resulting in better decisions. Researchers have found that the more sophisticated the preparation approach employed, the better the resulting performance.[51] Companies use goal setting and strategic planning because they generate results by infusing key objectives into the organization's psyche and increasing the likelihood of success.

The work I do today stems directly from two decades of corporate strategy work. Why was it that so many wonderful tools were relegated only to the business world when they had direct applicability to our lives as well? There exists an opportunity for people to take better advantage of sound business planning tools in crafting the personal lives of their dreams.

The link between goal setting and personal well-being is a case in point. People with goals have been found in many studies to be significantly happier.[52] Perhaps, it is because they know where they are going in life. Self-generated commitments that are personally significant are associated with happiness.[53,54] Goals that generate the most well-being have several consistent features. First, they are intrinsic including passions, interests, and personal growth, as opposed to extrinsic-relying on rewards, possessions, or titles.[55] Of the intrinsic objectives, intimacy, achievement, and/or altruism have been found to be most beneficial.[56] Second, healthy goals are self-determined not coming from others or society at large.[57] Third, positive goals provide a venue to leverage one's core strengths.[58] Collectively, great goals provide an important and often overlooked aspect of life—engagement and meaning.[59] Specifically, overarching life goals appear to play an important role in well-being.[60]

Plans are harbingers of dreams realized. Plans include the creative "what" of your goals and they set direction for the practical "how" of your actions. Plans provide meaning, purpose, and direction to life.

So what do you want to accomplish? If you already know, write it down. If you don't, take a stab at it. Draft a life plan. Avoid the urge to put it off. People often tell me they are hesitant to create a plan because then they will feel like they "have to do it." Uh, isn't that the idea? They are afraid of the very action of life planning because it may create some internal commitment. Yes it will. But it will also act to ensure you live a full life. People also worry that maybe they will get it wrong and would prefer to wait until their course is "clear." To get to a high-quality essay, every student knows several drafts are required. Life plans are no different. "You can't use up creativity. The more you use, the more you have" (Maya Angelou).

The best plans are those that stretch you, ones you don't know how to accomplish.

Isn't it much worse to miss out on life than to experience a little discomfort, awkwardness, and introspection? A good, long look at your plan requires it to be written and laid out before you. Only then can it be molded, shaped, and re-crafted until it feels right. The final say remains yours.

Your mature Wizard will let you know if you are on the right path. Your energy will rise and the goals and supporting actions will start to bubble up, creating pressure toward positive change. Contemplated long enough, the right plan will cry out for the chance to become real, the desire to have it will grow palpable in your heart.

To start the life planning process, complete Thought Expander 9.1, Life Plan. To start, rewrite your answer from the last row of Thought Expander 8.2, Life's Wish. Then detail at least three ways you might potentially go about achieving your wish. Include specific outcomes you want to accomplish, dates you want accomplish them by, and measurements that indicate you have achieved them. For example, you might want to become CEO of a technology company by age 40 or become financially independent by generating $100,000 a year in interest income in twenty years. Don't be afraid of rough starts. You can always revise and update your plan. It might make sense to treat your first pass of the exercise as a brainstorming activity where there are no wrong answers. Jot down whatever comes to mind; your imagination is your only constraint. Feel free to use more paper to think through this exercise for its scope can quickly become broad. There is no shortage of potential.

Thought Expander 9.1: Life Plan

The life I imagine:	Rewrite answer from last row of Thought Expander 8.2, <u>Life's Wish</u>.
How might I achieve my wish?	
Plan #1	
Plan #2	
Plan #3	

People often resist creating life plans. It can seem overwhelming. They simply don't know where to start. Not every plan needs to be world-changing. If you find your plans overwhelming, consider starting with more manageable goals that will still create significant value. That said, the best plans are those that stretch you, ones you don't know how to accomplish.

To get a more clear idea of where your best opportunities lie, complete Thought Expander 9.2, <u>Action Opportunities</u>. Write your biggest challenge in the header row (see Thought Expander 2.2, <u>Recurring Issues</u>, for a reminder). Be sure to present the issue in a positive framework, as an opportunity and not a constraint. For example, instead of focusing on a negative such as losing weight or exercising, state you want to get healthier or feel better about yourself. This shift will help generate motivation while making the value of your goal clearer. Identify at least two ways, Plan A and Plan B, by which you could capture that opportunity. From these, identify potential actions you could start or stop doing and place in the appropriate boxes. Ask yourself what thing, if you did it, would most advance your situation. Write it in the Start Doing box. Then ask yourself what thing, if you stopped doing it, would most advance your situation. Write this in the Stop Doing box. Feel free to repeat the process for other goals using the lined pages in the back of the book.

Thought Expander 9.2: Action Opportunities

The area of greatest opportunity:	Rewrite an answer from Thought Expander 2.2, <u>Recurring Issues</u>.	
Plan A:		
Actions	<u>Start doing</u>	<u>Stop doing</u>
Plan B:		
Actions	<u>Start doing</u>	<u>Stop doing</u>

Most people find the life-plan-fashioning process refreshing and fun. There are no wrong answers and you are only limited by the creativity of your Wizard. It feels good to let your imagination out to play. Like riding a bike, you get better with practice, and you never really forget how to do it. Work at crafting plans long enough across the various facets of your life, and soon you will have identified critical pieces to the puzzle of your life. As you assemble these pieces, look for over-arching themes. Often the areas of opportunity explored in Thought Expander 9.2, Action Opportunities, can be linked together to create a comprehensive plan leading to a well-lived life.

Ironically, people will work hard to protect a dollar, being sure to spend it wisely, but will invest the whole of their lives without a plan—the true definition of penny wise and pound foolish. Life is better lived on purpose through planning. Yet, how many spend more time planning a vacation or buying a car then they do conceiving their future?

> **Goals commit your spirit to action.**

Many CEOs feel this gap. With wealth, title, and well-established lives, they feel a nagging sense something is missing. What is missing is a loss of direction, purpose, and satisfaction. Plans fill this gap. Samuel Clemens's wittily noted: "Plan for the future, because that is where you are going to spend the rest of your life."

When I was in my early 20's, I drafted my first life plan. It included several long-term life goals as well as annual accomplishments and specific quarterly "to do" action steps. One of my early drafts laid out my dream to become a business CEO and have a million dollars in the bank by the time I was 50. Of course, I had no way to know how I would eventually accomplish this dream. Yet, I suspected that bringing it to life, by committing to the wish on paper, was an indispensable first step. How else could I think the dream through, massage it, and craft it exactly how I wanted it to be?

Almost immediately after drafting the plan, my life started to change. I became different. I found myself signing up for evening business classes and took a more high-profile job position where I was involved with innovative new products and novel, patentable technology. A few years later, I went back to school full-time getting a master's degree from one of the best schools in the country, Northwestern University's Kellogg School of Management, a feat of persistence in-and-of-itself as I didn't get accepted the first year I applied. Over the following years, I sought the prospects, followed the relocations, and took the jobs that would best position me to accomplish my plan.

Planning made clear what I could and should do to achieve my goals. It provided more sharply defined vision, allowing me to better identify the right opportunities and positioning me to capture them when they inevitably presented. The effort panned out. As a result of writing a life plan, I was able to accomplish all the major goals I set, years ahead of schedule. My written life plan provided both a destination point and a starting pathway. The goal setting process was responsible for the fact that, today, I am free to live my life how I choose.

By writing goals, you give them life, preordaining your desires to manifest.

Goal setting is surprisingly powerful. The act of writing down our ambitions engages a resourceful ally—the human subconscious. Scripting what we want to do in life provides an important directive to our brains. Goals commit your spirit to action.

No one fully understands the human subconscious, although that has not kept Freud and numerous other psychologists from trying to tease apart its inner workings. It is generally assumed that the subconscious mind is responsible for underlying, habitual, and instinctual thoughts and behaviors.[61] Remarkable things can be accomplished by engaging this mysterious part of our psyche. Hypnosis, suggestion, meditation, and visualization are techniques that have been employed to connect with it. The good news is that we don't have to know how the subconscious works in order to take advantage of it. To drive a car you don't need to understand the ways by which the explosive energy of combustion is converted into forward momentum. You only need to know how to get a car started, and point it where you want to go. The subconscious is no different. A life plan is a potent tool to convert and integrate a conscious idea into a commanding subconscious directive.

The subconscious is an aspect of your inner Wizard. Working in an unceasing and continuous fashion, our subconscious is believed to possess a greatly expanded processing capacity that has been argued to be millions of times more comprehensive than the conscious mind. Once engaged, the subconscious relentlessly seeks to solve the problem and deliver the desired outcome. The subconscious is thought to never sleep, and as a result, provides a never-ending stream of effort aimed at achieving any objectives placed before it.

Working 24 hours a day, 7 days a week, 365 days a year, the subconscious continuously strives to deliver your goals whether you are aware of its existence or not. Unlike the conscious, which sets goals, understands time, and is constrained by limited processing capacity, the subconscious is uniquely powerful managing our attitudes, values, and beliefs.

Evidence for the power of the subconscious mind regularly shows up in the lives of those who plan. A common realization among die-hard planners is a strong sense of compulsion. Planners regularly relay stories that describe being driven to do this, go there, or pursue that—all the while not being sure why. They feel an urgent push or necessary pull, only to realize at a later time they were actually striving to complete a goal created long ago and forgotten. They get a déjà vu sense that they have already completed the task on some level. Since visualization is the first step in all creation, they have started the completion process simply by planning it.

That happened to me when I left my CEO position. I found myself being drawn back toward additional education. First, I became an adjunct professor at the State University of New York teaching business strategy. Then, I enrolled in a philosophy class. After that, I took an online psychology course. Finally, I signed up for a Ph.D. program in psychology. I was unusually driven, particularly focused, and mildly obsessed. Why?

I was more than half way through my Ph.D. when I realized the answer. At that point, I found an old life plan created from when I was an undergraduate engineering student at Case Western Reserve. Clear as day it read, "Get a doctorate." Invoked, my subconscious was still actively trying to figure out how to achieve it some two decades later. The same goes for this book. Both the graduate degree and this manuscript were the result of plans I had crafted decades earlier. Each rose to the surface with fervent urgency, once I was in a place where I could properly act on them.

That is the genius of creating plans. Once written, plans take on lives of their own. It is almost as if by writing goals, you give them life, preordaining your desires to manifest. Through ideation, they become an intentional, real energy that eventually manifests in the physical.

It is important to mention that even with all its influence, the subconscious is not ultimately in charge. It acts on the directives you give it through conscious thought. In other words, your subconscious is governed by your King and directed by your Wizard. That means you have the ability to override and manage your subconscious, keeping it focused on that which is acceptable, valuable, and good. Like hypnotism, where subjects cannot be made to do something they don't want to do, your subconscious cannot run amuck, unless you allow it. This allows you to make future decisions in ways that optimize your changing desires in light of an ever-evolving environment. Enlisted with the right direction, your subconscious will entice you to think and encourage you to behave in ways that generate the dreams you hold most dear.

Lacking a plan, you will end up wherever you are headed.

"Declaring the end from the beginning" you accomplish what (you) want (Isaiah 46:10; ESV). Direction is necessary, because effort and courage are not enough to achieve success in life. Not knowing where you are going is problematic. Lost, directionless, wandering—no wonder so many people live a nominal existence. Lacking a plan, you will end up wherever you are headed.

An opportunity exists for you to create a meaningful life plan. Written plans with their detailed milestones and supporting activities work because they prioritize time, align efforts, demand personal responsibility, and monitor progress. To be effective, however, they need to be used. A good plan needs to be regularly reviewed, revised, and executed. Strong companies use their strategic plans as evolving documents to shape their actions throughout the entire year. They are actively employed and regularly appraised, updated, and modified to reflect changes in light of a myriad of influencing factors. Conversely, weak companies pull down their strategic plans once every year or two to dust them off, and update the budget numbers.

Life plans are no different. To maximize their value, they need to be reviewed frequently and adjusted. Superior life plans are expanded, modified, and tweaked. They are well-used documents that are regularly tailored to reflect meaningful changes in our environments, our situations, and ourselves. You don't need a life plan to enjoy life. However, you can't reach your full potential without one. "The heart of man plans his way, but the Lord establishes his steps" (Proverbs 16:9, ESV). Without a plan, it is impossible to choose the next best steps to success.

"The happiest people I know are those who are busy working toward specific objectives. The most bored and miserable people I know are those who are drifting along with no worthwhile objectives in mind" (Zig Ziglar). Those with written life plans are brave enough to commit to where they want to go and bold enough to expect they can make it. Life planners are an elite group—join them and tread the path of the accomplished. Lay out a life plan to capture your dreams, and you will be on your way to accomplishing them.

BEHAVIOR 10: ENVISIONING SUCCESS

"Far better is it to dare mighty things, to win glorious triumphs, even though checkered by failure... than to rank with those poor spirits who neither enjoy nor suffer much, because they live in a gray twilight that knows not victory nor defeat." — Teddy Roosevelt

See the win. To be effective, plans need to be created but they also have to be implemented. The first step toward working any plan is to formulate an image in your mind's eye of what success will look like. Plans get you where you want to go by allowing you to enjoy the final destination long before you get there. Holding a mental picture is the synergistic sister to drafting a plan. Envisioning, you picture the end from the beginning. Only when you can clearly see what you want, are you able to effectively go about obtaining your wish.

Holding a mental picture is the synergistic sister to drafting a plan.

Visualization is the portal to success. It is an essential, but often overlooked, step to goal accomplishment. Whatever you focus on expands, growing bigger and more likely. Visualizing is the process of forming a mental image of an outcome you desire—priming the mind. Benefits include improved clarity, increased self-confidence, and greater motivation. To get what we want, we need to be able to envision it first. En-vision means to see from within. The key to success is to picture things as you want them instead of how they are. In the creation process, God "Speaks of the nonexistent things...as if they already existed" (Romans 4:17; AMP).

There are several powerful forms of visualization that can facilitate goal achievement. These include vision boards, win writing, and active attention. Let's take each in turn.

Vision boards are a concrete form of imagining. A vision board is a pictorial representation of your goals, dreams, and desires. To create one, you might include pictures or words cobbled together from magazines, newspapers, and the internet, in a collage format. Collectively, the vision board is meant to clarify and inspire by engaging both our conscious and subconscious. Once assembled, the idea is to spend a few minutes each day looking at, thinking about, and reflecting on the imagery relative to your personal goals. Vision boards work best if they are kept in a place where they can be viewed regularly. The more emotional energy you invest, the greater your possibility of achieving the vision you hold.

As tools, vision boards clarify and shape our perspective and create great excitement. They illuminate what we want, while refocusing where we are heading. Providing insights into next best actions to make the goals reality, vision boards also allow you to see and feel the accomplishment long before it is actually achieved. I encourage you to create one.

> **Visualization is the portal to success.**

Win writing is another visualization technique. Win writing is an exercise where one completes a statement expounding on their future goals as though they are complete. The idea is to claim the still unseen outcome by detailing what you want it to look like. In win writing, one spends a short period of time, approximately five minutes, every day, exploring their future success. Often this is done by writing a few sentences or paragraphs in a journal. Details are particularly important in this exercise, so is variety. Over separate sessions, one might focus on a range of outcomes offering input from various perspectives. These might include writing detailed answers that showcase information regarding: "Who was present?", "When did it happen?", "What emotions did you feel?", and "How did you get there?" Creative answers to "What were your five senses experiencing?", "How did your life change?", and "What did it mean to you?" are also beneficial.

To awaken your Wizard's visionary state, take a few minutes to do the win writing exercise in Thought Expander 10.1, <u>Success Story</u>. It will seed your visualization process. Be sure to complete the statement from the perspective of having already completed the goal, achieved the desire, or accomplished the dream.

Thought Expander 10.1: Success Story

Aspect of Success	Describe in Answer
I am so happy and satisfied now that…	
When did this happen?	
How did you get there?	
What did this mean to you?	
How did you feel?	
How did your life change?	

The goal of win writing is to make the future life you dream of appear as vivid and real as possible. Therefore, practicing this consistently over a period of time can be particularly valuable. Rotating through different ways to look at your goals and assess possible futures, allows you to formulate the details of those lives while enjoying a forestallment on the outcome. It generates an indelible image of your success while generating clues on how you arrived at that destination.

A third visualization activity is developing active attention. Active attention lies on a continuum between vision boards and win writing. Exactly how it sounds, active attention is about focus. To develop a stronger focus, the goal seeker would review their goals regularly and reflect on them in a positive, affirmative fashion. Laminated pocket cards are ideal for active attention, although, anything written will do. On the back of a small piece of cardstock or index card, for example, one would write what they want to accomplish. The bottom rows of Thought Expander 7.2, <u>Preferred Course</u>, 8.1, <u>Life Desires</u>, and 8.2, <u>Life's Wish</u>, along with the plans developed in Thought Expanders 9.1, <u>Life Plan</u>, and 9.2, <u>Action Opportunities</u>, are good places to start. To practice active attention, the written objective is then reviewed several times a day and reflected upon. First thing in the morning, at lunchtime, after dinner, and last thing before bed are popular times.

The idea is to concentrate on the goal regularly throughout the day and to think about it constructively and optimistically. Some people also use the back side of the card to bolster their outlook by placing an inspiring piece of scripture or an inspirational quote to motivate them. By actively reflecting on your goals each and every day, you gain clarity about what you are striving toward and living for. Active attention provides meaning and purpose, while working to focus your efforts.

> By actively reflecting on your goals each and every day, you gain clarity about what you are striving toward and living for.

Visualization processes such as vision boards, win writing, and active attention, engage the imagination. The power of these exercises lies in their ability to get you to claim new things as though they were. All things are created twice—first in the mind and then in the world. Everything is first conceptualized and then realized.

Over time, envisioning reshapes your thinking. It refocuses your efforts, and subsequently, increases the likelihood your goals will be accomplished. Envisioning expands what is possible.

Personally held images are particularly influential. Most powerful among these are visions that stay with you. Pervasive ideas of where you want to go and who you want to be can act as strong rudders steering you over vast, seemingly landless stretches of ocean to your destiny. Such images can be intentionally crafted or they can occur passively through the equivalent of daydreaming or fantasizing.

Many of us hold visions of our lives that we can't seem to get out of our heads. These images please or interest us in some way, and we allow them to resonate, develop, and become part of our dreamscape. For me, this image reflected a long-standing desire I had to become a family advisor.

Shortly after I graduated with my engineering degree, my Wizard conjured up the perfect job. The vision held me as the point person for a family running a highly successful business. In this strategic role, I would coordinate a wide range of activities where my analytics, thoroughness, compassion, and loyalty would be highly valued. On the family front, this might include owner meetings, one-on-one coaching, financial planning, creating trusts, ownership transfers, and transitioning family members in or out of the business. On the business front, this could include board meeting facilitation, strategic planning, team building, leadership development, and preparing the business for sales. As a family advisor, I pictured myself becoming an integral part of the owners' lives by organizing services in a customized manner to meet their specific needs. This dream job came and went over the years, bouncing around in my head. To be honest, I never gave it any serious conscious thought, not even noting it in my journals or detailing it in my various life plans.

Hold a vision long enough and you compel it to materialize.

While a vision board approach would have likely caused this dream to more readily manifest, it turns out that any vision has power if held long enough. A few years back, I had just completed a corporate retreat when the CEO stopped me. She said that while they greatly valued the three day retreat we just completed, what they really needed was someone to help the family work better together, would I be interested? I was. It felt right, somehow.

Over the next seven years, I had the privilege of doing a portion of all the activities mentioned above and more. During this period, I gained a wonderful sense of satisfaction serving in a broad capacity, addressing key personal and professional issues, and acting as a partner to help the family make needed change. Seemingly out of nowhere, what I envisioned came to pass. My dream came to me, merely because I nurtured it in my mind's eye.

Visualization drives manifestation. It doesn't matter if it is intentional or not. Hold a vision long enough and you compel it to materialize. This occurs because what you see, how you think, what you believe, and how you act are influenced by the image you hold. For example, if you see yourself as fit and healthy, and hold that image long enough for it to be how you see yourself, you might find yourself exercising more, eating better, and relating to people who live more actively. So, what are you envisioning?

Your inspired Wizard knows that enormous potential lies within you. By visualizing, you shift your attention away from what you don't want and toward what you desire. In doing so, you provide for possibility, engaging in a mental experiment that provides access to a wonderful range of possible outcomes which you can enjoy as an installment in your future success.

Note, however, the final path traveled is seldom exactly as imagined. Success is further enhanced when you allow it to materialize in whatever form is most perfect. Making affirmations, for example, is a powerful technique that provides a wide breadth of possibility. Affirmations are a process of centering on your core values and closely held truths. For example, you might say the following out loud every morning, "This day, I will serve those around me, take concrete steps toward achieving my personal goals, and be kind, generous, and slow to anger." Scientists suggest affirmations work by shifting the point of concentration.[62]

In one study, researchers demonstrated that a positive statement can protect against the detrimental effects of stress related to problem solving.[63] In another, it was found that positive statements at the beginning of the school term boosted grades for underperforming students.[64] As a form of envisioning, affirmations work because they help identify and focus a person on the best of who they are. Like dreams, views of self are often muddled and unclear. Self-affirmations, such as, "I am a person who provides value to others," "My family and friends are most important to me," "I am a hard worker who can achieve my goals," or "I am a good person who follows God," provide clarity and motivation. Envisioning shifts us from limitation to possibility.

> The foundation of every success lies in the image held beforehand.

To create a useful affirmation, the first step is to identify a closely held personal value. As a self-driven achiever, you may hold accomplishment as paramount. As a godly person, kindness, service, or love might be in the top row. Place your answer in the top row of Thought Expander 10.2, Personal Affirmation. This value can be a truth you hold dear or it can be a perspective you wish to develop. The second step is to write a clear, comfortable, and compelling affirmation. What matters is that your affirmation honors your truth. If you are already a hard worker, your affirmation might honor this and affirm that continued efforts will deliver you the success you desire in life. Alternatively, if you want to grow in faith, for example, you might reflect on Bible quotes regarding God's many promises to his people.

Thought Expander 10.2: Personal Affirmation

Closely held personal value.	I value…
Create your affirmation.	I am …

Every accomplishment begins with a concept of what could be. That is true whether the potentiality is external or internal. The key is to hold a clear and compelling vision. "Let your eyes look straight ahead, fix your gaze directly before you…do not swerve to the left or the right" (Proverbs 4:25-27; NIV).

A clear focus on a value, way, or goal allows you to become highly receptive to stimuli that help move you in the direction of your desire.

Dream pursuit is how you avoid regrets.

The effectiveness of hypnosis in treating addictions and other dysfunctions is attributed, in part, to concentrated focus (Braid, 1843). In hypnosis, the individual focuses their attention in ways that make them more responsive to suggestion or direction. Similarly, through visualization and affirmation you cause your Wizard to refocus. The foundation of every success lies in the image held beforehand.

People without a vision tend to lead fallow lives. Not taking charge of your life has a cost—namely regret. Regret is an unhappy feeling that occurs when one senses they could have avoided, altered, or corrected a past mistake. It is about the "if only's" in life (e.g., "if only I could," "if only I was," and "if only I had"). Regret is an insight that the present situation would be better if you had acted differently, and this state of disappointment tends to be inversely related to well-being.[65] In general, regret increases when people feel they had more control than they used, and were better able to influence the outcome than they did.[66] Since most limits are self-imposed, each of us has enormous influence over our lives. As such, dream pursuit is how you avoid regrets.

Interviews of elderly people, at the end of life, support this idea. The number one thing people regret is the thing they always wanted to do but never did.[67] They regretted not pursuing their dreams. Beyond this, in order of importance, the elderly wished they had worked smarter, expressed their feelings more often, stayed in contact with their friends, and let themselves enjoy life more. Overall, people are most disappointed when they are not true to themselves. They regret living the life expected of them rather than the life they really wanted.

Your inspired Wizard understands that not following your dreams is what you will regret most. So what is it you will you most regret not doing? What can you do about it? Complete Thought Expander 10.3, <u>Opportunities Captured</u>, to explore your options.

Thought Expander 10.3: Opportunities Captured

Regret Area	Complete the following statements: "**I will** (insert item from left) **and avoid regret by...**"
Be true to myself	
Work smarter	
Express my feelings	
Stay in touch	
Enjoy life	

Scientific research provides additional insights regarding the sense of regret. Three separate studies found inaction to action regret ratios of 60:40, 63:37, and 75:25.[68,69,70] In these studies, failure-to-act regrets outnumbered regrettable actions by two to one indicating that most regrets result from a lack of action. Looked at another way, regrets from actions taken tend to pass quickly while inaction regrets persist.[71]

Don't lose the thrill of life by leaving your vision trapped inside you.

Several specific life domains were found to be prominent when it comes to the creation of regret.[72] Education, in particular, was most commonly lamented. People who missed out on getting the schooling they desired often regretted it for a lifetime. The next most significant areas were career, romance, parenting, and self improvement, in that order. Men tended to regret work choices and women regretted love choices. People are more likely to regret purchasing things while being disappointed with not purchasing experiences.[73] This is possibly due to the fact that experiences are often less recapturable than material items which can often be acquired later or replaced. In general, more regret is experienced with the greater the perceived loss.

I can think of very few things that are worse than getting to the end of life and realizing that you've missed out. Instead of letting life happen to you, make it what you want it to be. See yourself studying hard and doing well at school; write a vision of yourself thriving in your dream occupation.

Visualize your victory to secure it.

Picture yourself going to places you like and spending time with those you love. Imagine yourself becoming the person you were always meant to be. Don't lose the thrill of life by leaving your vision trapped inside you. By actively, enthusiastically, constructing your wish, you can be true to yourself. "An average person with average talents and ambition and average education, can outstrip the most brilliant genius in our society, if that person has clear, focused goals" (Mary Kay Ash).

Your inspired Wizard knows you craft your life. You mold it and shape it to the form of your desire by following your spirit, looking far ahead, dreaming big, creating a plan, and envisioning triumph. Ultimate success is a direct result of your ability to glimpse goals as already accomplished. In order to create something, you must first be able to envision it. Visualization is a potent tool that conjures in the mind's eye an end result from the onset. In so doing, it creates possibility, manifesting reality from shapeless imaginings. To skip this valuable process is to risk living a lesser life, one with regret. For the ability to fashion your own life is fundamental to fulfilling your destiny. Visualize your victory to secure it.

THE WIZARD

Your Wizard discerns that success comes from following your spirit, looking far ahead, dreaming bigger, creating a plan, and envisioning success. Developing an inspired and savvy Wizard is essential to identifying and creating the life you want. Yet, the story of success has just begun. Even as your King grows to think better and your Wizard grows to craft your live anew, accomplishment is possible only with the ability to convert these ideas into outcomes. This next aspect of success is invaluable in that regard, for it breathes life into both your King and your Wizard making the successful life possible through action...

War·ri·or [war-ee-er]. A soldier or fighter with experience; a courageous combatant. A brave, specialized performer.

ASPECT III: THE STRONG WARRIOR

The Warrior is the part of you that takes action. It can be thought of as the tactical part of each person's psyche. Your Warrior gets things done. It does so by optimizing the effort put forward and always focusing on doing what it takes to accomplish a winning outcome. When mature, the Warrior is effective and efficient, filled with great energy and capability. It makes life's journey possible. This part of you provides strength to progress and moves you forward. Finished goals, realized outcomes, and personal accomplishments are manifestations of your Warrior.

The Warrior's doing balances out the Monk's being. It leverages the King's understanding and implements the Wizard's plans. The Warrior aspect of success moves you from where you are to where you want to be. It secures desires and works to make dreams a reality.

If this aspect of success is weak, meek, or immature, success will be impossible. When things look too hard; when you regularly procrastinate, can't finish things, or let others take advantage of you, it is an indication that your Warrior is underdeveloped. In this state, your Warrior is not able to properly do the things that will bring you the outcomes you desire. Conversely, when you are uncaring, treat others poorly, are explosive, or act in other rude, inconsiderate, or uncaring ways, it is an indication that your Warrior has become aggressive. Here, you are over-relying on your Warrior at the expense of other more appropriate behaviors available from your King, Wizard, or Monk.

To see where your Warrior stands, do the following exercise. Check up to ten items from any of the three boxes below that best describe emotions you most commonly experience, or one's that you find most challenging and problematic. Consider not only what you think, but take into account what others who know you well say about you.

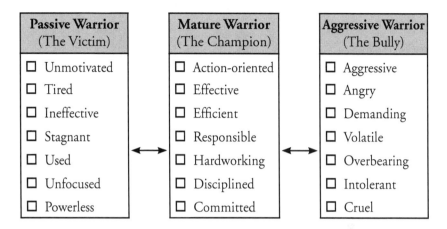

Passive Warrior (The Victim)		Mature Warrior (The Champion)		Aggressive Warrior (The Bully)
☐ Unmotivated		☐ Action-oriented		☐ Aggressive
☐ Tired		☐ Effective		☐ Angry
☐ Ineffective		☐ Efficient		☐ Demanding
☐ Stagnant	←→	☐ Responsible	←→	☐ Volatile
☐ Used		☐ Hardworking		☐ Overbearing
☐ Unfocused		☐ Disciplined		☐ Intolerant
☐ Powerless		☐ Committed		☐ Cruel

Now look at where most of your marks reside. If there are more items checked on the left-hand side of the graphic, then your Warrior is probably underdeveloped. A passive Warrior, or Victim, tends to be weak and immature. Fully embraced, this section of the book will help you develop a strong Warrior.

Alternately, if most of the circled items tend toward the right-hand side of the graphic, your Warrior is probably heavily relied upon and used to the point where it is counterproductive. An aggressive Warrior, or Bully, tends to compensate for unaddressed weakness in the King, Wizard, or Monk. While this section will most certainly be of value, it is important that you also identify which other aspects(s) might be suboptimal. Strengthening these aspects will level and restore balance, thereby, reducing the need and tendency toward overreliance on your Wizard in ways that do not fully serve you.

To be successful in life, your inner Warrior must be both strong and mature. As such, your Warrior knows how to execute a direct order from the King or implement a plan from the Wizard so you can later bask in the appreciative energy of the Monk. It can figure out what needs to be done next, based on where it is and where it needs to go. Courageous, a well-trained Warrior can rank and prioritize options, assess risks and potentialities, and execute. Developing a strong Warrior is essential to goal attainment and, ultimately, to achieving success in your life.

Like the King and Wizard, there are five core behaviors to a strong

Warrior. Your mature Warrior knows how to (11) take action, (12) embrace work, (13) manage time, (14) focus efforts, and (15) do the next best thing. We will explore these five behaviors, in turn, throughout the pages of this section.

BEHAVIOR 11: TAKING ACTION

"A vision without action is a dream. An action without vision passes time.
A vision with action can change your world."
— Joel Arthur Barker, adapted

D o it now. Get going. Whatever your dream, seek it, strive for it, dare
to live it. Action is essential to every accomplishment, and victory is
impossible without it. You need to takes steps early and often if you want
to realize your goals. Attempt, persist, and try, try again. Effort precipitates
achievement, for the successful life is one of action. Physics, the science of
action and movement, demonstrates this well.

According to Newton's third law of motion, for every action there is an
equal and opposite reaction. To realize an alternate outcome, the law states
that some form of energy must be applied.
Life is no different. Every desired outcome
requires some input for it to materialize. Due
to a lack of action, many people leave great
reservoirs of potential unexplored. They suffer from low inertia.

The successful life is one of action.

In physics, inertia is the tendency of an object to continue in its current
manner unless it is influenced in some way. Every person is either moving
toward their goals or they are moving away from them—often stagnating
while quietly, imperceptibly falling behind. People with low inertia often
find it difficult to gain any impetus. They feel as if life is passing them by.

So, how do you rectify the negative symptoms of personal inertia? The
simple fix is to add energy to the system. Action is the essential, missing
ingredient. Like rolling a boulder down a hill, momentum is gained by
pushing over and over again. With sequentially applied action, the boulder
begins to move and then accelerates. Rolling faster and faster, at some point
the boulder becomes difficult, if not impossible, to stop. With enough en-

ergy, the boulder will actually gain a life of its own such that incremental pushes will no longer make a noticeable impact on its speed. At this point, you need only shift from propelling the boulder forward to steering it where you want it to go.

Success in life is no different. Action builds momentum generating positive inertia toward goal attainment. Additional exertion works to increase the speed of progress. Regular, consistently applied effort can create so much forward energy that it can become impossible to stop the forward progress, making the desired outcome not a question of "if?" but a question of "when?"

> Action builds momentum generating positive inertia toward goal attainment.

Action precipitates success. To become an accomplishment, every aspiration must be acted on. Otherwise, your dreams will stay just that. Progress in life is similar to driving. A car has to be moving for you to steer it. Action allows you to avoid obstacles and navigate twists and turns on the way to accomplishing your goals.

Your inner Warrior recognizes that exertion is of fundamental import. The benefits of action as a method of progress can be found in a wide range of disciplines including business, psychology, sociology, spirituality, and philosophy. When I was doing merger and acquisition (M&A) work, there was a phrase bantered amongst strategists who, after buying a new company, needed to integrate it with existing operations. It says, "Fast and good trumps slow and perfect." These executives recognize a certain genius in action, and understand the corrosiveness of indecision. When people don't know what is going to happen, they tend to assume the worst. As a result, a good acquisition integration plan implemented quickly was found superior than a polished one put into action later. "Decisiveness is a characteristic of high-performing men and women. Almost any decision is better than no decision at all" (Brian Tracy).

Indecision can significantly damage progress. During an acquisition, good employees are more likely to leave because they tend to be most marketable. Customers are likely to become frustrated when faced with unclear changes and expectations. In general, when people don't know what is going on, they fill in the blanks with their worst fears. "Inaction breeds doubt and fear. Action breeds confidence and courage. If you want to conquer fear, do not sit home and think about it. Go out and get busy" (Dale Carnegie).

The M&A "fast and good" mantra is action-oriented. Successful practitioners realize they are better off adjusting direction and resetting the course as they proceed, optimizing as they go. In a very real sense, doing is the primary means of control.

According to planned behavior theory (Ajzen, 1985), a sense of control also improves motivation to act. In this way, planning and action are interrelated. As seasoned military practitioners well know, plans and action occur simultaneously, each shaping, reinforcing, and building on the other. Maybe this is why General and President Dwight D. Eisenhower quipped, "In preparing for battle, I have always found that plans are useless, but planning is indispensable." You plan, then you take action, and the outcome reshapes your plans, delineating the next best action.

Success is a byproduct of doing. Only action can take you where you want to be. The trick is to create a good, reasonable plan, and implement it

Doing is the primary means of control.

promptly. Avoid waiting for the plan to be perfect—it never will be. You can always change course, but, to do so, you must be going somewhere. It is the forward-moving action of an airplane that allows it to generate lift and take off. Likewise, it is the forward-moving action in your life that allows you to rise up to achieve your goals. "No matter how carefully you plan your goals they will never be more than pipe dreams unless you pursue them with gusto" (W. Clement Stone).

Where might your best opportunities for action lie? To get you moving, write one of your goals in the top row of Thought Expander 11.1, Action Plan (see Thought Expander 9.1, Life Plan, and 9.2, Action Opportunities, for ideas). Next, identify various actions you could take to build momentum toward accomplishing your goal. Consider what you could do over various periods of time. Write your action possibilities in the lower row of the Thought Expander. If they seem overwhelming or feel out of reach, break them into smaller and smaller actions until they seem realistic and doable.

Thought Expander 11.1: Action Plan

Goal:	
Timeframe	**Actions**
Today	
This Week	
This Month	
This Quarter	
This Year	

You now have a plan for accomplishing your goal. Get started on it today. Stop waiting for the stars to align. "He who observes the wind will not sow, and he who regards the clouds will not reap" (Ecclesiastes 11:4; ESV). Seize every chance to capture the opportunity that resides in the common day. As you proceed, remember to update your actions and plans as your situation evolves.

You can always change course, but, to do so, you must be going somewhere.

Your strong Warrior understands that a good plan executed today is vastly superior to a great plan implemented someday. Your Warrior lives for action, understanding that life is motion. Precise, efficient, effective, the mature Warrior intrinsically understands the value of doing, knowing it is fundamental to success.

Inaction is a bigger problem than most people realize. In fact, it is implicated in many psychological dysfunctions. Depression is a good example.[74] Among U.S. adults, women experience depression twice as often as men.[75] Some psychologists now believe that this gender difference in depression is the result of different coping mechanisms between the sexes. Women have a preference for ruminating, while men lean toward action.

Rumination is the contemplative act of reviewing and reconsidering a situation, event, or outcome. Rumination, it turns out, plays a role in creating negative feelings that can lead to depression while action tends to mitigate it.[76,77,78] Ruminators think

> Seize every chance to capture the opportunity that resides in the common day.

about, stew on, and replay events over and over again in their minds. These are usually negative events. In ruminating, these people tend to reinforce and exaggerate the importance of events, overemphasizing the meaning in them and exaggerating the impact on their lives. They stake out an internal place where they dwell with their negative reflections and counterproductive thoughts. This occurs at the expense of doing something, anything.

Men, more commonly, employ a different strategy. They lean toward responses of action. They get drunk, punch the wall, see a sporting event, or play cards with their buddies. Over bigger issues they may quit their jobs, get divorced, move to a new city, or start life anew. Although not always productive, men tend to prefer doing over reflecting. It is suspected that as a result of this "doing" bias, adult men experience half the rate of depression that adult women experience.

The point is clear. Action is synonymous with living well. Even pointless action may be beneficial. Take "distr-action" for example. Distraction is a combination of the words distracted and action. It is a method by which to disengage from your ruminating thoughts by doing something, anything. Even pointless, meaningless, and inane activities done for their own sake have been found to reduce depression.

Depression is a problem not only among adults but also among young people. In a study of children and adolescents, increased levels of rumination also related to higher levels of depression and anxiety, however, increased levels of distraction did the opposite.[79] Distraction acted to reduce negative thinking and valueless reflection while enhancing well-being.

I call this distratifaction–the positive feeling that comes from getting out of your head and doing something, anything, to engage yourself. Action is so important, that even without a purpose, it appears to be more valuable than no action at all.

Rumination, like worry and hopelessness, works to convince people that productive options are not available. That is never true. There is always a course that can be pursued, a stride that can be taken, something that can be done. The challenge with counterproductive, self-focused thinking is that it only ends when you either take action to prove the idea wrong or you give up.[80] Quitting is a lousy option as it guarantees a suboptimal outcome. You can't score if you don't shoot. Accepting failure or embracing a hopeless outlook drains vigor and stunts life.

Action is synonymous with living well.

Genius lies in doing. As Ralph Waldo Emerson said, "Do the thing and you will have the power." Doing that "thing" shifts you from doubting to trying, from worrying to growing, from fantasizing to accomplishing. Action is the cure to worry. Personal power arises out of the courage of doing. In doing, we realize that reservations are unfounded, and that our desires are obtainable.

Americans today are in a great depression, and this is not a reference to recent economic turmoil (i.e., the great recession). Despite development of a modern health care system to identify mental illness and a plethora of new drugs to treat it, depression rates for men, women, and children in the United States sit at epidemic levels. It may be that depression is a natural survival adaptation used to conserve resources in situations where action appears futile.[81] Specifically, lifestyle changes during our recent shift toward industrialization may lie at the root of the dramatic rise in depression.[82]

Modern humans have radically fewer opportunities to pursue effort-based rewards—tangible objectives obtained through direct efforts like fishing, weaving, and building—that provide their own unique gratification. As such, they are receiving less frequent rewards thought to be essential for healthy psychological function. The use of automation and the proliferation of services in daily life have removed effort-based rewards—a sense of accomplishing something concrete.

Increasingly, we are asked to focus on the abstract such as completing business reports, creating fiscal budgets, devising marketing strategies, and servicing customers. Vast reductions in physical activity have been associated with less brain activation in areas responsible for pleasure, motivation, problem-solving, and coping. Such changes can lead to reduced mental resilience upon exposure to stress and an increased unhappiness. Researchers suggest that finding work that requires physical activity and generates a tangible reward may mitigate this trend and reduce depressive tendencies. Cutting firewood to heat your home, growing your own vegetables, building or fixing things around the house are several examples. Starting your own business, hiring employees, buying a building, and restoring a hot rod are larger ones. The changes in brain chemistry that result from effort-based rewards are one reason that exercise is commonly used as part of treating depression. Irrespective of what kind of action it is, an active, physical engagement toward accomplishing tangible outcomes can generate increased feelings of fulfillment and satisfaction. If such activities are lacking in your vocation, as they are with many, you can benefit by adding them to your personal life.

> It is a practical truth that, to achieve, you must do.

Action is essential to success. People who take action are more likely to receive attention, be appreciated, improve goal progress, and experience greater well-being.[83] Beyond psychology and physics, spirituality also espouses action. "Ask, and it will be given to you; seek, and you will find; knock, and it will be opened to you" (Matthew 7:7; ESV). Notice the strong action verbs that are required for success—we need to ask, seek, and knock to get what we want. "Even so, faith, if it has no works, is dead, being by itself" (James 2:17; NAS). Action is synonymous with life.

It is a practical truth that, to achieve, you must do. Theodore Geisel is an excellent example of this law. He spent his life writing. Theodore wrote extensively, plying his trade at length in a variety of ways so that he could become a better writer. He wrote and wrote. However, he never took the risk to do the thing he really wanted to do. Theodore never wrote the next great American novel—his lifelong dream. The lesson lies in his action and inaction, as both played to their logical conclusion. You probably know Theodore Geisel better as Dr. Seuss. While learning to become a writer of enough caliber, Dr. Seuss wrote over sixty children's books, all as practice. His hard work and efforts went on to lead him to critical acclaim as he sold over half a billion copies! All the while, he worked to develop the talent and experience he thought necessary to follow his dream. However, he never attempted the novel he always dreamed of writing. Who knows what might have been?

My favorite Dr. Seuss book was published toward the end of his career and addresses this point directly. The perfect graduation present, *Oh, the Places You'll Go!* is a funny, poignant story about the journey of life. In it, Geisel speaks of the "waiting place." It is a place where things do not happen, a location free of action. I have spent more than my fair share of time in the waiting place. Of my thirty years in corporate America, I spent more than twenty of them looking to do something more fulfilling. Years went by as I waded through a psychological morass of having strong interests without knowing how to live them.

We all visit the waiting place. You know you reside there when you start telling yourself "I will be ready to do X once Y happens…" (fill in the X and Y variables with what you are waiting on and for). Examples include: "After the next promotion," "When the kids graduate", "When we have enough money," "When I have things under control," "Once things improve," "When this problem is resolved," etc.

Geisel had this issue too. Action led him to extraordinary success and inaction left him with a "What if?" question regarding his lifelong dream. He was always waiting and working to become a serious writer. But he never followed through. Ironically, his recommendation in *Oh, the Places You'll Go!* is to not stay in the waiting place. "Everyone is just waiting. NO! That's not for you! Somehow you'll escape all that waiting and staying. You'll find the bright places where Boom Bands are playing." Geisel encourages the reader to quickly find a way to escape inaction and move on to places where things are happening. In advocating action, he identifies a crucial choice to achieving success.

One of the most destructive things you can do is to spend your life waiting. "Action is a great restorer and builder of confidence. Inaction is not only the result, but the cause, of fear. Perhaps the action you take will be successful; perhaps different action or adjustments will have to follow. But any action is better than no action at all" (Norman Vincent Peale). Even people with lofty aspirations get distracted by the vagaries of daily experiences and too often place their dreams in the waiting place.

So what are you waiting for? Do you want to stay where you are? If not, what can you do? To gain clarity, write a major goal in the header column of Thought Expander 11.2, Action Drivers (see Thought Expander 11.1, Action Plan, if needed). Next, identify various actions you could take toward that goal. Consider the easier and harder, both smaller and bigger options, and place them in the left-hand column. For each action, identify some possible benefits and write these in the right-hand column. Next, consider what will likely result if you don't take any action. Write the negative consequence of inaction in the footer row at the bottom of the table.

Thought Expander 11.2: Action Drivers

Goal:	
Actions	**Benefits**
Likely Result Without Action:	

Frequently, people believe they have valid reasons to not act, to wait. Often, these are just excuses or effort-free choices. Waiting seems easier than working to get what you want out of life. Action requires time and resources, making lingering seem palatable. However, in delaying, you are loitering on the curb of life, watching it, not living it. For inaction is not free. Like doing, waiting also consumes a slice of your life energy leaving less pie in the future.

There is a joke about a fellow in dire trouble. His business has gone bust, and he is so desperate that he decides to ask God for help. He begins to pray. "God, please help me. I've lost my business, and if I don't get some money, I'm going to lose my house as well. Please let me win the lotto."

Lotto night comes, and somebody else wins. Again the fellow prays. "God, please let me win the lotto! I've lost my business, my house and I'm going to lose my car as well." Lotto night comes, and he still has no luck. Once again he prays. "My God, why have you forsaken me? I've lost my business, my house, and my car. My children are starving. I don't often ask you for help, and I have always been a good servant to you. Please just let me win the lotto this one time, so I can get my life back in order." Suddenly, there is a blinding flash of light as the heavens open and the fellow is confronted by the voice of God, himself.

If you fail to act, you act to fail.

"Hey, come on now, you are going to have to meet me halfway on this. Buy a ticket."

There is always something you can do irrespective of circumstances. At minimum, you can plan for the future you want. More specifically, you can start preparing the boat, baiting the hook, or casting the line in preparation for your next journey. The wisdom of action is demonstrated even among the smallest of insects. "Go to the ant, O sluggard; consider her ways, and be wise. Without having any chief, officer, or ruler, she prepares her bread in summer and gathers her food in harvest" (Proverbs 6:6-8; ESV).

The Warrior aspect of success recognizes that a life of waiting is a life not lived. Inaction is costly both to what you get and how you feel, leaving you empty and unfulfilled. Action is your Warrior's default state. Only action yields forward progress. Action builds up, reinforces, and increases likelihoods. It informs, expands, and generates possibility. Inaction wears down, weakens, decreases, and limits. Your strong Warrior knows that purposeful action is essential for success.

Your Warrior is courageous. Like a mature soldier, your Warrior will execute a well-conceived plan, even if afraid. Focusing effort on activities that generate the most value, your Warrior avoids taking so much risk that you might explode, risking ruin, while also avoiding so much safety that you don't move at all. A well-developed Warrior is able to maintain and manage the precarious balance between doing what is scary and pursuing what is justifiable in order to achieve that which is worthwhile.

"Create a definite plan for carrying out your desire and begin at once, whether you're ready or not, to put this plan into action" (Napoleon Hill). If you fail to act, you act to fail. Whatever your hearts desires, take action toward it. It is in doing that you become.

BEHAVIOR 12: EMBRACING WORK

"It is not work that kills men, it is worry. Work is healthy."
— *Henry Ward Beecher*

Experience the joy of doing. Work is not a distraction or inconvenience; it is a conduit for the vital energy of life. It is a pathway to the self. Toil is a sacred part of existence, enabling the diligent to rise above the self and the industrious to achieve a greater purpose. Work harmonizes life. A wishbone and a backbone are essential to success. "So I saw that there is nothing better for a person than to enjoy their work" (Ecclesiastes 3:22; NIV).

Unfortunately, work gets a bad rap. It has been villainized. Set aside as something bad, society often portrays work as an event to be avoided. It is drudgery, a chore to be suffered through until retirement or death. Viewed this way, it is no surprise that many people are dissatisfied. Look for the bad in work, and you will find it embedded within a gambit of discomforts and challenges ranging from task drudgery to office politics. As a result, work for many seems alienating.

We need to think differently. Work is a soul-filled exercise replete with its own dignity. Quality work is a reflection of personal excellence. It is an enterprise from which we learn and grow. We see what we are made of when we labor. For the man, the woman, who does something, is something. They may experience toil, but they are the ones who learn, grow, and achieve.

> A wishbone and a backbone are essential to success.

In reality, work is profound in its excellence. Thomas Carlyle stated that, "Work is the grand cure of all the maladies and miseries that ever beset mankind." Are you maximizing the benefits of work in your life? There is an opportunity for every person to work with gusto and live more success-fully.

How do you think about work? In what ways can you improve its val-ue? To increase its value, take a moment and complete Thought Expander 12.1, Work Benefits. For each category in the left-hand column, identify perspectives you could hold or actions you could take to increase the ben-efit of work in your life. As an example, for the first row entitled "See life as a positive," you might write "Work makes me realize that through effort I can achieve my goals."

Thought Expander 12.1: Work Benefits

Category	How does/could work help me to (insert category)?
See life as a positive	
Achieve better results	
Show respect for others	
Take responsibility	
Grow myself	
Show appreciation	
Demonstrate commitment	
Be more positive	
Contribute to the world	
Honor myself	

Work is the motor of life's journey. Embrace the work of life and you can accomplish any dream. For "No thoroughly occupied person was ever found really miserable" (Walter Landor). There are many subtle, yet salient benefits to your industriousness. Most importantly among them, work fuels possibility. Each of us can labor in ways that help to transform our spirit. There is no shortage of evidence that a more enthusiastic work attitude translates into more productive outcomes such as increased diligence, enhanced responsibility, superior performance, and even improved relationships.[84] Pride in our labors reinforces personal worth, ultimately enhancing satisfaction and happiness.

Work is essential to living well.

Your inner Warrior understands that work is a fundamental element of living successfully. It is neither something to be avoided nor something to be feared. Work is a natural and important part of human life. Work is needed to thrive. For "Work and you will earn a living; if you sit around talking you will be poor" (Proverbs 14:23, GNT). Work is essential to living well.

However, this is not what most are led to believe. Hollywood perpetuates the idea with respect to love, fame, and wealth—each being depicted as complete and permanent wins, if achieved. Riches in particular are portrayed as the ultimate goal, providing access to infinite relaxation, joy, and peace. Once we are rich, we will have it made; we will be happy. Unfortunately, it doesn't work like that.

Some of the wealthiest CEOs I work with have tested the life of leisure out. They found that a pleasure-filled life is a rather empty existence. As a result, most return to work long after the need to create wealth has been satisfied. Why? They don't quit working, in part, because infinite recreation is untenable. Non-productive free time results in boredom, stagnation, and sometimes trouble.

Energy is a vital part of the life process. At the start of each day, you, along with everyone else, get an allotment of energy. You then decide how to channel this crucial life force. You could spend it pursuing baubles or use it to change the world. You could use it responding to what life brings you or invest it to get what you want out of life. One way or another, you allot your daily energy to something. It is the effectiveness of this expenditure that matters.

Workaholics, for example, go overboard in their allocation of energy used for work. They tend to overspend, borrowing the needed energy from the next day or other vital areas of life. Over long periods of time, this can result in serious problems. As anyone who owns a rechargeable device knows, if you run the batteries all the way down and leave them that way for any period of time, damage occurs. The cells will no longer take a full charge and their ability to dispense the same is permanently impaired. Life is no different. If one's batteries run too low it can hurt, leading to burnout, illness, and unhappiness.

One way or another, you allot your daily energy to something. It is the effectiveness of this expenditure that matters.

A life of leisure is similar but occurs on the opposite end of the scale. Here, people tend to under-spend their energy, letting it build day after day. While renewal during weekends, vacations, and sabbaticals is necessary, all things in excess are problematic. Done too excessively, relaxation can backfire, leading to low motivation, disengagement, and slothfulness resulting in a life without meaning. Revisiting the prior simile, charging a battery all the time will also ruin it. It will lose its functionality and, over time, not be able to properly dispense the charge. Energy will no longer flow through the battery. Damage occurs, impairing its normal function. We are no different. If our energy gets trapped long enough, we no longer work properly. Our ability to work is damaged, our perspective unhealthy. We can eventually lose interest or develop unproductive habits, becoming disillusioned and lost.

Too much or too little work is a problem. A successful life is the result of a healthy expenditure and recapture of energy. Batteries were designed to have energy course through them, to ebb and flow, to charge and discharge in a process of continuous flux. Life is similar. Too much or too little work creates an imbalance putting people out of accord with their natural needs. Such discord and lack of ease combine to create dis-ease—a lack (dis) of flow (ease). Sickness is the result of not living in equilibrium. To live well, you must find a healthy balance with work. Accomplished people play at work and they work at play.

Work, to be productive, needs to be applied resourcefully. Effort must also be spent in a disciplined way to achieve success. Discipline is an essential action that allows you to be efficient with your life energy and effective in your endeavors. Success requires a regimented Warrior who is willing and able to show the control necessary to appropriately prepare, postpone, and persist. Let's consider each of these three essential "Ps" of discipline in turn.

First, disciplined work requires preparation. In facing life, you are either proactive or reactive. By construction, pro-active means something that leans toward (pro) getting things done (active). Likewise, re-active means to again and again, after the fact (re), to get things done (active). Reactive people are mired in repetition of tried responses while the proactive prepare, running their lives

> **Accomplished people play at work and work at play.**

from a position of creativity and newness through the exertion of will. They don't need to wait for an opportunity to go and get it. As a result, the proactive approach is far superior.

In the business world, proactivity and success are inextricably linked. During the Great Depression of 1929, Post was the largest cereal company in the world. They dominated the marketplace. Kellogg Cereal was just one of a number of want-to-be competitors. As the economy stalled, Post cut their costs by dropping their advertising. They shifted from seeing the situation as an opportunity to viewing it as a problem—one requiring preservation—so they hunkered down.

Kellogg, however, took a different view and decided to continue to strategically invest in key areas like advertizing. As a result of their foresight, Kellogg emerged as the market leader ahead of Post when the economy finally recovered. Today, some 80 years later, Kellogg remains the largest producer of cereal in the United States.

Additionally, to the extent proactivity yields profit, reactivity generates costs. Many years ago a friend of mine had a loose muffler on his car. He didn't bother to take care of it leaving it to drag underneath his vehicle. He figured it would just fall off, why bother. One day on the way to work, his muffler hit a pot hole at the perfect angle such that the front lip of his muffler caught. Thrusting the unit upward, the muffler punctured his gas tank. His car immediately exploded into flames. To hear him tell it, it was less than ten seconds from impact until the car was engulfed in fire. He barely stopped and got out alive. He watched as his wallet, briefcase, and other personal effects went up in a thick cloud of black smoke on a busy

Illinois freeway. Thank goodness, it was his wife's day to drive his young son to school.

An unprepared approach to life is risky. Left alone, small problems can become major disasters irreparably altering our lives. Experienced corporate strategists know this well. Many CEOs create annual plans to lay out their business direction over the upcoming year(s). Most such plans assume that things will continue in a general direction with some consideration for likely upside and downside estimates. It is the rare plan that has a forecast that doesn't show growth attainment and target accomplishment—in large part because leaders don't

Discipline allows you to be efficient with your life energy and effective in your endeavors.

wish to be fired. However, reality is often very different. To address this, the best strategic plans include what is called a contingency plan. Executives explore what events could cause their plans to go significantly wrong, and they develop a method to identify them early, and the executives develop a course of action to thwart, mitigate, and minimize such possibilities before they happen. Preparing in this way, executives help ensure business longevity. Preparation is also an essential action to achieving success in life.

The second of the three P's of discipline is postponement. Accomplishment often requires delayed gratification. The ability to forgo today for a better outcome tomorrow is a strong indicator of success. One famous study is the Stanford Marshmallow experiments, where in the late 1960s and early 1970s children who were able to wait longer for rewards, such as marshmallows, were found to do better in many areas of life.[85] Delayed gratification, the ability to postpone a benefit now in exchange for a larger gain later, foretold higher test scores, more academic achievement, and other positive outcomes decades later in life.[86,87] Successful people, it turns out, are those who are self-disciplined and patient. They are adept at postponing gratification. As such, they have learned to overcome its nemesis—temporal discounting.

Temporal discounting (Mazur, Snyderman, & Coe, 1985) is the process of undervaluing payoffs that are further away in time, in favor of more imminent rewards. In the marshmallow experiment, temporal discounting occurred among children who could not wait to eat a snack (marshmallow, cookie, or pretzel) placed right in front of them even though they would receive two of the same if they waited approximately 15 minutes. More relevant examples might include eating the donut now and promising to start your diet tomorrow, or buying a luxury on credit knowing that you can't readily pay it off. In both cases, the "now" benefit appears to exceed the benefit in the future—even though an objective review of these situations suggests that is not the case.

Techniques to improve the negative impact of temporal discounting include assessing immediate negative consequences, conceptualizing long-term benefits, and finding productive ways to let time pass.[88] Achievers are people who get good at exchanging near-term gratifications in return for long-term gains. Successful people are willing to sacrifice in the current day for the promise of a better tomorrow.

The third of the three P's of discipline is persistence. Napoleon Hill, the author of *Think and Grow Rich*, notes that, "There may be no heroic connotation to the word persistence, but the character is to the quality of man what carbon is to steel." Success is born of endurance; the secret is to keep trying. Persistence is the continuous act of placing effort toward what could be instead of accepting what is.

> **Be willing to sacrifice in the current day for the promise of a better tomorrow.**

Persistence is powerful stuff, often trumping ability. Take intelligence for example. Decades of scientific investigation has found that an emphasis on perseverance outperforms a focus on personal aptitude.[89] Students who see intelligence as the foundation for their success often become fearful of any challenge that threatens to unseat their perceived superiority. As students advance and information becomes increasingly complicated, those with a fixed mindset of intelligence are left more vulnerable to stress and failure. Alternately, students who focus on persistent effort and enjoy hard work experience the opposite. Embracing a growth mindset allows them to meet adversity as an opportunity for personal growth.[90] "You're never beaten until you admit it" (George Patton). Students who adopt this philosophy understand that while intelligence might be helpful, effort is essential. Persistence becomes a harbinger of success.

Even geniuses and savants are not born accomplished. Mozart, Curie, Da Vinci, Einstein, Darwin, and many, many others had to take their innate talents and cultivate them through tremendous, sustained effort. Giftedness doesn't translate directly into achievement. Most everyone knows a very intelligent or gifted person who has little to show for their lives. We also all know a tenacious, committed person who is wildly successful beyond their acumen. The difference between them is merely their persistence.

Accomplished people are dedicated and committed to work. They fully capitalize upon whatever abilities with which they are endowed. As a result, they are more likely to achieve their goals, and they experience greater well-being and happiness in the process.[91,92] Actor Harrison Ford reflects this stating, "I realized early on that success was tied to not giving up. Most people...gave up... If you simply didn't give up, you would outlast the people who came in on the bus with you."

> Failure is a resource— a valuable indicator of how to next proceed.

Persistent people have hope. They stick with a course of action because they expect their efforts can influence outcome. They try and try again because they are driven to achieve their goals and refuse take no for an answer. "He who has a 'why' to live can bear almost any how" (Fredrick Nietzsche).

Conversely, people who don't expect to succeed do not persevere. Researchers see this in tests on animals who no longer take action, even when it will benefit them, because they, presumably, have come to perceive their situation as hopeless.[93,94] Termed "learned helplessness" (Seligman, 1975), this behavior results from experiencing repeated failure, and it is observed in people, as well as animals.[95] People who have learned helplessness try less, if at all. When they do try, they do so for shorter periods and they give up more quickly. Not surprisingly, reduced levels of effort cause them to succeed less frequently and fail more often. A vicious cycle of quitting, failure, and passiveness is born from the conviction that their effort won't make a difference. Beliefs have a powerful affect on a person's ability to adapt and accomplish.

Your mature Warrior knows to persist in the face of failure. "Many of life's failures are people who did not realize how close they were to success when they gave up" (Thomas Edison). Failure is a resource—a valuable indicator of how to next proceed. There is always a way to accomplish your goal. Take the behavior of ravens for example. They have been observed getting drinks from narrow containers by dropping in small pebbles to raise the water line. Similarly, water consistently dripping in one spot will eventually cut a hole right through stone. Continual effort in the direction of your dream is needed for a successful life.

Persistence not only trumps intelligence but it also beats out short bursts of intense, raw effort. Too much effort expended at one time can damage and overwhelm. Consider exercise, for example. It does no good if you head to the gym and lift so many weights in one day that you can't go back again for several weeks. Similarly, eating nothing for a week and then going back to your old ways won't get you where you want to be weight-wise either. Perpetual effort is a far superior approach to accomplish goals. Success is a result of small efforts consistently applied over long periods. Consider this—a lake is filled one raindrop at a time.

Small labors constantly applied can generate amazing results. I call this approach to accomplishment persistent incrementalism. Take Thomas Edison, for example. He tried more than a thousand times before coming up with the right filament material to create the incandescent light bulb. When asked about his chronic "failures" by a reporter, he clarified stating "I didn't fail a thousand times; the light bulb was an invention with a thousand steps." This is persistent incrementalism at its best and yielded Edison some 1,093 U.S. Patents. Bet on the persistent person every time.

Starkly evident among many of the highly successful people is the pattern of failure and its role in persistence. Failure has an unfair, negative connotation. Rightly employed it is a powerful tool. Failure is life giving us feedback about our efforts; persistence is our response to that lesson. Accomplished people have lives interwoven with both failure and persistence. Thomas Edison was once sent home from school with a teacher note indicating he was "too stupid to learn" and was fired from his first two jobs for being "nonproductive." Walt Disney was fired from a newspaper for "lacking imagination." J. K. Rowling overcame twelve publisher rejections of Harry Potter while Colonel Sanders was told "no" by over a thousand restaurants before launching his fried food empire. Michael Jordon was cut from his high-school varsity basketball team, Winston Churchill failed sixth grade, and Einstein was classified as an "unteachable fool." Even one of our greatest presidents, Abraham Lincoln, had ten major political defeats on his way to the presidency. Failure and persistence appear to be essential ingredients to accomplishment.

So many wildly accomplished people have failure in their backgrounds, that it appears as if defeat might be a required component of success. However, what they did with their defeat is what mattered. George Bernard Shaw used it to motivate, noting: "When I was young I observed that nine out of ten things I did were failures, so I did ten times more work." Failure, setbacks, and delays fuel an essential life giving process that leads to growth and, eventually, accomplishment. Provided it is perceived valuable in some way, some of the most traumatic experiences can lead to the most significant personal development.[96]

Be willing to burn the bridges behind you, and make success your only option.

Instead of resisting failure, take advantage of it. Expect it will happen and leverage it. Failure is life's way of telling you to modify your course, and try something different. Often, each shortfall provides insights on where to go and what to do next. The trick is to treat each disappointment as a valuable learning experience. Failure plus persistence equals accomplishment. "I can't change the direction of the wind, but I can adjust my sails to always reach my destination" (James Dean).

Success is the result of capturing opportunity as it comes, like making jelly when your efforts yield sour fruit. People who demonstrate flexibility in response to adversity are not only more likely to achieve their goals, but they also tend to experience greater mental, physical, and social well-being.[97] You may need to change tactics or alter the path you're on, or you might not—the secret is to never quit pursuing your dream.

Be willing to burn the bridges behind you, and make success your only option. This doesn't mean you should permanently damage relationships or act in irresponsible, dangerous ways. It means you should be willing to pursue actions where retreat is no longer an option. As an example Firdtjorf Nansen said, "I demolish my bridges behind me - then there is no choice but forward." Accomplished people are irrevocably committed. They utter phrases like: "Damn the torpedoes, full speed ahead" (Admiral David Glasgow Farragut).

Collectively, preparation, postponement, and persistence are cornerstones to an effective work ethic. Each is a skill that can be developed and mastered. Consider your life. Are there opportunities for you to work in a more disciplined manner? To explore your options, complete Thought Expander 12.2, Effort Options. In each cell, indicate ways you could become more prepared, things you might be better off postponing, and areas where persistence could payoff.

Thought Expander 12.2: Effort Options

Category	Prepare	Postpone	Persist
Home			
Family			
Work			
Coworkers			
Body			
Mind			
Spirit			

Every obstacle between you and your goals is also an opportunity; you are only a victim if you choose to be. Don't let any situation destroy your hope for a successful future. Use it as an occasion for self-examination and personal growth. Avoid letting negative thoughts about the current situation sabotage your opportunity to get what you want in life. Your attitude is up to you.

How bad do you want your goal or dream? The difference between successful people and everyone else is that they are deeply driven to accomplish their goals. Successful people are committed to succeeding. Accomplished people follow the recommendation that: "whatever your hand finds to do, do it with all your might" (Ecclesiastes 9:10; NIV). This approach is both effective and rewarding.

There is no reason for anyone to work with more enthusiasm than you.

When I was an engineering student at Case Western Reserve University, I joined a fraternity. Zeta Beta Tau (ZBT) was comprised of a great group of guys and provided a wonderful backdrop to the college experience. I learned many things during my fraternity years that continue to serve me well. One of them had to do with how new members were selected. Most recruiters and human resource professionals hire the most talented or qualified person. As my fellow CEOs know, this isn't always the best measure of actual, on-the-job success. At ZBT, we had another metric. The young men who were invited to join were admitted exclusively on one overriding factor. You might guess it was looks, smarts, athletic ability, or some other similar factor. It wasn't. Members were selected solely on their desire to become a "Zeeb." The fraternity had long since realized that those people who most wanted to join were the same brothers who cared and contributed more. Innovative thinking like this kept our fraternity at the top of the social and academic heap year after year.

Your inner Warrior appreciates that a successful life requires doing. There is little you can do about people who are smarter and more talented than you—but there is no reason for anyone to work with more enthusiasm than you. Your strong Warrior understands that commitment combined with a devoted work ethic is an unstoppable combination. Disciplined effort is impossible to thwart, for even in failure, valuable insight is obtained toward achievement. Winning is a product of doing. To work with enthusiasm is to live fully.

BEHAVIOR 13: MANAGING TIME

"Do not squander time for it is the stuff life is made of."
— *Ben Franklin*

Use time well. It does not care how thin, rich, or good looking you might be. Time is the great equilibrator. No respecter of persons, time is neither friend nor enemy, except you make it so. Successful people get more out of life because they use time better. In any given day, we all get the same amount of time. The person who masters time wins.

Today our lives seem to be busier and more hectic than ever. As a result, many people feel stuck, unable to find the time to figure out how to use their time better. Ironically, many people are simply too busy to make the needed changes as to how they use their time. They are too tired and run down from letting time manage them, and they can't make the effort.

In reality though, there is more than enough time. You just need to find it. According to the A.C. Nielsen, the average American watches more than four hours of television each day.[98] That equates to 28 hours per week or 2 months per year. A total of 11 years of a 65 year life (1/6th) is spent "glued to the tube." Worse yet, the A.C. Nielsen numbers don't include screen time spent surfing the web, answering e-mails, or using a cell phone. Other surveys put total American time looking at an electronic screen at closer to 8.5 hours per day—almost double the television estimates.[99] As a result, many stand waist deep in a fresh lake of time, parched with thirst.

Eliminating television, alone, would free up 95,000 hours of time, the equivalent of 43 years working a second full-time job. At an average American rate of $25 per hour, that equates to an additional $2.4 million in income in a lifetime. Alternatively, assuming the average Ph.D. takes six years at 2,000 hours per year—one could achieve the highest educational credential obtainable by carving out a little more than half their screen time. Each of us can be smarter in how we consume time.

So, what would happen in your life if you reallocated just 30 to 60 minutes of your screen time each day to accomplish something more productive? What could that mean to your life over the next month, year, or decade? What could you build, accomplish, achieve? An enormous resource lies before you. A small cup of seeds planted each day could generate a plentiful harvest. You just need to start planting.

I have tapped into this river of possibility many times in my life—always amazed at the results. For example, when I moved from Chicago in 1999, I was growing increasingly uncomfortable with the enormous amount of time television consumed in my life and the limited benefit derived. In changing jobs, I had just lost access to a corporate gym. Concerned with staying fit and hoping to keep off those thirty beer-and-pizza pounds I lost since college, I instituted a new rule. There would be no television in any given day unless I exercised first. If I didn't want to work out, no problem, but also no television—not even the news. It was a good decision, and I found myself working out regularly again.

The person who masters time wins.

Over time, the decision evolved into only watching television while I worked out. First, it was live television or recorded shows on VCR; now it is DVR's, Net-Flix, and DVD/Blue-Ray movies. This arrangement accomplished several things. It got me to exercise. It made the training easier, distracting me during long runs and helping time to pass more quickly. It also practically eliminated my time on the couch, freeing up time to pursue other interests.

Today, the efficiency of combining a low-value activity (television) with a high-value activity (exercise) allows me to capture approximately 500 hours a year of my life. Over the last sixteen years, I estimate that this decision has equated to over 7,000 hours, or three full-time work years. I have found a novel way to use time better.

How about you? What are your best options to use time better? Do you want to carve out 30 minutes a day to read a good book, run on the treadmill, call old friends, pray, or start the next great American novel? The possibilities are endless. However, every success begins with a reallocation of time.

How you spend your time matters. Everyone can make improvements that help get them from where they are to where they want to be. It only takes a creative approach. There is an old joke where two guys are camping in the woods and they hear a bear. The first guy quickly takes off his boots and laces up his running shoes. The second guy chastises him saying "Dummy, don't you know you can't out run a bear." The first guy replies slyly as he dashes away "I don't need to out-run the bear, I just need to outrun you." The well-lived life is very much like this. Successful people are better stewards of their time.

> **Small changes have a dramatic impact over time.**

Small changes have a dramatic impact over time. Consider a plane's global positioning system (GPS) trajectory. If a plane leaves Buffalo for Cleveland and the GPS system is off by one degree, chances are it will still find Hopkins International Airport. However, if the same plane leaves for Los Angeles, it is a likely to miss LAX completely, arriving in the ocean or desert. Incremental efforts accumulate. Investors who earn just 1% more than their peers end up having double the wealth over a life time. Small, positive adjustments compound and generate enormous gains resulting in significantly different outcomes over time. That is the power of using persistent incrementalism, explored in Behavior 12, Embracing Work, to your advantage.

Consider your own time spent. What activities do you want to start doing or spend more time on? Which should you spend less time on or stop doing entirely? To get a better idea, take a few minutes to complete Thought Expander 13.1, Time Optimization.

Thought Expander 13.1: Time Optimization

Activity	
Add:	Stop:
Increase:	Reduce:

If you find this exercise challenging, you can reference the <u>Improvement Areas</u> Table that follows. It includes typical comments collected from years of coaching.

Improvement Areas

Area	Add	Increase	Reduce	Stop
Relational	• Fun weekend with kids each month • Eat breakfast with kids • Weekly date night	• Spend 30 min./ day talking with spouse • Have monthly lunches with friends	• Owning things that take my time • Time spent with people don't enjoy • Internet/phone time	• Making chores more important than kids • Focusing on own needs • TV at dinner
Mental	• Visualize goals for five minutes daily • Meditate or other awareness exercise	• Pray regularly • Appreciation exercises • Paying it forward	• Filling mind with pop culture, politics and entertainment • Rumination	• Doing work at home after dinner • Binge drinking
Personal	• One activity of passion a quarter • Take two justifiable risks per year	• Seek first to understand • Study self-improvement daily	• Judging others • Email checking to four times a day • Gossiping	• Doing entire "to do" list. Pitch half. • 24/7 work availability
Physical	• Eat two servings of vegetables each day • Join gym or put TV in front of treadmill • Weigh self daily	• Exercise three times a week no excuses • Weights and aerobic activity in regimen • Exercise with others	• Meat consumption to once per day • Junk food to one item per day • TV to one hour per day	• Snacking after dinner • Drinking soda • Using cell when driving
Vocational	• Assume everyone is doing their best • Active listening	• Meeting effectiveness • Delegation	• Decide immediately, handling demands only once • Distractions	• Multitasking • Doing personal work at work
Spiritual	• Attend a personal development retreat	• Give 10% of time, talent, and treasure	• Worry and fear by developing faith	• Swearing and using God's name in vain

All of us have things we should do more or less of. We all have things we need to start or stop doing. Scripture cautions each of us, "Look carefully then how you walk, not as unwise but as wise, making the best use of the time" (Ephesians 5:15-16; ESV). But as we know all too well, this is easier said than done.

The Greeks have a word for this challenge, "akrasia" (ə'kreɪzɪə), which means knowing the best course of action but not doing it. Often this is the result of deeply engrained heuristics, or habitual ways of acting. Engrained tendencies, in order to be useful over long periods of time, are, by design, hard to change.

Successful change, therefore, requires consistent effort over a significant period. A general rule of thumb is that to create a new habit, the new behavior needs to be done for at least a month. Researchers have found that, in reality, it takes much longer. The average time to create a new habit was 66 days, or just over two months. Looking at introducing new routines such as jogging or eating better, it can even take up to nine months before the new activity is unchangingly automatic.[100] It takes time to use time better.

> **It takes time to use time better.**

When compared to creating better habits, eliminating bad habits is even more difficult. This is probably because we end up focusing on what we don't want, and that, as your King knows, brings more of it into your life. A bad habit is like a stray cat, feed it, and it will keep showing up. Psychologists have found three ways to moderate the challenge of making change.[101] First, it is easier to tweak than eliminate a bad behavior. Second, it is easier to change habits when they are done more consciously. Third, it is easier to change things which provide smaller benefits.

To successfully make change, they suggest following the three R's: replace, regulate, and reward. Poor practices are easier to correct when they are replaced with other behaviors.[102] For example, people who bite their nails have had better success when the chewing habit was replaced with the related activity of manicuring. People who talk too much gained more ground when they focused on attentive listening instead. Regularity matters, too. Behaviors are more quickly replaced when they are done consistently.[103]

Rewards play a role too. It is easier to correct undesirable practices when the new practice results in an equal or greater sense of benefit.[104] If eliminating sweets is the goal, the replacement behavior will be more successful if it makes the person feel soothed some other way. By finding alternate ways to placate the reward system (for example, sacrificing television time, where most snacking occurs, to take a walk with friends), your brain will use the benefits (socialization and exercise) to reinforce and more quickly develop better patterns.

Eliminating bad habits and developing new, improved habits is an invaluable practice. Good habits use time better. They allow one to become more efficient and effective through better time management.

> Eliminating bad habits and developing new, improved habits is an invaluable practice.

As a field, time management is a well-studied science that creates real value. Best practices include planning activities and scheduling time. One way this can be accomplished is by creating "to do" lists for the days, weeks, months, and even years ahead. The Franklin Covey® system, for example, encourages people to rank and prioritize their daily activities in terms of importance (ranked A, B, C, or D) and order of execution (1, 2, 3, etc.) to better manage time. Similarly, time quadrants (Covey, Merrill, & Merrill, 1994) promote goal-related actions be pursued based on their importance and urgency. This shifts people away from overemphasizing immediate demands and toward actions of longer term value. For example, answering low priority e-mails and doing mundane tasks can all too easily consume peak cognitive time that could be better used planning or doing. In many instances, narrowed efforts yield material progress. Known as the 80:20 rule (Pareto, 1895), a study in economics led to the realization that in many cases the first 20% of our efforts produce 80% of total value possible, with each additional effort yielding a diminishing marginal return.

The best approach is to do more of what will best move you toward your goal and less of everything else. In engineering, this is known as the critical path—the process that constrains a project's progress. Chemists more commonly refer to chemical reactions like this as having a limiting reagent, a chemical that restricts the extent to which a reaction can take place or how quickly it occurs. Both the critical path and limiting reagent constrain progress by limiting the outcome. Identifying and focusing on these constraints is central to making your Warrior efficient and effective.

Every goal contains within it a mission-critical path where managing the bottleneck of activities is essential to success. As one proceeds toward their goal, the trick is to identify barriers to the desired goal and mitigate or eliminate them. The idea is to generate the best likelihood of achieving the objective through an effective and efficient deployment of time.

Time management conserves an essential limited resource—one your mature Warrior guards with zeal. Consider for a moment the activities that make up life. Some of these are undoubtedly important while many other are less so. Even if we don't spend our time optimally, most people are pretty good at prioritizing that which is significant. However, the real value surfaces when we compare our activities against our life objectives. Many things are important in life, yet not all of them align with our goals.

To gain clarity on this idea, fill out Thought Expander 13.2, Activity Alignment. Select a meaningful life goal, and write it in the box in the top left-hand corner of the Thought Expander. Next, think of a typical week. Identify the top ten things you spend time on, or wanted to spend time on, during that period. Insert these items into the appropriate box for each, based on how well they align with your goal. Activities that align well with your goal are inserted into the right-hand column and activities that are necessary to living well are placed in the bottom row.

> **Every goal contains within it a mission-critical path where managing the bottleneck of activities is essential to success.**

For example, if housework is a top ten item, it would likely be in the upper left-hand box because it is seldom aligned with big life goals and it rarely sits in the way of accomplishing them. Conversely, if spending quality time with your spouse or children aligns strongly with your goal of having better family relationships and you haven't been investing the time, it would be listed in the lower right-hand box. Writing this book was in the lower right-hand corner for me, and it is what I focused on while weaving in activities important to my well-being and health like meditation and exercise which lay in the lower left-hand corner because they are not directly aligned with my overarching goal. Finally, compiling a list of people interested in this book, hiring an editor and designer, and seeking out agents were all non-necessary activities, when compared to writing, but were still aligned with my goal of publishing, so they would be placed in the upper right-hand quadrant.

Thought Expander 13.2: Activity Alignment

Goal:		

	Alignment with Goal	
	Low	**High**
Not Necessary	Avoid:	Weave:
Necessary	Stage:	Focus:

Now look at your grid. Don't be frustrated if you don't have many activities driving you toward your goals—you are not alone. Notice the large grey words in the background of the four boxes, avoid, weave, stage, and focus. To increase the likelihood of success in attaining your goal, these watermarks provide a plan of attack. The idea is to move toward doing actions that will help you achieve your goals while managing the others. Clearly, items not on the critical path and poorly aligned with your goal should be avoided (upper left quadrant). This can be accomplished by delegating, hiring out, or by simply not doing these activities. Activities high in alignment but not on the critical path are ideally woven into your life when practical (upper right quadrant). They are done, but when time allows and in ways that do not slow or impede our primary directive. Conversely, activities low in alignment, but on the critical path, need to be staged into your life as soon as practical (lower left quadrant). Staged items are done in rank order with the most important items completed first—ahead of the Avoid and Weave Quadrants. The goal is to concentrate efforts on activities that align with your goals and facilitate movement along the critical path (lower right quadrant). To be more successful, you need to better align your efforts with your goals.

At this juncture, your inner Warrior is probably starting to get excited about getting things done—excellent. Effective time management takes you to the boundary of personal accomplishment. In addition to helping achieve valuable goals, such productive value-oriented activities often result in enhanced feelings of well-being and happiness.[105,106] Used well, time is life itself.

Time management skills are also an excellent investment. "For to the one who has, more will be given, and he will have an abundance; but from the one who has not, even what he has will be taken away" (Matthew 13:12; ESV). Philosophers and sages have applied this phrase to money, success, and wisdom. It also applies to time. Efforts spent to use time better result in the availability of more free time which then provides additional opportunity to spend time better. In this way, a virtuous cycle of productivity and accomplishment is born.

> **Successful time management is the art of doing the right things first.**

Too many people are wasting time. Ironies abound in modern life. Look at your jobs, houses, yards, and activities. Most people spend a lot of time on things that do not really matter, consuming enormous amounts of time on low value, unproductive activities. The lowest hanging fruit to living more successfully is often located by looking at how you currently use your time. Successful people fill their lives with activities that move them along the critical path to their goals. Busyness is opportunity ignored, while procrastination is opportunity delayed. Both are self-inflicted wounds that drain your life energy. Every day, millions of people get further and further behind because they are doing unimportant things first, while putting off what they should really do. Successful time management is the art of doing the right things first.

Napoleon Hill wryly notes, "Procrastination is the bad habit of putting off until the day after tomorrow what should have been done the day before yesterday." When asked, procrastinators consistently tell me they delay action to use the fear of an impending deadline as motivation. Delays become increasingly urgent, and as the apparent importance of meeting the deadline worsens—and the risk of failure becomes overwhelming—they are increasingly incented to act. The criticality of the situation ferments until action become imperative. Procrastinators don't manage time, they let time manage them. The implications of this approach are noteworthy.

When teaching as an adjunct professor at the State University of New York, I noticed a dramatic difference in the quality of work and the learning realized between students. Procrastinators sacrificed both. Researchers have found that procrastinators consistently get lower grades.[107] They seem to miss out on more of the critical "digestive" time needed to think about their work product, than more effective time mangers who enjoy more polished outputs. Starting early also provides more time for the subject matter to be reflected on, absorbed, integrated, and retained. Overall, schedulers perform better because they invest time proactively, not reactively. While some procrastinators argue they do, in fact, use less time, the question is at what cost? Clearly, a good education that molds your mind, one that helps you understand yourself and the world around you while positioning you to contribute to society, is an important aspect of a high quality life. To what better purpose is a procrastinators' time being allocated? As a CEO with 500 employees and as a leadership development coach, I have seen the same problem among the adult workforce, as well.

Master time, and life will serve you.

According to Wayne Dyer, "Procrastination is one of the most common and deadliest of diseases, and its toll on success and happiness is heavy." The negative impact is due to an intentional shift in power. While a scheduler maintains control of his life and its various activities, a procrastinator sacrifices his opportunity to shape the outcome, preferring to wait upon the environment. Instead of proactively effectuating their situation, they prefer to react placing themselves beyond the point of direct influence. As such, they experience significant stress and worry.[108] The damaging effects of stress, both physically and mentally, are well-documented. People who procrastinate are less healthy, earn less, and have lower levels of well-being.[109]

Doing things last minute also increases nervousness and feelings of victimization, making projects seem harder than they are. By not starting early, procrastinators end up becoming further demotivated. Their avoidance breeds ambiguity, worry, and fear which results in a downward spiral of yet more procrastination. As time passes, the importance of action in-

creases until the risk of failure becomes overpowering. Ultimately, procrastinators are less successful, because they give up control over an important
Warrior aspect of their lives—managing time. Procrastination, which starts
as a choice, becomes a way of life. Important things are delayed and a more
successful existence passes by. Martin Luther saw this stating, "How soon
not now, becomes never" and Proverbs 20:4 (NIV) tells us that, "Sluggards
do not plow in season; so at harvest time they look but find nothing."

Interestingly, procrastination is seen as being similar to an addiction.
People who put off doing what is important have been found to do so in
order to pursue short-term gratification. A lack of action is the result as
procrastinators accept a "pay for it later" approach to life so they can feel
good now.[110]

Sadly, immediate rewards are the way of many. Take financial debt
for example. The average American family has almost $16,000 in person-
al credit card debt.[111] As a country, we have a national debt standing at
$53,088 per person, greater than the $52,762 an average household earns
in a year.[112,113] Since there are 2.6 people per household the national debt
equals $138,028 per household.[114] As
a country and a people, we consume
more than we can afford. Likewise, we
are also the most overweight nation
on earth when compared to other advanced economies.[115] We eat too much
because it is enjoyable and exercise
too little because it seems like work.
This occurs in spite of overwhelming
evidence regarding the long-term impact. People have a tendency to delay
important action irrespective of the consequence.

> Everyone has the same amount of time; successful people simply use it better.

Many people look for the easy way out and, left unchecked, it will cost
them their success. Successful discipline starts with how you spend your
time. Lord Acton said, "A wise person does at once, what a fool does at
last. Both do the same thing; only at different times." Success lies in your
use of today. Master time, and life will serve you; don't, and you will be a
slave to it.

Everyone has the same amount of time; successful people simply use
it better. They strive to be more productive recognizing that enormous
amounts of sub-optimally used time are available. Accomplished people
are time management soldiers who harness the moment and concentrate

on actions that align with their goals. They don't wait until tomorrow to do what can be done today.

Your inner Warrior doesn't want to waste time. To honor that, strive to be more efficient by developing better habits and more effective by concentrating your efforts on the right activities. Your strong Warrior knows that goals are achieved by consistently pursuing the most valuable activities. Be willing to do what needs to be done, and you will achieve the life you want.

BEHAVIOR 14: FOCUSING EFFORTS

"Where we put our focus is the direction we tend to go."
— Peter McWilliams

Pursue what matters. Success is more accessible to those who focus their efforts. By concentrating your efforts toward a primary goal, you are more likely to arrive at it. Focused effort accelerates the course traversed.

Early explorers understood this. When crossing new lands, they would start the day's journey by picking out a landmark in the distance, like a large tree, a mountain peak, or a gap in the horizon that aligned with the direction they wanted to go. Then, they would steer toward it during the day's journey.

Naturally, the marker would come in and out of sight, but it remained the primary objective for that day. Reference points worked to lead explorers steadily from where they were to where they wanted to go. These reference points kept them from getting unintentionally diverted and kept small missteps from compounding into larger navigational errors.

To get the most out of life, stand guard against distraction.

Likewise, today, successful people keep their eyes on the prize. Knowing that they end up going where they look, they pay particular attention to what they focus on. Accomplished people concentrate on important long-term goals. They focus on possibility and avoid anything that doesn't support their quest. Consciously avoiding distractions, accomplished people create opportunities for more of what is good in life to take place.

Your strong Warrior realizes that focus is essential to success. For you always head the direction you face. To get the most out of life, stand guard against distraction. Accomplishment is the result of narrowed toil. Success requires a stingy approach to diversion and a firm commitment to living as desired.

Aesop's fable is a wonderful example. Let's revisit the tale.

The Tortoise and the Hare

The Hare was once boasting of his speed before the other animals. "I have never yet been beaten," said he, "when I put forth my full speed. I challenge any one here to race with me."

The Tortoise said quietly, "I accept your challenge."

"That is a good joke," said the Hare; "I could dance round you all the way."

"Keep your boasting till you've won," answered the Tortoise. "Shall we race?"

So a course was fixed and a start was made. The Hare darted almost out of sight at once, but soon stopped and, to show his contempt for the Tortoise, lay down to have a nap. The Tortoise plodded on and plodded on, and when the Hare awoke from his nap, he saw the Tortoise just near the winning-post and could not run up in time to save the race.

Then the Tortoise said: "Slow but steady progress wins the race."

There are two very different perspectives contained in this tale. Consider the goals of both the Tortoise and Hare. At first blush, their objective appears identical. However, a deeper examination reveals an interesting discrepancy. How many goals did the Tortoise have? One—he concentrated exclusively on winning the race. How many goals did the Hare have? He had not one but two goals. Like the Tortoise, he wanted to win the race. However, he also wanted to embarrass the Tortoise as a way of showing his contempt. It is this difference that resulted in him losing the challenge. Why? The Hare lost because his focus was bifurcated. Taking two disparate actions, going fast and then stopping to nap, the Hare's efforts conflicted, ultimately impairing his progress. The Hare lost the race because he was trying to do too many things at once. "A double-minded man is unstable in all his ways" (James 1:8; KJV).

I call this phenomenon distractive dilution, and it is running rampant today. Distractive dilution is the excessive, over-inclusion of non-value-added activities that act to shift our focus away from what is most important resulting in diminished goal progress and marginalized life advancement. The epidemic is evident in the behavior of our kids, our leaders, and everyone in between.

Take my work for example. CEOs partner with me to help them

achieve their personal and professional objectives. Some time back, I was speaking with a business owner who complained that his team was not making progress toward their major corporate goals. He showed me a list of twelve initiatives that his team was working on. Many were major undertakings and included activities such as replacing the computer system, achieving manufacturing quality certifications, entering new markets, and developing new products. I inquired which of these was the most important. He looked at me with an air of undisguised incredulity and declared "They all are!" He went on to mention that no material progress had been made toward these items over the last few years. To address this, he would simply add new items to the list each year. There you have it. That was his solution—to keep adding things expecting the increased pressure would help get something done. It never did.

So, how many "A" priorities do you have? To get an idea, complete Thought Expander 14.1, Top Priorities. List the major things you are trying to accomplish in life in the two "A" Priority columns. Next, rank each in order from 1 (most important) to 10 (least important).

Thought Expander 14.1: Top Priorities

Rank	"A" Priority	Rank	"A" Priority

What did you realize? How does this prioritization exercise stack up to your current use of time? If you could only work on one priority until it was completed, which would it be? Success results from effort focused.

A caveat is necessary here. There are those who argue that they hold two or more goals equally. For example, some argue that both their families and their work are "A" priorities. As mentioned in Behavior 2, Taking Responsibility, you can certainly pursue them both equally, embracing their various conflicting pulls in a state of paradox. But you will sacrifice some level of performance with each. In reality, one is preferred over the other. "No one can serve two masters. Either you will hate the one and love the other, or you will be devoted to the one and despise the other" (Luke 16:13, NIV). Recognizing and being honest about your most-valued goal, better allows for prioritizing while bringing a sense of personal peace.

The problem with a more-is-better approach is that it doesn't work. It is challenging if not impossible to build momentum toward accomplishing any objective when a significant demand for attention exists in other areas. Resources spread thin become ineffective.

Supporting this notion, psychological researchers collected evidence indicating people are lousy at multitasking.[116] Their findings show that performance dramatically declines when distraction is inserted into people's lives. Distracted drivers, for example, have been found to be just as dangerous as drunk drivers.[117] Similarly, multitasking has been observed to impair achievement both at school and at work.[118,119] Across a wide range of tasks, distraction hampers performance.[120]

Unfortunately, people tend to believe the opposite is true. They see multitasking as a good idea—one that will improve their efficiency. They believe they perform better when they do two things at once. Researchers in one study found that 70% of people proclaim to be better than average at multitasking. Yet, researchers have found that only 2.5% of people can successfully multitask—only 1 in 20.[121] Clearly, there is some questionable thinking going on since 97.5% of the population (pretty much everyone) is living in ways that reduce their productivity without even knowing it.[122] Multitasking is a problem because it dilutes effort.

The impact of such behavior is significant. In one study, researchers found that distractions increased mistakes, thereby reducing accuracy, by 20%.[123] That's enough impairment to make a B-minus student (80%) a failure (64%). In another study, researchers found productivity declines of as high as 40% due to the act of multitasking.[124] The issue is that every diversion reduces productivity, consuming valuable time in order to get back on task.

When I was a child, one of my favorite field trips was going to the Natural History Museum in Cleveland. There was a planetarium where a replica of the nighttime stars was projected on a large, domed ceiling. While the instructors dimmed the lights, the anthropologists would tell how people used the stars to mark the seasons, tell time, and predict the future. The only caution instructors gave was that flash photography was absolutely not allowed, and any violation would end the event. Kids being kids, it would happen that every few years someone would test the limits and flash their camera in the middle of the presentation. The outcome was dramatic. You couldn't see anything, not a single star afterwards. In response, the instructors would immediately end the show by turning on the lights and ushering us out. Why? After exposure to a bright light, it takes the human eye 20 to 30 minutes to fully readjust to the dark.[125] Due to this "dark adaptation" there just wasn't enough time to start the show over.

> # Every diversion reduces productivity.

Life distractions are comparable to a bright flash in a dark theater. Scientists have found that the typical information technology office worker gets only 11 minutes between each interruption, after which it takes an average of 25 minutes to completely return their focus to the original task at hand.[126] Obviously, this results in the workers almost never being able to fully focus on their work. How many jobs are like this today?

It is no wonder that so many people are frazzled, for they are now working in environments filled with so many distractions that it hurts their performance. Interruptions might include not only interpersonal matters, but increased demands originating from phones, e-mails, texts, and the like. Modern communication technology, for all its benefits, is a tool that needs to be better managed.

This is no easy task. Researchers observing several hundred students in their normal study environments (e.g., bedroom, library, or den) told them to work on an important school assignment for 15 minutes. Even knowing they were being watched, the students couldn't resist texting or using social media.[127] The average limit on their self-control was a meager six minutes, with signs of declining on-task focus occurring around the two minute mark. Overall, only 65 percent (2/3rds) of the time was used on schoolwork and 35% (or 1/3ʳᵈ) was lost to multitasking. In exploring Success Behavior 13, Managing Time, you explored the amazing value that could be created if you regained 10% of the time in any given day, yet you now waste over 30% of it, due to distractions.

By allowing the less valuable to take up your mind space, you make it harder to hold more valuable things front and center. Known as inattentional blindness (Mack & Rock, 1998), psychological researchers have found that your focus significantly influences what you see, allowing you to miss material events in your environment as seen with the moon-walking bear discussed in Behavior 3, Focusing Attention.[128] It is not hard to imagine how in certain situations, the attentive differences due to multitasking could wind up being catastrophic. Further, a distraction-allowing approach can make it more difficult for people to concentrate and focus, impairing their cognitive ability.[129] Regular interruptions can have a long-term, systemic, negative impact on your ability to think well. The efficiency reductions appear to be a result of energy lost from switching from one activity to the other and the associated cognitive ramp-up time it takes to make that transition.

By identifying and concentrating on what is really important, you are more readily able to accomplish it.

Chemists and chemical engineers have a saying that, 'The solution to pollution is dilution.' Analogously, successful people know that dilution is not the solution, it is the problem. To employ an electrical circuit reference, success is more easily accomplished in series than in parallel. That is, it is much better to do a series of things one at a time than it is to do everything at once. Focus matters. "Any intelligent fool can make things bigger and more complex...it takes a touch of genius and a lot of courage to move in the opposite direction" (E. F. Schumacher).

To get a practical handle on this, let's explore your multitasking activities. Take a minute to complete the Thought Expander 14.2, Multitasking. For each life area, identify areas where you multitask. These might include all the things you do while you are doing something else. Take spending time with your spouse, for example. You may eat dinner, watch TV, go through the mail, or respond to texts. At work, you may read e-mails, talk on the phone, eat lunch, and write your monthly report during a meeting.

The idea is to become aware of where distractions exist so you can get an idea of where you might be selling your career, relationships, dreams, or happiness short. Feel free to add additional life areas like friends, commuting, puttering, and any other area that resonates as important in the blank, bottom row.

Thought Expander 14.2: Multitasking

Area	Activity 1	Activity 2	Activity 3	Activity 4
Work/School				
Home				
Family				
Life Goal				
Other				

Success results from effort well-focused. Substantial value lies in discovering and removing well-engrained, distracting activities that waste energy and consume time. Getting a handle on distractions allow you to get things done more quickly and with better results. "Let your eyes look straight ahead; fix your gaze directly before you. Give careful thought to the paths for your feet and be steadfast in all your ways. Do not turn to the right or the left" (Proverbs 4:25-27).

Your inner Warrior understands that doing one thing at a time is more effective. When strong, your Warrior avoids distractions and stops engaging in them the moment they are realized. Instead, your accomplished Warrior concentrates efforts to win the battle at hand, before moving onto the next task. Fighting more than one adversary at a time is risky business.

In what area of your life, would mitigating distractions benefit you? To find out, select one of the areas from Thought Expander 14.2, Multitasking, and write it in the top row of the Thought Expander 14.3, Focus Assessment. Next, in the left-hand column, list the various distractions related to this area during which you multi-task. For each diversion, identify the benefits and costs. Consider how each activity adds to or subtracts from the overarching personal goal in this area. For example, if relationship with your spouse is the area of importance, you might stop working on the computer while talking to him or her. You might think that you are getting more done, but the cost could be that you are not listening fully, or that you are sending a message of unimportance. Here, multitasking impacts the desired strong relationship with your spouse.

It is often advantageous to be a responsible quitter.

Thought Expander 14.3: Focus Assessment

Area:		
Distraction	**Benefits**	**Costs**

This exercise helps to clarify what actions you should be doing and those you might want to think twice about. Every distraction is an opportunity. In many cases, our actions detract from our most important goals, similar to the Hare in Aesop's fable. Fragmented efforts are personally expensive because they dilute our ability to perform effectively in life.

A focused approach yields superior outcomes. This is true in all areas. Success is the product of effective action, focus its catalyst. A centered mind is genius. By identifying and concentrating on what is really important, you are more readily able to accomplish it and more quickly able to move onto the next goal.

One way to get more targeted is to become an honest, astute, and clear-eyed quitter. As an act, quitting is significantly underrated. Pursuits that keep you from achieving your goals or becoming all you can be make up a significant portion of people's lives. These pursuits need to be dropped. You cannot strive for greater if you don't stop pursing the lesser. Just as there is no shortage of people willing to take your time, there is also no shortage of people willing to use your time—whether it is listening to their gossip, performing trivialities with or for them, or helping them to accomplish their goals. Some of this is normal, but when the demands of others start to stand in the way of you living the life you want to live and achieving the goals you hold dear, better time control is needed.

Human resource managers understand the importance of not waiting to fix something that isn't

Progress is the product of effort focused.

working, quipping that, upon reflection, they have "never fired anyone too soon." Of course, they are referring to problematic people with some underlying performance issue or interpersonal problem.

Typically, leadership long since knew something wasn't working with the employee in question, but took their time to ensure it was the right decision. Time and time again, the decision period ends up being way too long. In helping hundreds of CEOs make needed change, I have never heard anything to the effect of, "Wow, I wished I had waited longer." Instead, I regularly hear "Wow. That was definitely the right thing do to; why didn't I do that long (weeks, months, years) ago?"

Likewise, it is often advantageous to be a responsible quitter. Don't wait to get on with life. When you realize you are involved in things that don't serve you, walk away. As a fine steward of your limited years, you will notice, on occasion, that what you are doing is no longer helping you achieve your goals or fulfill your potential. The solution is simple—cease and desist. Too many people are wasting their lives doing things that don't feed their passions or make them feel alive. They are engaged in the suboptimal in order to feel needed, keep busy, or pass the time. Inane and counterproductive activities are often left to linger much too long. One can't pursue the salient trapped in the mundane. Learn to move on. It's okay. Setting healthy boundaries means you appropriately value life.

To more readily accomplish your goals, concentrated efforts are required.

Several people important to me challenged my decision to leave a $350,000 per year career. My peers couldn't understand why someone would walk away from the CEO title, power, and pay. My parents thought it was fiscal suicide. But the job was in conflict with my spirit and what I really wanted to achieve in life. It weighed me down and slowed me up. For seven years, I lived a life that wasn't right for me, not having the courage to walk away from a situation that wasn't working.

I am not alone. Many people stay in a situation long after it's become untenable, permitting an issue to fester into a crisis. Like me, they allow the state of affairs to continue until the pressure becomes so intense they are forced into action, either of their own volition or at the hand of someone else. Others are not so fortunate to reach such inflection points; instead they languish in situations that have long since stopped serving them.

Progress is the product of effort focused. Numerous objectives, simultaneously sought, are more likely to fail. Worse yet, the shortfalls occur in innocuous, subtle ways leaving you to wonder at the cause of your disappointment. Even the spiritual seeker can be thrown off by cross purposes. "And when you fast, don't make it obvious, as the hypocrites do, for they try to look miserable and disheveled so people will admire them for their fasting. I tell you the truth, that is the only reward they will ever get" (Matthew 6:16; NLT). It is all too easy to lose focus as struggles around the use of time, effort, and attention often play out in the background. To be properly accomplished, every goal requires a conscious alignment of effort optimal to its completion. The addition of every objective significantly increases the possibility of perturbence.

Think of it as a physics problem. Waves in a pool extend symmetrically around a single point of entry. However, throw one or two more stones in the water and the beauty of symmetry is quickly replaced by a jumble of waves banging against and interfering with each other. Such crisscrossing force vectors amplify, diminish, and distort the outcome of the original effort.

Likewise, the efforts and outcomes of multiple goals often conflict. As with the Tortoise and the Hare, this often occurs in ways that are not readily obvious. The more objectives you pursue, the greater the chance for inconsistency, each additional goal increases the likelihood that efforts to achieve it will cancel out. As more and more goals are added, the risk of a negative impact increases exponentially.

Your inner Warrior knows that, to more readily accomplish your goals, concentrated efforts are required. Granted, this not always the easiest approach; it takes discipline, but the payoff is substantial. As Zig Ziglar points out: "If you do what you ought to do, when you ought to do it, the time will come when you can do what you want to do, when you want to do it."

Accomplished people focus their energies. They understand that distractions and multitasking work to dilute effort and stymie performance. To avoid this, you can avoid activities that don't move you toward the life you want, instead endeavoring to pursue higher-value enterprises. Putting important things first, your strong Warrior works to keep your energy narrowly targeted. Like a magnifying glass that can turn sunlight into fire, success is the result of effort well applied.

BEHAVIOR 15: DOING THE NEXT BEST THING

"More and more research is showing that those who have purpose and gain direction in their lives are the ones who get ahead." — Zig Ziglar

Move smartly forward. Don't wait to chase your dreams; the time will never be perfect. Start right where you are and merely begin. Action is essential to success.

Successful people are serial doers. Biographies of famous people demonstrate this tendency. As a result of unremitted action, the protagonist is eventually found doing the right thing at the right time, yielding the accomplishments now worth reading about. Accomplished people are doers who persist in the face of adversity and advancement alike, until they eventually triumph. That is, no doubt, why biographies are inspiring and many people like to read them. Biographies contain many of the success principles around which this book is written.

Successful people are serial doers.

However, if you want to apply all the same steps that led the author to greatness, you will most likely be disappointed. For example, if you wanted to be a successful inventor like Thomas Edison, you would be unable to replicate his advances in any significant way. He was in the right place at the right time with a proclivity that allowed him to leverage his natural talents and interests and deliver a bevy of impressive technical innovations. Individual success is like a fingerprint—unique to the person, time, and place—never to be exactly replicated. The trouble with biographies is they are impossible to copy directly as they cannot specify what, specifically, you should do next in order to accomplish your life goals.

Yet, there is a theme. Successful people throughout the ages are consistently observed doing the next best thing. They are doers who spend their time in ways that will most likely generate progress toward their goals. Accomplished people consider the infinite number of options before them, and they choose those that will best move them forward. They have strong Warriors and irrespective of circumstances, have a default tendency toward action. So regularly do they expend energy in this manner, that the force of success builds in their lives like waves buffeted by the wind, propelling them toward their objectives. Benjamin Franklin understood this when he quipped, "Energy and persistence conquer all things."

The challenge with this approach is that most people, especially hard-charging, Type-A personalities, do not like the ambiguity involved. Outcome uncertainty in this next-best-thing approach sometimes breeds anxiety, depression, and resentment.[130] People want to know, before expending too much energy, how it will all work out. They want to understand how the next best thing will result in their goal being achieved, and they are reluctant to take action unless they can clearly envision the result. People want assurances without faith.

> **Consider the infinite number of options before you and choose those that that will best move you forward.**

Life doesn't work like this. No one knows the end from the beginning. That is a good thing. If we knew how everything would work out, life would be unbearably dull and boring. A detailed itinerary would remove the adventure, stifling the joy and smothering the excitement. Think about it. If the outcome from every action was clear and the result obvious what would be the point? We would be just going through the motions—marionettes to a preordained life. There would be neither the agony of defeat nor the thrill of victory.

Instead, life is a lump of clay to be shaped and molded with our hands and baked in the kilns of our hearts. The results are not foretold by the Fates of ancient mythology. Each of us contours and forms our outcome based on our decisions and actions, understanding the final product is unknown until it isn't.

To succeed, you must avoid quicksand thinking, sidestepping the mire of wondering how it will work out. Confusion, ambiguity, fear, and inaction reside there. Goals spend most of their time lurking around the next bend. To reach them, the secret is to continually do whatever moves you toward them. Don't concern yourself with the how you will succeed, concern yourself with what is the next best step. Instead of wondering, "How can I possibly do this?" ask "What should I do next?" Focus on what can be done, and progress is yours.

Achievement is ultimately the result of placing trust in your actions. Life responds to what you do, continually revealing new possibilities from which another choice must be made. Every effort pulls back the curtain a little further, making the stage a little more visible. By trusting in the active pursuit of your dreams, the universe is compelled to provide the next steps.

There is a joke that humorously drives this point home. An elderly woman goes to see her doctor to treat an ailment. After spending some time in the lobby, she is escorted into a private examination room. The doctor asks her what is wrong with her and she responds, "Doctor, I need your help. You see, I have a terrible gas problem. I am always passing gas—while visiting my friends, when shopping, and even during church. Just now, while waiting in your crowded lobby, I passed gas at least a dozen times. The good news is that my gas is silent, and it never smells. In fact, I have passed gas twice already while talking with you, but you would never know it." After careful consideration, the Doctor gives her some medicine and asks her to return in two weeks. Right on time, the elderly woman returns telling the doctor, "I don't know what you gave me, but it is not working at all. I'm still passing gas as often as ever, but now it smells really terrible. I was mortified having to wait in your lobby, painfully trying to hold my flatulence. The good news is those few that snuck out were silent, so nobody had any idea who was stinking up the place. I am so embarrassed. Doctor you need to do something else to help me out." The doctor replies, "That is excellent news. Now that we have fixed your sense of smell, let's work on your hearing."

Have a default tendency toward action.

Like the old lady, often you don't know all the challenges that lie ahead. To be successful, you must be willing to dive headlong into life. Only then can you understand where you are and what you can do about it. For the accomplished life is composed of a continuous series of course corrections. These are not always expected, but they are always necessary for progress. You must focus on what you can do in the current day. "Take therefore no thought for the morrow: for the morrow shall take thought for the things of itself" (Matthew 6:34, KJV).

Your mature Warrior continually strives to do the next best thing. As each action dissolves into an ever-morphing life canvas of potentiality, the resulting actuality brings new options to bear. Successful people leverage this cycle, optimizing it throughout life. They consistently find the next best thing, and then they readily do it. They seize opportunity when it arises or prepare for it when it doesn't.

> ## Life is a lump of clay to be shaped and molded with our hands and baked in the kilns of our hearts.

It was a "do-the-next-best-thing" approach that allowed me to achieve success in my career. During college, I had dreamed of running a business and becoming a millionaire. When I graduated, I moved to Michigan to take a job as a chemical engineer where I spent three years formulating and compounding adhesives in a laboratory. Not surprisingly, there was no one available who could advise me on what to do to best achieve my long-term dreams. So, I took a straightforward approach.

To accelerate progress toward my goal, every day I would look at the various options before me and take action toward the most promising one. Among countless other steps, I asked to join a new product development research team that was focused on commercializing new technology. I also started going to night school for business. These decisions paid off. I ended up being a part of the team that developed more than a dozen adhesive chemistry patents, while also gaining important business exposure. The inventions and business experience were pivotal in getting me into one of the best business schools in the country. It should be noted that this possibility was not foreseen when I started toward my goals of running a business and becoming financially independent.

Later, when I graduated with a Master's in Management from Northwestern, I kept on optimizing. I continued a regular process of identifying and executing the next best thing. At each stage, I made decisions most likely to lead me where I wanted to go. The grades I got, the schools I attended, the jobs I took, the companies I worked for, the relocations I accepted, and the hours I worked were all guided by this process. By holding a vision of what I wanted to achieve in front of me, I was able to identify crucial criteria, and determine a superior course of action.

Over the decades that followed, I made thousands of next-best-thing decisions with my goal as a guide. When life handed me gold, I put it in my pocket; when life produced coal I used it to warm myself. Along the way amazing things happened.

By trusting in the active pursuit of your dreams, the universe is compelled to provide the next steps.

The universe responded to my intention, providing me a path forward as I went. Life consistently delivered me opportunities I had not originally contemplated and possibilities I could never have fathomed. In doing the next best thing, my goals were accomplished with expectations exceeded. I went on to become CEO of a $100 million global company at age 35—some 15 years ahead of plan. I also achieved my financial target, for the first time, at age 36. That is the promise of doing the next best thing.

Of course, I had no idea that my goals would lead me to change jobs seven times, relocate three times, and work in more than a dozen different industries. Had I waited to understand how it would all work out, had I insisted on knowing, I would have done nothing and success would have been sacrificed.

Reasoned action theory (Fishbein & Ajzen, 1975) proposes that by perceiving that next action will productively lead you in the direction of a goal, you are more motivated to perform it. Successful people believe their efforts are linked to greater achievement. That is the reason they often appear to push harder than the average person. They do so because it works. "Let us not grow weary of doing good, for in due season we will reap, if we do not give up" (Galatians 6:9; ESV).

How about you; what is your best course of action? Let's find out. In the left-hand column of Thought Expander 15.1, Valuable Action, take a few minutes to list the most important things you are planning to do today or tomorrow, based on what is going on in your life right now. If you are like most people, few of these will relate to your long-term goals. Then, think about what you most want to accomplish in life. Refer back to prior exercises as needed.

From here, consider a range of possible actions that you could take today that would have the best chance of moving you toward an important life goal. Write these in the right-hand column. No matter how small, there is always something you can do next to move yourself closer to your goal. The idea is to come up with specific things you can do toward accomplishing your dreams.

Thought Expander 15.1: Valuable Action

	Important "To Do's"	Goal-Oriented "To Do's"
1.		
2.		
3.		
4.		
5.		

To effectively progress toward your goals, it is imperative that you center attention on the most important things first. Homeowners know this well. They must be smart about what projects they tackle. There are numerous changes and improvements that can be done to a property. Some increase the value much more than others. For example, while kitchens and bathrooms provide a handsome payback, so do basic features like siding and dry basement, roof, and windows.[131] They do so because they are important to a well-functioning house. Office remodeling, back-up generators, swimming pools, and finished basements perform poorly in comparison.[132] This is probably because these improvements are not as essential. The trick is to do the next one thing to your house that best improves the

> It is not about what you could do, it is about what you should do.

overall value derived.

Your inner Warrior appreciates that to be successful your most-valued goal must be pursued first. Daily activities can be thought of as being like rocks, pebbles, and sand where the rocks reflect the most important opportunities and the sand the least important with pebbles being neutral. Continuing the simile, life, therefore, is like a Mason jar. If you spend your time on the less important things, filling your jar with sand and pebbles, you will find that you can't fit the rocks, the important things, in later. No room is left. However, by leading with the important things, you place the rocks in jar first, leaving plenty of room for the pebbles and sand. In focusing efforts on what is most meaningful first, more can be accomplished in life.

Repeating this process again and again is the equivalent of honing your Warrior's sword. A sharp blade does a superior job with much less exertion. Likewise, taking the best action entails less overall effort while also bringing goals to fruition more quickly. In both cases, less energy is expended, more progress made.

Important goals need priority.

It is not about what you could do, it is about what you should do. Focused action is more efficient and more effective. On their death bed, people do not wish they spent more time maintaining their stuff, organizing, cleaning the house, reading the news, checking e-mails, surfing the web, or watching TV. Your inner Warrior knows these things are the sand and pebbles of life and should be done as filler only on the heels, or in the wake, of more value-laden efforts.

What is your next best action? To gain clarity, look back at the Thought Expander 15.1, Valuable Action, and circle one action item in the right-hand column that, if implemented, would best move you forward. The action chosen should be the one most likely to create momentum in the direction of an important goal and move you toward the life you want to live. Ideally, it is linked directly to your dreams.

Your action items do not have to be, and realistically won't be, big all the time. Often they will seem small and incremental like researching how something works, exploring various options, or making that call. To make a difference, they only need to be activities that facilitate progress in some way. They may vary from day to day based on yesterday's outcomes. The next best action will change based on what happened last, how your environment responded, what you learned, and who you are growing to become. The key is to focus on what will be most worthwhile and then to do it next. Small, incremental steps consistently taken are exceedingly powerful. The most impressive and courageous human journeys are completed this way.

How about you? What is your life calling you to do? What one thing should you do next? Take a minute and write it in the top row of Thought Expander 15.2, <u>What One Thing</u>. Try to compose an actionable response—identify something tangible that you can reasonably accomplish. Then answer the four questions provided. Detail your options. When completed, the action you pursue should be big enough that, once completed, it will leave you satisfied that the day was a useful contribution, a good investment, toward your dream.

Thought Expander 15.2: What One Thing

Describe what one thing you could do that would make your day worthwhile:	
Question	**Answer**
What do I need to do exactly?	
Why? (be specific)	
What are the benefits?	
How will I get it done?	

To flourish, this process must be repeated regularly. To be successful you need to ask yourself "What one thing, if accomplished today, would make the day most worthwhile?" Then you need to give it priority ahead of everything anything else. Often, that means doing it first. Implemented habitually, doing the next best thing places you on an intersection path with success by keeping you from filling your days with things that matter less.

Important goals need priority. To ensure they don't get lost in the vagaries of daily existence, they need to be managed differently. Take exercise, for example. Many people work out early in the morning. They don't select this time because they are most awake, energetic, or least busy. They do it first thing to make sure it doesn't get lost in the noise of the day. That way they are sure to capture its many benefits including increased well-being.[133,134] Likewise, to effectively save money you need to give it priority. Financial experts suggest you pay yourself first before any other expenses so you have money saved for the future.

> **Consistently take smart action toward your goals without knowing how they will ultimately be accomplished.**

Imagine for a moment what your life would be like if every day you did the most important thing before anything else. Working with people who have incorporated this powerful practice into their lives and by living this way myself, I know firsthand the result. Life becomes unbelievably amazing!

By taking the next-best step you gain forward momentum toward your goals. Progress might appear slow at first, but with consistent action applied, your progress would accelerate over time. The positive progress made and victories achieved will serve to motivate you, encouraging you to try harder and focus even more on goal-oriented actions. Over time, a self-reinforcing process is established, enabling you to accomplish any dream.

A strong Warrior is pivotal to every action that facilitates progress. Your Warrior understands that the practice of doing the next best thing will shift you from victim to victor. One proverb says, "How do you eat an elephant? One bite at a time." Likewise, you achieve even the most monumental goal the same way—one well-placed effort a time. By breaking every goal down into smaller, actionable parts, the largest of dreams becomes possible.

Sometimes, the action needed is ridiculously easy, and other times it can be incredibly hard—and yet both are infinitely preferable to no effort at all. If you don't swing the bat, you are guaranteed to never hit a home run.

Too many people fill their days with activities that consume their time without propelling them toward their dreams. Successful people do not. At work, accomplished people allocate their best hours to focus on important, long-term, strategic initiatives, not administrative tasks. At home, they put family ahead of trivialities. In life, accomplished people give priority to their dreams. Accomplished people consistently take smart action toward their goals without knowing how they will ultimately be accomplished. They trust their efforts will pay off, and they do. As such, they invoke a valuable, self-reinforcing process that propels them forward.

Keep walking toward your goals, and they will come into view.

Success is garnered by acting in the smartest possible way. As with any journey, you can't know how it will work out. But, you don't have to let your limited view stand in the way of high-quality action. Embrace the exciting adventure ahead. Keep walking toward your goals and, eventually, they will come into view. Realize that, while everything will not work out as expected, success will invariably result. Before you, innumerable possibilities lay. Pick wisely from these and proceed. Right effort results in better progress. Enjoy the journey, recognizing that every worthwhile destination is achieved through a thousand well-taken strides. Success shows up when you do the next best thing each and every day.

THE WARRIOR

Your Warrior understands that success comes from taking action, embracing work, managing time, concentrating effort, and doing the next best thing. Developing a strong Warrior is essential to accomplishing your goals and securing the life you want. However, great accomplishments by your Warrior are meaningless without an ability to appreciate and enjoy them. Victory void of satisfaction is failure. Being able to fully welcome, appreciate, and enjoy the wonder of life is an equally important component of success. As such, your Warrior can only achieve real victory with its complementary aspect...

ASPECT IV: THE CONTENTED MONK

MONK

Monk [muhNGk]. A person of virtue and benevolence. One who commits themselves to spiritual goals and living in ways that are holy.

ASPECT IV: THE CONTENTED MONK

The Monk is that part of us that embraces the awe and wonder of life. It can be conceptualized as the element of each person's psyche that respects, values, and enjoys. It is where peace, love, and happiness reside. Aware in the current moment, a mature Monk values and appreciates what is good about life, savors experiences, and lives judiciously, blessing and being blessed by others. The Monk assesses life's journey as worthwhile. Optimistic, your Monk trusts possibility, living fully in faith. The perceived quality of your life resides with the maturity of your Monk.

Spectral opposites, the Warrior and Monk represent the "do" and "be" aspects of life, respectively. Complementary bookends, the doing of the Warrior represents embracing the flow of action while the being of the Monk reflects the awareness and self-presence that allows you to fully experience the wonder of life. A complement to the Warrior, the Monk is the reflective, growth-oriented, and spiritual part of you. It strives for harmony, proving reflection as a balance to action and enjoyment a product of striving. The Monk enhances the King's understanding and the Wizard's creativity.

If this aspect of success is passive, weak or immature, real success is not recognized. If you find that you are not enjoying life, you are unaware of your feelings or have none at all, if you can't appreciate what is good, or feel detached and isolated, it is an indication that your Monk is underdeveloped. In this state, your Monk is not able to properly represent you by appreciating and valuing what is good in life. Conversely, when you regularly seek escapes, stimulation, or over-indulge in pleasures, when your emotions take over or you live in constant drama exaggerating event implications, it is an indication that your Monk has become aggressive. An over-reliance on your Monk comes at the expense of other, more appropriate aspects that exist in your King, Wizard, or Warrior.

To see where your Monk stands, do the following exercise. Check up to ten items from any of the three boxes below that best describe emotions you most commonly experience. Consider not only what you think, but what others who know you well say about you.

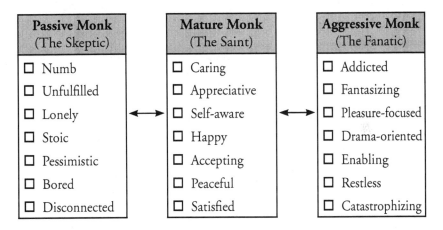

Passive Monk (The Skeptic)	Mature Monk (The Saint)	Aggressive Monk (The Fanatic)
☐ Numb	☐ Caring	☐ Addicted
☐ Unfulfilled	☐ Appreciative	☐ Fantasizing
☐ Lonely	☐ Self-aware	☐ Pleasure-focused
☐ Stoic	☐ Happy	☐ Drama-oriented
☐ Pessimistic	☐ Accepting	☐ Enabling
☐ Bored	☐ Peaceful	☐ Restless
☐ Disconnected	☐ Satisfied	☐ Catastrophizing

Now look at where most of your marks reside. If there are more checked items toward the left-hand side of the graphic, then your Monk is probably underdeveloped. A passive Monk, or Skeptic, tends to be frail and immature. Fully considered, this section of the book will help you develop a more contented Monk.

Conversely, if most of the circled items are located on the right-hand side of the graphic, your Monk is probably heavily relied upon and used to the point where it is counterproductive. An aggressive Monk, or Fanatic, tends to compensate for unaddressed weakness in your King, Wizard, or Warrior. While this section will most certainly be of value, it is important that you identify which other aspects(s) might be suboptimal. Focusing and strengthening these aspects will level and restore balance thereby reducing the need and tendency toward overreliance on your Monk in ways that do not fully benefit you.

To be successful in life, your Monk must be mature and open-minded. As such, your Monk knows how to live well and is aware of that which is positive, beneficial, and good. A healthy Monk maintains healthy levels of physical and psychological energy and comprehends what is needed to grow. Your Monk understands that achievement and happiness are less about outcome and more about perception. In other words, gleaning wisdom from any experience results in a more Monk-like appreciation of life—yielding love, peace, and joy. Developing a contented Monk is essential to happiness.

Like the other previously explored aspects of success, there are also five important behaviors that lead to a contented Monk. Your mature Monk knows how to (16) renew yourself, (17) serve others, (18) expect good things, (19) have faith, and (20) enjoy the journey. We will explore these five success behaviors, in turn, throughout the pages of this section.

BEHAVIOR 16: RENEWING YOURSELF

"If one advances confidently in the direction of his dreams...he will meet with a success unexpected in common hours." — Henry David Thoreau

Become all you are capable of being. People who commit to becoming their best selves are the personification of success. They have set out to achieve the ultimate goal—excellence—and live a life of continuous personal expansion. Self-development is powerful fuel accelerating anyone who pursues it in earnest down the road of accomplishment. "Today's excellence is tomorrow's mediocrity; so keep pushing boundaries and pursuing excellence in everything you do" (Dr. Hisham Abdalla).

Once basic needs such as food, clothing, and shelter are met, humans seek higher-order needs. In order, these include safety, belonging, and self-esteem. Motivation theory proposes that there are a series of need stages. Of the five stages, the lower levels include satisfaction of physical and safety needs followed by belonging and self-esteem stages. The highest level is self-actualization (Maslow, 1943), where people strive to realize all that is possible for them. "What a man can be, he must be," noted Abraham Maslow. Self-actualization is considered to be the highest human motivation, one that provides a sense of connection with life as a greater whole.[135]

Beyond motivation theory, another way that psychologists assess growth is through eight progressive phases of development. The highest stage of personal development is represented by generativity (Erickson, 1950). Generativity is the desire to nurture or create something that will outlast you for the benefit of others. Examples include meaningful work, contributing to society, guiding or mentoring others, volunteering, or even writing a self-help book. In this penultimate stage, the goal is to produce worthwhile outcomes for others as a continued process of reaching and striving to become all you can be.

People ultimately desire an existence where purpose—set by the King, created by the Wizard, and achieved through the Warrior—is paramount.[136] To craft a life of meaning and fulfillment, your Monk solicits these three aspects of success to meet all your basic needs, and once completed, leverages them in an effort to help you become self-actualized. Self-actualized people achieve success in the broadest sense of the term. They tend to be both highly accomplished and deeply satisfied. Not only do they appear comfortable with themselves and confident in life, but they are able to transcend the distractions and focus on what is really important. Self-actualized people are wise. They show a range of well-developed perspectives that include independence, serenity, and a love of mastering themselves.

> Many people lack the exhilarating sense of challenge and joy that comes with striving to become all they can be.

To what degree does this describe you? Are you self-actualized? To get an idea of where you stand, complete Thought Expander 16.1, Self Actualization, by circling the answer that best fits each question. (Note: The Self Actualization Scale is for general insight and is not scientifically validated.)

Thought Expander 16.1: Self-Actualization Scale

Adapted Scale	Strongly Disagree	Disagree	Agree	Strongly Agree
1) I am realistic and not threatened by the truth or the unknown.	1	2	3	4
2) I accept myself and others as they are without prejudice.	1	2	3	4
3) I am serene, without damaging guilt or shame.	1	2	3	4
4) I am responsible for myself, a self-starter, making work play.	1	2	3	4
5) I remain composed and objective during adversity.	1	2	3	4
6) I am spontaneous without unnecessary inhibitions.	1	2	3	4
7) I am autonomous, independent, and comfortable being alone.	1	2	3	4
8) I resist conforming to culture, determining my own views.	1	2	3	4
9) I am living my life to the full with frequent peak experiences.	1	2	3	4
10) I am motivated toward continual growth.	1	2	3	4
Grand Total = ← Totals				

Total the scores, by column, for each circled answer, then add all the columns to get the grand total in the far left-hand column. A fully, self-actualized person would theoretically score a perfect 40. Most people score closer to a 20. Since life is a personal development journey, self-actualization is a process that is never complete. Learning, therefore, is a continuous, lifelong practice that is never really finished. That is, of course, unless you stop.

According to Henry David Thoreau, "Most men lead lives of quiet desperation." Silently, they bear lives that are less. Not fully satisfied, they feel something is missing. What is it that so many are lacking? Many people lack the exhilarating sense of challenge and joy that comes with striving to become all they can be. As a result, they live lesser lives.

Embracing change, rather than avoiding it, is critical to living successfully.

This process often follows a familiar path. Early in life, a significant number of people are willing to do what it takes to become successful. They work hard, taking appropriate risks, understanding that doing so will yield commensurate rewards. They labor, eventually capturing some level of achievement that often includes power, recognition, wealth, or a specific, desired accomplishment. The process is then repeated by a select few throughout life as a pattern of striving and arriving.

Many more, however, leave this practice behind. As the years pass, they shift from the highly creative process of exploring possibility and striving, to a staid and stale process of maintaining what they've built and shielding what they have. Wealthy, they transition from pursuing to protecting. The process is slow, subtle, and insidious. Learning and growing are given lower priority as they seek to maintain and defend what they have accumulated.

This approach comes at a cost. The very behaviors that generated success have now stopped, placing continued growth and additional accomplishment in jeopardy. Science supports the idea that such a shift in objective can alter performance. In one study, researchers found that students who sought to protect did significantly worse in school than those who wanted to learn and grow.[137] The problem is that as people shift from seeking growth to protecting, the natural creative process of building up and tearing down, of starting and ending, terminates. Growth ceases. As a result, Les Brown, in *Beyond the Secret* finds that "Nine out of ten people will die rather than change."

The strategy is untenable. The world is neither static nor stable. Things around us are changing all the time. According to the Greek philosopher Heraclitus "Change is the only constant." To protect anything in life, to maintain its stability and keep it in place, ever increasing levels of effort are required. As you grow your roles and needs change in life. Embracing change, rather than avoiding it, is critical to living successfully. It is better to transform before you have to.

Another way to look at this is to consider people as being either promotion or prevention focused.[138] Promotion-focused individuals seek advancement, are comfortable taking risk, like to work quickly, think creatively, and dream big. Prevention-focused individuals seek responsibility, they are risk adverse, like to work methodically, are thorough, and accurate. Neither is inherently better than the other, and both are useful in certain instances. The problem occurs with both groups, when the known becomes preferred over the possible, and when security becomes desired over development. "Anyone who stops learning is old, whether at twenty or eighty. Anyone who keeps learning stays young" (Henry Ford).

Physicists use the term momentum to describe an object's motional energy. It is the product of an object's mass and velocity traveling along a vectored trajectory. According to Newton's first law of motion, bodies in motion tend to stay in motion while bodies at rest tend to stay at rest. Such inertia reflects the tendency of an object to continue in its current manner unless it is influenced in some way.

> **Fulfillment lies in becoming the best you possible.**

Similarly, you have growth momentum. Unless some external force is applied, the direction you are heading is likely the direction you will continue to go. If you allow societal pressure, the comfort of wealth, past successes, or a general malaise to bring you to a personal development stop, you will tend to stay at rest.

Instead of allowing yourself to lose momentum, you need to recognize that creative change is essential to your happiness and your success. To take advantage of this, you must continually be willing try new things, and strive to become better. "By your endurance you will gain your lives"

(Luke 21:19; NAS). Fulfillment lies in becoming the best you possible. "There are no such things as limits to growth, because there are no limits on the human capacity for intelligence, imagination, and wonder" (Ronald Reagan). To realize your full potential, you must continually learn, grow, and change. Anything less sells life short.

Ironically, you get regular assistance in this regard. Life is a great teacher, readily bringing before you whatever lesson you most need to learn. Take any situation or trouble that persists. The reason it continues is because the lesson contained therein has not yet been learned. If unhealthy relationships crowd out your joy, the message has yet to get through. If you are unhappy with your life, the tutorial remains incomplete. Life consistently challenges you to change. This occurs in both your inner and outer worlds. Unfortunately, there is only so much you can change external to yourself. Changing others, for example, is folly. Moving to a new town and taking a new job might solve the problem, but it might not, because you take yourself with you everywhere you go. When you can no longer satisfactorily change your state of affairs, you are challenged to dig deep and change yourself.

Most opportunities for transformation lie within. Personal development is not a self-focused, selfish endeavor. Quite the opposite, it is one of generosity. It is the foundation on which all progress is built. In helping yourself, you help others. A sick mother will find it difficult to raise her children properly. An unhappy person will find it hard to maintain healthy relationships. A doubting minster will be challenged to marshal the necessary resources to guide his flock. Helping yourself, as a way of giving back, is underappreciated and overlooked. A moderate investment in the self can often generate abundant returns that start with you and go on to benefit others. You can only give what you have. Matthew 7:3 (NLT) chides us in this regarding stating, "Why worry about a speck in your friend's eye when you have a log in your own?"

> **Life is a great teacher, readily bringing to you whatever lesson you most need to learn.**

To be successful, it is necessary you master yourself. For only the wholly-developed person is in a position to take full advantage of what life has to offer. Good advice requires that you be wise; helpful guidance requires that you have commensurate experience; and real compassion requires love of self.

Your mature Monk understands that self-mastery is one of the best gifts you can give the world. For only a person who is self-aware, satisfied, living in integrity, maintains healthy boundaries, and is able to love is well-positioned to raise the collective consciousness.

> **When you can no longer satisfactorily change your state of affairs, you are challenged to dig deep and change yourself.**

Self-actualized people teach by both direct instruction and indirect example. They are better able to teach others, raise children, build strong relationships, council friends, and guide society. Beyond those helped directly, the fully-developed individual is noticed as different. People look to them and emulate what they do as role models, in hopes of becoming like them. In this way, becoming all you can be raises the character of the world.

Personal growth is generally categorized as having two components. The first is acquisition of knowledge. Learning, understanding facts, processes, relationships, and methodologies are included in this type of development and reflected in your King. The second is acquisition of consciousness which lies squarely in your Monk. Understanding, integrity, compassion, and appreciation comprise consciousness. By and large, knowledge-based growth consists of learning about the world while consciousness-based growth is concerned with self-mastery. Both are important, complementary approaches to achieve success.

So what personal development opportunities lie before you? How do you plan to renew yourself? Complete Thought Expander 16.2, Development Opportunities, to explore your options. The challenge is to identify at least six personal development goals that you would like to pursue. To do this, identify three knowledge-based and three consciousness-based goals. Knowledge-based examples include anything learned such as getting that degree you always wanted, studying scripture, or learning a foreign language of your favorite destination. Consciousness-based examples might include practicing mindful awareness, reflection exercises such as journaling, learning to meditate, or engaging in prayer.

Thought Expander 16.2: Development Opportunities

	Knowledge-Based (Learning and experience goals)	Consciousness-Based (Psychological development goals)
1.		
2.		
3.		

Few people fully value personal development. Among the hundreds of CEOs I have worked with, most spend a thousand times more money on transient things than they do on becoming their best selves. They buy second homes, put in swimming pools, and drive fancy cars. Yet, they can't understand why they often feel lost, sensing something is missing in their lives. "We act as though comfort and luxury were the chief requirements in life, when all that we need to make us really happy is something to be enthusiastic about" (Charles Kingsely).

Only the wholly-developed person is in a position take full advantage of what life has to offer.

The problem is that things don't satisfy. Paradoxically, it is opportunities pursued that provide the greatest personal satisfaction and, when missed, result in the largest regrets. Researchers have found that education, in particular, is implicated as the most significant culprit. Missed opportunities to achieve knowledge-based goals are the number one thing people wish they had done differently.[139] Consciousness-based goals also appear essential to achieving healthy psychological function and overall well-being.[140,141] In general, both forms of self-development goals generate more personal value than objects external to the self.[142] As a result, people who live in ways that allow them to grow are more likely to flourish.[143]

So how much should be invested in becoming a better self? Applying the real estate formula to a human life, you will need to spend 0.5-4.0% of its value, annually.[144] According to the Environmental Protection Agency, the statistical value of a life is $7.4 million in today's dollars.[145] Combining the two statistics equates to an investment of $37,000--$296,000 per year is required to maintain a healthy self. At the low end, the ideal investment in developing ourselves is right in line with the cost of a good college education at $50,000 per year. Understanding that spending such funds is out of reach for most, the point remains clear—irrespective of the amount of discretionary funds available, many people dramatically under invest in themselves.

> **Few things are more valuable than an investment in you.**

This short-sighted approach is ironic for several reasons. First, you earn what you learn. There is a strong correlation between the levels of education a person achieves and the income they earn. Second, the benefits are timeless. Like milk, all material things have an expiration date. Physical things decay, rust, and fade away, but investments in the self are permanent, durable, and not subject to the ravages of time. They do not depreciate, their value isn't subject to external factors, and no one can take them away. Third, self-improvement generates excellent returns. Investing in a better you creates a stream of benefits that compound, each continuously building on itself and yielding increasing value over a lifetime. Interest on this asset generates income every day of your life. As a result, few things are more valuable than an investment in you.

Like all the ideas in this book, I have taken the idea of personal development to heart in my own life. There were many periods where I was unable to practically influence situations that were not working. For example, I spent decades feeling unfulfilled while working in corporate America. However, I did not have the resources to do what I wanted, or the know-how to make needed changes. It was during these periods that I turned inward. Unable to influence my external circumstances, I chose to improve myself both in knowledge and abilities. Shortly after moving to Midland, Michigan in 1987, I signed up for evening business classes at Central Michigan University. A few years later, I left Dow Corning and went back to school full-time, eventually getting my Masters in Management from

Northwestern University's Kellogg Graduate School of Business—a degree that to this day remains invaluable.

In 2008, I again found myself taking a philosophy class at the State University of New York; only to use it as a spring board to toward a psychology PhD the next year. In the years I wasn't pursuing knowledge-based growth, I read and studied a broad range of personal development and self-help books. I attended retreats, hired a life coach, and became a certified trainer, facilitator, and coach myself. I held the idea that if I wasn't growing in my current environment, I could at least be growing personally. More than anything, I attribute these self-investment efforts to allowing me to now live the life I always dreamed of.

Your contented Monk realizes that a life of personal growth has many benefits beyond the obvious factors of career advancement and earnings potential. It centers your actions and focuses your efforts on things of real value. Self-improvement creates a series of positive outcomes. It can start an upward, virtuous cycle of success or stop a downward cycle of problems and failure. Becoming all you can be works to improve *all* areas of life, while simultaneously enhancing the lives of everyone around you. Imagine what your life would be like if you took steps to regularly expand your capabilities. You would grow tremendously, almost unimaginably, over a lifetime. As a result, contentment, peace, wisdom, riches, and success would be yours.

A life committed to personal development can be thought of as a train route circling up and around a very tall mountain. The higher you progress the better the view, the cleaner the air, and the brighter the sun. On the Growth Rail Road Line there are always new trains coming, and you can get on or off at any time. The fare is reasonable. Many of us know people who got off the train early, while it was still at the bottom of the mountain, to make money, or get married, start a family, or avoid school. Some got back on, many didn't. As the train ascends, there are noticeably fewer and fewer people onboard. Of course, this is because people continue to disembark in greater numbers than those who board. The terrain is of gradual slope making progress almost unnoticeable. However, after riding further and further, you come to realize that not only is the view fresh and inspiring, but those remaining on the train headed to "Successville" are noticeably different. They are capable, accomplished, and content. Although a little haggard from the extra travel effort, they are more confident, peaceful, and happier than the average traveler. The result of maturing in their King,

Wizard, and Warrior, long suffering travelers come into a place where they can fully experience growth in their Monk.

How about you? What personal development is needed to help you further along in your journey? To gain clarity, take a few minutes and complete Thought Expander 16.3, Intrinsic Growth. Instead of focusing on extrinsic goals like accumulating wealth, title, or possessions, consider pursuing intrinsic goals. These might include knowledge-based goals such as finishing college, pursuing an advanced degree of interest, achieving a professional certification, or gaining understanding or experience that will enable you to start a new career. On the consciousness-based front, they may include becoming a better spouse, getting a handle on your anger, winning your children's hearts, understanding yourself better, addressing addictions or fixing other behaviors that get in the way of you being your best self. Flip back to Table 12.2, Improvement Ideas, for additional ideas, as needed. List each intrinsic goal in the left-hand column. Then for each, identify specific actions you can take next. These could be research appropriate schools, register for a class, read a book, research the topic online, find a person who has accomplished your goal and discuss it, hire a coach, or go to counseling. Add these in the right-hand column. The possibilities are endless. What is important is that you are actively pursuing some form of personal growth.

Thought Expander 16.3: Intrinsic Growth

Intrinsic Goal	Ways to achieve

Now pick one and do it. Success requires that you actively pursue a better you. Think of your many options as different tools sitting in a box. Which one you pick depends on the situation at hand. It is a never ending, ever-cycling process of picking the one that works best.

Anyone who has worked at a Fortune 500 company has experienced this tool de jour approach. Corporations pull out different tools based on the challenges they are facing. These include new methods, philosophies, or systems. Each tool holds promise and builds excitement and energy as it is first rolled out through the organization. Most work well for a time or season. Eventually, however, every tool reaches a point of diminishing marginal returns, falling to the wayside, requiring an ever-evolving process of step-wise improvement.

Successful people select the training, education, and experiences that they need most.

This occurs for four reasons. First, situations change. As corporations apply a tool, their environment continues to morph and shift. As result, what works now won't work later. Second, companies adapt. A sales group that shifts from a regional focus to a product-line focus will eventually incorporate tool-specific behaviors that take advantage of the new structure. Such changes necessarily come at a cost as new situational dynamics result while the older, regional-effective strategy is ignored. Third, blind spots always exist. As companies concentrate on the strengths of a tool, they take their focus off other important factors which this tool doesn't address, allowing other problems to grow in an unforeseen manner. Fourth, overuse dampens effectiveness. Over time, any overused tool will become dull, its effectiveness waning. To be high performing, companies need to continually identify and introduce the next best improvement opportunity. To be successful, businesses must continually pursue improvement.

Individual development is analogous. In the background, your situations, your thinking, and your behaviors continually evolve. To accommodate, successful people select the training, education, and experiences that they need most. Done consistently, positive change and transformative growth are the result. Ultimately, healthy personal development is an actively managed process of learning and self-exploration. "When you're finished changing, you're finished" (Ben Franklin).

You now know that a commitment to becoming the best possible you undergirds a successful life. Standing still doesn't honor your spirit. Your circumstances, perspectives, and interests are always changing. You either grow through them or you languish because of them. The accomplished person's natural state is one of expansion not of maintenance, of development not protection. It is through continuous transformation, born of the creative expression of new ideas, exploration of new pursuits, and experience of new discovery, that you fully become.

Your contented Monk recognizes that to live well one must commit to a life of renewal. Success requires both a solid knowledge of the world and a deep consciousness of the self. To achieve this, the individual must embark on a path of continuous self-development. All accomplishment and progress result from the fertile grounds of inner triumph. An improved understanding and enhanced self-awareness are powerful, durable assets that pay dividends throughout life. Your Monk understands the world is the way it is because you are the way you are. In renewing yourself, you allow yourself and the world to fully become.

BEHAVIOR 17: SERVING OTHERS

"All joy in this world comes from wanting others to be happy,
and all suffering in this world comes from wanting only oneself to be happy."
— Shantideva

Look beyond yourself. Fulfillment comes from being other-centric. Goals that focus on benefiting others, achieving a greater good, or improving the world move you beyond yourself. Other-centric activities provide meaning and purpose while yielding a more satisfied and fulfilled existence. While it is true from Behavior 16, <u>Renewing Yourself</u>, that sometimes the way to help others is to first improve yourself; every well-lived life also includes ambitions for something bigger than the individual self. "The meaning of life is to find your gift. The purpose of life is to give it away" (Pablo Picasso).

Billionaires around the world understand this, which is why many are committing to the Giving Pledge. Making this pledge, participants agree to give away at least half their wealth, although many choose to give much more. The richest people on the planet give because they realize the importance of serving others. "As each has received a gift, use it to serve one another" (1 Peter 4:20; ESV).

To capture real success, view your purpose as one of service.

To capture real success, view your purpose as one of service. You need to find a way to create value for others. Success is garnered by giving yourself. Anything you do to make the world smarter, safer, healthier, or better off will act to benefit all. Through engagement, you become reawakened, reenergized, and renewed. True happiness, therefore, comes as a result of moving beyond the self toward something greater. In helping others, you help yourself. "Give the world the best you have, and the best will come to you" (Madeline Bridges).

There is an old Latin phrase "incurvatus in se" (pronounced incurva-toos-in-say), meaning turned inward on oneself. It is represented by a small "c" letter. Believed to come from the writings of St. Augustine, it represents a self-centered life lived focused inward, as opposed to a generous life focused outward. The idea, from the early Christian Church, is that life gains meaning and purpose when it is not about you. Religious philosopher John Caird agrees noting, "There is provided an escape from the narrowness and poverty of the individual life, and the possibility of a life which is other and larger than our own, yet which is most truly our own. For, to be ourselves, we must be more than ourselves. What we call love is, in truth . . . the losing of our individual selves to gain a larger self." The good life is other-centric.

> Experiencing well-being, or happiness, in life is the result of striving for something beyond that which benefits you alone.

Psychological science researchers concur. There are many different ways to assess the amount of "c" curvature, or self-focus, a person has. Self construal theory (DeCicco & Stroink, 2007) proposes that people see themselves as some mix of the contracted "me," the mutual "we," and the expanded, holistic "all." Individuals with a fully expanded sense-of-self tend to see themselves as a part of everyone and everything. They tend to interpret others' successes as their own, seeing humanity's problems and triumphs as impacting them directly. As such, their life perception is more empathetic and they tend to experience more joy and greater life satisfaction.[146,147]

The increase in well-being resulting from a shift in focus away from one's self and toward others is a pattern found in psychological science. Self-determination theory (Ryan & Deci, 2000) proposes that other-serving (versus self-serving) goals and generative actions (instead of personal striving) work to bolster well-being.[148] Compassionate goals theory (Crocker, Olivier, & Nuer, 2009) asserts that an eco-centric (external) rather than an ego-centric (internal) focus facilitates well-being.[149] Values-in-action theory (Peterson & Seligman, 2004) purports that use of transcendent strengths such as meaning and love toward others is related to greater levels of well-being.[150] In these examples and others, theorists support the proposition that shifting focus away from one's self plays an important role in a person's well-being and, therefore, their success.

The lesson is consistent and clear. Experiencing well-being, or happiness, in life is the result of striving for something beyond that which benefits you alone. The importance of one's goal-orientation can be found by considering the "happy hermit" and "miserable saint" dilemma. It appears that both individuals violate the idea that more self-expansive views result in greater happiness. Certainly, if it were true, that an external focus was responsible for well-being, then you would expect the hermit to be unhappy and the saint to be joyful. A closer look, however, reveals that their focus, not the role they play in life, is what matters. The happy hermit may be alone, but that says nothing about the greater good he or she may pursue. He could spend his time developing his mind, advancing human understanding of spirituality, or furthering fundamental scientific theories of the universe. As such, the reclusive appearance masks a focus beyond the self. Conversely, the miserable saint may appear to be giving towards others, but may really be striving for worldly recognition, which can lead to a wretched existence. The service-oriented role hides his self-focus. Happiness is ultimately a matter of purpose.

The good news is that purpose is of your own making. To increase your well-being and success in life, you don't necessarily need to quit your job, get divorced, or move away. Instead, you only need to shift your focus outward. Take a moment and think about some of the things your Monk might want to strive for such as developing spirituality, expanding positivity, becoming self-actualized, or growing closer to God.

Detail these major goals in the left-hand column of Thought Expander 17.1, Ways to Serve. Then for each, describe how it will potentially benefit you. It should not be a surprise if this middle column is easy to complete as most goals are about you. Next, however, consider how you could accomplish your goal while benefiting others or serving the greater good. Examples could include mentoring someone, caring for another, loving your enemies, or assisting those who are less fortunate. How might a change in focus make the goal about something instead of you from which you stand to benefit even more? Write your answers in the right-hand column.

Thought Expander 17.1: Ways to Serve

Category	My Goal	How it Benefits Me	How it Serves Others or the Greater Good
Personal			
Career			
Family			
Life			
Other			

Does your focus really matter? It matters immensely. Small, subtle changes occur when you take yourself out of the equation. Goals shift, motivation increases, fear declines, performance improves, and happiness grows. This can be accomplished in your current life by broadening your goals to include a purpose beyond yourself. Actions that advance science, create beauty, assist others, improve the human experience, or transform the world, expand the scope of your life's meaning. There is no shortage of ways to move beyond the self, start simply by giving of your time, treasure, and talent. Accomplished people hold a mindset of service.

How do you know you have other-centric goals? One way to tell is to ask if the goals would still exist and matter if you weren't here. If they would, then they are externally focused goals. For example, the goal to eliminate cancer has value whether you are alive or not. Thought Expander 17.2, Selfless Pursuits, can help you start thinking in this way. Assuming money, time, and ability are not issues, how might you help others or make the world a better place?

Thought Expander 17.2: Selfless Pursuits

Social Areas	Ideas	Global Areas	Ideas
Family		Health	
Team		Welfare	
Group		Humanity	
Church		Innovation	
Institution		Economy	
Community		Environment	
Country		Greater Good	
World		Spirit	

Altruistic goals generate feelings of purpose and meaning. They create a sense of engagement. Goals focused beyond the self make your life count for even more. Researchers in one study of approximately 13,000 adults who had completed online surveys found that meaning and engagement were chief drivers of well-being.[151] People with compassionate goals tend to feel closer and more connected with others, while those with self-focused goals are more likely to experience conflict, be lonely, and feel confused and afraid.[152]

Usually, goals beyond the self are related to greater life satisfaction while self-image goals are associated with more distress.[153] Altruistic goals include activities geared directly toward the benefit of others and actions designed to improve the greater good.

In general, the degree to which people engage in virtuous, value-laden activities is directly related to their happiness. Such productive engagement, either paid or unpaid, generates improved well-being, an

Giving of the self is central to having success in life.

increased sense of usefulness, better aging, and an enhanced overall life quality.[154] Poet and philosopher Hakim Sanai notes that: "As long as you cling to yourself, you will wander right and left, day and night, for thousands of years; and when, after all that effort, you finally open your eyes, you will see yourself, through inherent defects, wandering round itself like the ox in a mill; but, if, once freed of yourself, you finally get down to work, this door (to God) will open to you." Ultimately, giving of the self is central to having success in life.

It was for me. As mentioned previously, a few years after leaving my CEO position, I was given the opportunity to partner with a private, family-owned business to assist in a wide range of activities. This included: improving communication and working relationships between various family members and among the executives, transferring the business in a tax effective way, installing a professional management team, and preparing the company for sale. To do this, an equity stake in the business was offered along with a long-term retainer. Over the next three years, we completed a series of intricate and fundamental changes to the business and its structure that improved performance while providing increased freedom to the family owners.

Significant value was created in this process. In fact, the impact to both the family and me was considerable. The actions we took captured millions of dollars in value, helped the business successfully navigate a downturn in the marketplace, and allowed the family to successfully exit daily operations. By serving this family business well, I also benefited. Not only did I achieve personal satisfaction, my net worth was significantly improved. By effectively serving the needs of others, I prospered.

Successful entrepreneurs know this well. The secret to earning significant wealth is straightforward—do things that produce value for others. The greater the value, the more you will earn. Wealth generated in life is directly related to the good created. The whole world rushes to those who serve it well. The fastest way to joy is to solve another's problems.

The fastest way to joy is to solve another's problems.

Your mature Monk realizes this is true in matters of spirit, as well as matters of accomplishment. You get what you give. If you want love, give it. If you want someone to help you, help them. If you want to achieve, help another accomplish. If you want a better life, improve other's lives. Putting yourself in the energy of that thing you want, while making it happen for others, increases its propensity to show up in your life. "Whatever one sows, that will he also reap" (Galatians 6:7; ESV).

Conversely, you also lose what you take. Consider entitlement, for example. Entitlement programs were never created as an excuse to avoid work or as a relief to the pursuit of self-betterment. There exists an evolving belief that one can gain by taking. The recent explosion in social security disability cases supports the possibility that many people seek, and are getting benefits, they do not deserve.[155] Many government programs, and more generally our legal system, are being exploited. Getting on long-term social security disability is seen as just short of winning the lotto. What else could explain the fact that once on social security disability 99% stay on until retirement age?[156] The problem is that by taking we don't gain, we lose. While social programs are an important safety net, entitlement is a dangerous success-deadening trap. Eventually, getting something for nothing causes the recipient to become helpless, stuck, and unhappy as time further distances them from achieving their full potential.[157]

When people are able to develop the skills necessary to provide for themselves, they achieve what psychologists refer to as self-efficacy (Bandura, 1977). Self-efficacy is a person's confidence in one's own ability to complete tasks, reach goals, and succeed in various situations. People with high levels of self-efficacy believe they can perform well, and they tend to live in a manner that leverages their ability to achieve. They view challenging tasks as opportunities for growth rather than something to be avoided. As a result, they approach their work and their lives differently.

Your inner Monk understands that a successful life is based on giving of yourself. Serving others advances personal progress. The Monk is inspired to commit acts of kindness and undertake philanthropic ventures. One of the best ways to create value is in service to others or life as a greater whole. In making the world a better place, we become connected, involved, and vested in what is good. For "The sole meaning of life is to serve humanity" (Leo Tolstoy).

Socialization is core to human well-being. Positive emotions, in particular, are thought to be an adaptation which acts to reinforce social-oriented behaviors, enhancing our survival as a species. The broaden-and-build theory (Fredrickson, 1998) supports the proposition that positive emotions encourage people to behave in pro-social ways, while negative emotions push them to separate from others for safety. People who strive to create value for others have been found to experience greater levels of well-being while also realizing improved cognitive, behavioral, and emotional outcomes.[158] As a result, living a life of service tends to generate the good feelings and personal satisfaction necessary to call any life a success.

Acts of generosity demonstrate this point. One study found that spending $5/day on someone else makes one happier than if one spends it on one's self.[159] Such happiness is self-reinforcing in that it further increases willingness to invest in additional pro-social activities.[160] Pro-social behaviors, like generosity, are thought to build social capital during good periods that could prove valuable during more challenging times.[161]

To test this, researchers studied undergraduate students using a computer game. Results show that people with lower subjective assessments of their economic class were actually more, not less, generous.[162] The findings are in direct contrast to expectations generated from economic theory where those who have less were expected to give less. Authors speculate that lower economic classes have an increased disposition toward egalitarian values and a better ability to relate to economic hardship. This occurs because such groups are more likely to benefit from, and have a greater future need for, the social capital that such behaviors create.

Adversity can lead to a sense of compassion. Tony Robbins remembers as a child, his family not having money to buy food and the deep sense of appreciation when another family gave them a meal. Now he pays it back by funding millions of free meals annually. In summary, positive actions toward others increase well-being and the good feelings that result in an increased desire to help others through a process that can build upon itself over time.[163]

But where do we start? How can we go beyond ourselves and serve others better in our daily lives? Often overlooked opportunities to serve exist in our daily interactions. These include how we view and interact with others. Take respect, for example. Respect is defined as a feeling of admiration for another person based on their qualities, abilities, or achievements. It contains the assumption that there is something good, valuable, and worthy about the other. It is a form of appreciation. Conversely, disrespect contains the belief that there is something bad and worthless about another. It is a form of contempt. Respect and disrespect are both judgments. Judgments are often premature and biased, such that the level of quality and worth of another is determined ahead of full knowledge. Such pre-judgments are assumptions from which our word prejudice is derived.

Often overlooked opportunities to serve exist in our daily interactions.

Prejudice starts early in life and can be found everywhere. Recently, I overheard a principal in my daughter's middle school explaining, wisely, that "Children with physical handicaps, birth defects, or learning disabilities didn't deserve labels like 'retarded' or 'slow.' "What they deserve," he went on, "is our respect." Bravo. They do deserve our reverence, and so does most everyone else.

Every interaction provides an opportunity to show respect. Seeing the value in everyone is a mark of service. Service in your daily life is realized in how you treat others. For in seeing the good in your fellow man, you recognize the good in yourself. Service creates compassion.

Another often underappreciated way to serve is evidenced in how you communicate. There are four general steps to serve through communication: listening, accepting, inquiring, and responding. First, you serve by listening. Listening shows respect, projecting a sense of valuing another.

The key to real listening is to dampen the instantaneous knee-jerk need to respond. You have one mouth and two ears for a reason; you are made to listen twice as often as you speak. Ironically, people who listen more and speak less are perceived as better conversationalists. It is difficult to learn anything while talking.

Every interaction provides an opportunity to appreciate another.

Second, you serve by accepting. Not to be confused with condoning, accepting is allowing. Clearly, there are many different stages of life, each shaded by an infinite number of perspectives, desires, and environments. Acceptance asks you to permit people to be who they are, where they are, with the issues they have—all without trying to change them. You honor another by delaying conclusions until you can appropriately evaluate them. "Do not judge according to appearance, but judge with righteous judgment" (John 7:24, NAS).

Third, we serve by seeking first to understand through effective inquiry. Each person has a unique song playing in their heads that others can't hear. Therefore, adept questioning is essential to gain clarity before you are in any position to share. Great queries include: "How do you feel?", "What do you want?", "What have you tried so far?", "What is the likely outcome?", and "How can I help you?" to name only a few.

Fourth, you serve in how you respond. Words have incredible power to build-up and inspire. The most effective responses are those that reflect your own experiences. Such replies are most reverential since they carry no obligation on the part of the recipient to copy them and no promise of their effectiveness. Service-oriented responses share experiences that help others take advantage of your successes and avoid your failures—framed in positivity.

The least effective responses are those that direct or tell. To give advice is to "should" on another. Shoulding, as a response, is disrespectful and says much about the speaker—none of it flattering. The shoulding party takes the higher ground which ultimately suggests they are smarter and better able to make a decision. Doing so, the teller inadvertently professes to be better able to assess the underlying facts, feelings, and needs of the other while confidently prognosticating the ultimate outcome. Sounds ludicrous, doesn't it? How could anyone know enough about another's situation to make a better decision? Yet, this approach is a staple of many interactions and relationships.

Every interaction provides an opportunity to appreciate another. Successful people use their interactions as a chance to identify, explore, and learn from another's excellence. Something about each and every person is good, valuable, and worthy. Not surprisingly, relationships where this is assumed, flourish. People like and value people who like and value them, reflecting the unique talents, special gifts, and aspects of genius that reside in everyone. You create value in your own life when you identify and appreciate another's wisdom. In discovering the worth of another, every interaction becomes an accelerated step along your journey toward success.

Service is an important part living well.

In some more enlightened, new-age circles, the ancient Sanskrit word "Namaste" is used as a greeting. It is a beautiful blessing extended to show deep respect. Namaste means the spirit in me honors the spirit in you. When spoken, it is often accompanied by a nod or a small bow. The greeting is a conscious recognition of the sublime which resides in all life. People are more accommodating when they recognize that they are in the presence of another spirit. By learning to see others this way, you honor and love all around you. For as Galatians 5:13-14 (NIV) reminds us, "You, my brothers and sisters, were called to be free. But do not use your freedom to indulge the sinful nature; rather, serve one another humbly in love. For the entire law is fulfilled in keeping this one command: Love your neighbor as yourself."

You inner Monk understands that service is an important part of living well. Selflessness expands accomplishment. In loving others, you fully become while also establishing a sublime connection with the divine. If you value others, they will value you. Treat them well, and they will support you. Appreciate their genius, and they will help you find yours. Serve them, and they will help you accomplish your dreams. Author and leadership guru Og Mandino said it this way. "Extend to each person, no matter how trivial the contact, all the care and kindness and understanding and love that you can muster, and do it with no thought of any reward. Your life will never be the same again." Your contented Monk knows that to be successful you must move beyond yourself.

BEHAVIOR 18: EXPECTING GOOD THINGS

"Words can never adequately convey the incredible impact of our attitudes toward life...life is 10% what happens to us and 90% how we respond to it."
— Charles Swindoll

To thrive, be more positive. Humans have a unique ability to choose their way of thinking. Each of us shades the expectations of our lives with a color. At opposite ends of the spectrum are the rose-colored sunglasses of optimism and near-black shades of pessimism. Each perspective, positive or negative, influences what you see, driving how you behave, and, ultimately dictating what shows up in your life. Positivity, born of optimism, tends to generate better outcomes while negativity, derived from pessimism, tends to dampen possibility and thwart accomplishment. To be successful, you must look inside and adjust your attitude. Successful people assume good things will come—and, as a result, they do.

Your attitude affects every aspect of your life.

Your attitude affects every aspect of your life. Often you are unaware of the impact your outlook has. The influence can be significant, either leading you to more readily achieve your goals or pushing them further out of reach. As David Schwartz notes, "Believe it can be done. When you believe something can be done, really believe, your mind will find the ways to do it." In general, an optimistic attitude constructively enhances achievement, while a pessimistic outlook is destructive and thwarts accomplishment.

Think about an optimist you know, someone who always seems positive, looking on the bright side. How would you describe them? What level of happiness, fulfillment, or satisfaction do they possess? Most optimists appear healthy, competent, kind, and productive. They tend to be people who go the extra mile, willingly take responsibility, are attentive, nurture relationships, and work hard. They often have jobs they enjoy, spouses they love, and friends by the bushel. They are also more successful.

This is not coincidental. A person's perspective is either constructive or destructive. For how you see the world greatly influences what you do next, and actions taken are directly related to the outcomes achieved. Researchers have confirmed this relationship, observing that a person's expectations influence both their performance and success. This leads to a more positive outlook in a process that builds on itself in a positive, self-reinforcing, upward, virtuous cycle.[164] So powerful is the effect of expectation that the quality of a person's smile in their high school yearbook picture can be used to predict their well-being some three decades later.[165] Be it conscious or not, people often get what they expect.

Teacher expectations are one area where this has been analyzed extensively. Numerous longitudinal studies have found that teachers' expectations significantly affect student learning. Looking at students across a wide, socio-economic spectrum, researchers found that inaccurate student expectations (i.e., those with differences between perceived skill and actual ability) materially impacted their test scores. This not only occurred in the current year, when the student was with the teacher, but the impact persisted even ten years later.[166]

Expectations impact outcomes.

In the landmark Oak School study, eighteen elementary school teachers were told that 20% of their classes contained students classified as "intellectual bloomers." But in fact, these "gifted" students were randomly selected and actually represented the average student. By year end, 47% of these children gained more than 20 points on standardized tests versus 19% of the non-bloomers.[167] In another study, researchers monitored 11,000 students over five years and found a significant correlation between teacher expectations and student performance.[168]

In general, teachers that expected a higher or lower quality product from a student got it. Positive expectations enhanced performance in what is known as the Pygmalion effect, coined from the play of the same name by George Bernard Shaw. Negative expectations diminished performance in what is known as the Golem effect. These various studies indicate that expectations have a significant impact on outcomes.

But how do a teacher's expectations work to influence the performance of the students themselves? Either the teachers are causing the outcome by unconsciously treating the students differently, or the students are performing differently based on the expectations placed upon them, or both. It can be readily argued that student's internalized perspectives of themselves must play a role since they are the ones taking the tests. However, another experiment sheds light on the amazing role the teachers play in the outcome by shaping student's internal perspectives. In this study, the students were replaced with rats.[169] Undergraduate students tasked with training rats were told that some rats were "maze bright," while others were "maze dull," even though the rats assigned to each group were randomly selected and were no different on average. Researchers found, at

> **Optimists are not blind to the donut around the hole.**

the end of the training period, that the maze-bright rats learned the mazes significantly faster than the maze-dull rats indicating that the trainer's expectations played an important role. Assuming rats are not able to act on their own expectations, differing trainer expectations appear to be a pivotal factor in the learning process.

Collectively, these studies and others, demonstrate the tremendous power of expectation on the world around you. Expectations permeate all you think and all you do. Confidence, one way or the other, exerts a profound impact on both our own and other's life outcomes. "The thoughts that you think and the statements you make, regarding yourself, determine your mental attitude. If you have a worthwhile objective, find the one reason why you can achieve it rather than hundreds of reasons why you can't" (Napoleon Hill).

How you go about framing a situations matters. Sir Winston Churchill wryly noted that, "A pessimist sees the difficulty in every opportunity; an optimist sees the opportunity in every difficulty." Optimists are not blind to the donut around the hole. While not conclusive, the preponderance of research indicates that optimism conveys many advantages.[170] Being in a positive frame of mind improves performance at both school and work, resulting in better grades and enhancing task outcomes.[171] Optimistic people have better relationships and people want to be around them more often.[172] Such people feel more connected, are liked better, and have been found to exercise more and sleep better.[173] Not surprisingly, they are seen as more attractive and experience better health.[174,175] Optimists tend to be more resilient and better able to overcome adversity and trauma while experiencing greater levels of well-being and personal success.[176,177,178] It appears that positive expectations penetrate many facets of the successful life.

Conversely, people with low expectations tend to experience impeded performance.[179] Negativity puts you in defense mode, narrows the field of vision, and shuts off receptiveness to new possibilities. Diminished expectations result in less success.

By shifting your expectations, you expand the level of achievement possible.

In both cases, the outcomes reflect the expectations. Adverse outcomes resulting from suboptimal viewpoints convince pessimists they are correct while encouraging outcomes resulting from advantageous perspectives assure optimists they are right. Expectations generate results of a like kind, each reflecting the outlook held. Over time, related outcomes become a self-fulfilling feedback loop.

To understand why such differences exist, it is helpful to look at the very different ways optimists and pessimists frame their point of view.[180] Optimists look at good events as being the norm, happening often, and as a result of their own efforts. They see bad events as being unusual, infrequent, and due to specific external causes. Pessimists, on the other hand, frame the world in exactly the opposite manner. They see good events as being uncommon, temporary, and due to factors beyond their control. They frame bad events as being common, frequent, and due to them.

How might your framing be helping or hurting you? Take a moment to identify some aspect of life that you tend to think negatively about such as a challenging economy or difficult relationship. Consider a long-term issue that has been a regular annoyance. Write it in the Personal Challenge box of Thought Expander 18.1, Positive Shifts. Next, identify negatives you tend to see in the situation. Place your answer in the Pessimistic View box. After that, consider the possibility that your perspective is incomplete and explore how the situation might align with a more optimistic perspective. Craft an answer that puts a reasonable, but more positive spin on the situation. This is often most easily done by converting the challenge into an opportunity. Write your answer in the Optimistic View box.

Thought Expander 18.1: Positive Shifts

Personal Challenge:	
Pessimistic View (permanent, pervasive, and a result of general factors often related to myself)	
Optimistic View (temporary, infrequent, and due to specific external causes)	

Once the personal challenge is analyzed, identify a personal win you have not properly appreciated, and write it in the Personal Win box of Thought Expander 18.2, <u>Appreciative Shifts</u>. This might be an important success, meaningful accomplishment, or a good thing in life that you take for granted or that has not been fully appreciated. Next, identify how you might be under-appreciating the situation. Place your answer in the Unappreciative View box. After that, consider the many positive aspects that resulted from your personal win. Write your answer in the Appreciative View box.

Thought Expander 18.2: Appreciative Shifts

Personal Win:	
Unappreciative View (permanent, pervasive, and a result of general factors often related to myself)	
Appreciative View (temporary, infrequent, and due to specific external causes)	

Did you notice a shift in your perspective of each situation? Outlook alters the energy around a situation. Positive reframing constructively repositions perspectives so they are more beneficial. In this way, every situation can become a tool to drive our success rather than a difficulty that impedes it. Einstein knew this stating, "Problems cannot be solved by the same level of thinking that created them." By moving from the suboptimal, habitual thinking of the subconscious toward a more optimal, intentional view that we consciously manage, you have the opportunity to take more control over your life.

The following story drives home the point. George was always in a good mood with something positive to say. Every day, upon waking, he would tell himself that he would not be a victim to life but would choose the positive. He believed success was about choices, and he always picked the good over the bad mood, the constructive versus the destructive interpretation, and the optimistic ahead of the pessimistic outlook.

George managed a pawn shop on the bad side of town. He knew to take precautions including always keeping the back door locked. However after years of vigilance, one day he forgot to secure the door and was held up at gunpoint by two men. Shaking, while trying to get the cash, he spooked the armed robbers who shot him in panic. As he lay on the floor, he realized that he could choose to live or die.

Fortunately, George was found quickly and rushed to the hospital. Not surprisingly, he was frightened. But what scared him most was the look on the faces of the paramedics and doctors. In their eyes, he saw that he was a dead man even though their words said he would be fine. He knew some positive action was needed.

During surgery prep, there was a big, burly nurse shouting questions at him. She asked, "Are you allergic to anything?"

George responded, "Yes."

Activity in the operating room came to a standstill as the triage team silently awaited his reply.

"I am allergic to bullets!" he cried. "But, I am going to live," he told the team. "I'll be really mad if I don't survive." The energy in the room shifted, and all dug in to make that happen.

George lived. While no one would dispute that the skill of his doctors served him well, it is also a possibility that his attitude played an equally important role. It reset expectations and expanded possibility.

No one is suggesting turning a blind eye to problems or living a Pollyanna-ish life. Reality needs to be dealt with. "When weeds come up in your garden...(they) aren't going to disappear until you get on your hands and knees and pull them out" (Nick Ortner). Problems can't be allowed a foothold, reinforced by adverse thinking. Doing so will fertilize negativity, giving it deeper roots and a stronger hold. Negative thinking creates a pattern of adverse expectations that keeps us from better options and outcomes. "What I feared has come upon me; what I dreaded has happened to me" (Job 3:25; NIV). Instead, negative perspectives need to be recognized, managed, and replaced with more productive alternatives.

Your words are the seeds of your future harvest.

Consider a few of your negative expectations. When are you a Debbie-downer? These are the things that make you unhappy or upset. You don't like them because they take away your joy, possibly acting as long-term sources of annoyance. Take a minute to write down a couple of persistent negative thought patterns in the left-hand column of Thought Expander 18.3, Better Expectations. Next, consider more positive alternatives. Craft more favorable expectations, and write those in the right-hand column. For example, you may be frustrated that your teenager doesn't readily do what you ask and shows disrespect. To some degree, you have come to expect this of him or her. You may get angry and show it, or you may give up at times, counting the years until they leave for college. Yet you know that if left unchecked, your child's lack of respect could leak out into other important areas of your child's life. It could cause them to perform less well at school, have fewer friends, and even damage your long-term relationship with them. Instead, you could reframe the behavior positively noting that it isn't personal, but a natural part of growing up. It is a process that needs to be managed not a problem in and of itself. You might then realize that while you can't really control anyone but yourself, you can set clear, fair, and firm boundaries, and then enforce them consistently. Additional topical ideas to consider when completing the following Thought Expander could include negative judgments of others, adverse self opinions, and unfairness in life outcomes, among many others.

.:gative Expectations | Positive Expectations |
|---|---|---|
| 1. | | |
| 2. | | |
| 3. | | |

Now look back on your list. Which column feels better and is more likely to help you achieve? Know for every negative expectation in life, there is another more compassionate option. The goal to living successfully is to find more constructive viewpoints so we can better pursue possibility instead of being roped in by limitation. For every negative expectation you hold, there is a more productive alternative. For your attitude is simply your thought life turned inside out; where your heart shows up in your approach to life. Therefore, "Make a game of finding something positive in every situation. Ninety-five percent of your emotions are determined by how you interpret events to yourself" (Brain Tracy).

Expectations matter. By shifting your expectations, you expand the level of achievement possible. One way expectations become readily transparent is through your words and deeds. Take what you say for example. Words speak volumes about what you really think. Like a poker player's "tell," the subtle unconscious clues he projects about his cards, your words disclose to others in great detail what you expect out of life. Freud, the famed psychologist, believed there were no verbal mistakes just words that come from your subconscious that you are unable to repress—hence the term Freudian Slip. In a nutshell, your words give you away, clearly detailing what you really think, believe, and expect.

My unique background became the topic of conversation regularly, during my years of advisory work. The engineering degree impressed some, the top-tier masters degree in business strategy and the CEO stint gave credibility to others, but it was always the psychology Ph.D. that drew the most notable reaction.

Still today, upon learning that I have psychology training, some people are taken aback. A few quietly try to sneak away; others put their hands over their mouths and go quiet to avoid inadvertently giving up any more information. While many want to learn about themselves, others are concerned that I might be able to learn a lot about them, understand things that sometimes they don't even realize about themselves. To a significant degree, I can. By listening attentively to what is said, and asking the right questions, I can subtly glean meaningful insights. Given enough time, anyone can figure what you are thinking simply by hearing what you say and watching what you do. It cannot be otherwise.

Your words are clear reflections of your inner thoughts, beliefs, and expectations. As such, they are precursors to every physical manifestation and outcome in life. Words have the power to create or destroy, either building up or tearing down. The Bible tells us that we need to tame our tongue, for although small, it can have a great impact on our lives and the lives of those around us. "A great forest is set on fire by a small spark" (James 3:5; NIV). Your words are the seeds of your future harvest. Positive words bless. They are "Sweet to the soul and healing to the bones" (Proverbs 16:24; NIV). Like good seeds, affirmative views grow to provide the food needed for a successful life. Crops include accomplishment, fulfillment, and blessing. Conversely, negative words sow damaged seeds that are stunted and fail to grow to their full potential. Great power and influence reside in every verbal expression.

Your inner Monk realizes that words are clues to the soul and an avenue to success. For what you say acts like a tidal current setting the course for what will come into, and go out of, your life. While a skilled sailor knows how to use the wind to transit the best course, the underlying tidal currents must be considered as well, since they can radically alter the boat's trajectory.

Words are no different. If you speak in ways that support your best efforts, your progress will be bolstered. What you say opens wide the gates to great possibility or keeps them ajar, limiting access. As such, you must exercise great caution with this most powerful tool—your mouth.

If you wish to be more successful in life, speak more optimistically. Be positive about what has happened and what will come to be. Appreciate your many blessings and note the good in others. Dole out a steady stream of positivity on your situations and the people in your lives.

It is this latter point that is often challenging for top executives. Many CEOS are not comfortable with positive words directed at their employees. CEOs argue that they only like to praise people when "They deserve it." As a result, compliments are few and far in-between. Explaining themselves, they worry that if they give praise too often, their employees will get the idea they are doing well enough and stop working hard. Praise in many companies, therefore, is kept at a minimum.

What the CEOs forget is that praise is only one type of positive interaction. Employees find appreciation for work done, help with personal problems, and feeling "in on things" to be more valuable than wages, job security, or even promotion and growth.[181] Showing interest in people's personal lives and finding common ground beyond work are both strong, positive interactions. Good executives know that relationships are pivotal to their achievement as a leader and the company's success as a whole. Accomplished people use their words productively.

> **Words reveal your underlying desires, expectations, and beliefs, influencing what you achieve.**

Words reveal your underlying desires, expectations, and beliefs, influencing what you achieve. Science supports this idea. Measured by a positivity ratio (Fredrickson, 2010), researchers have found that the number of positive to negative interactions directly reflects a relationship's quality. In the business world, flourishing teams were found to say at least three positive things for every negative utterance.[182]

Couples, too, are impacted by the quality of their verbal exchanges. Marriage experts have found that they can predict with over 90% accuracy from a 15-minute conversation which couples will stay together over a ten year period by assessing the ratio of positive to negative interactions.[183] Couples headed for divorce had positivity ratios of 0.8:1, or less, while healthy relationships are closer to 20:1. Even during arguments, couples who stayed together remained affirmative, generating five positive comments for every negative one. Collectively, better relationships are a result of more positive language.

Every relationship is either getting stronger or weaker as a result of the words used to fertilize it or poison it. For "Death and life are in the power of the tongue" (Proverbs 18:21; NAS). Words give you the life you want or they take it away. Wisdom dictates that you cultivate more positive interactions.

My mother regularly admonished, "If you don't have anything good to say, don't say anything at all." The corollary is that if you think of something good, affirmative, or helpful, say it. Every positive utterance is a confirmatory expectation. Words are barometers of your psyche, indicators of opportunity.

It is likely that no one talks more negatively to you than you talk to yourself. Too often you are your own worst enemy, treating yourself in ways you would never dream of treating others. It is valuable to learn to silence this inner critic. "The last of one's freedoms is the ability to choose one's attitude in any given circumstance" (Viktor Frankl). Evolving our internal dialogue from one of criticism to one of encouragement provides a platform for a more successful life.

> **Every success is preceded by hopeful anticipation.**

To reduce the frequency of negative thoughts and replace them with positive alternatives, there are many useful exercises. One of them is to write down the negative thought on a piece of paper and then tear it up, burn it, or throw it away. The combination of writing followed by an action directly focused against the thought sends a striking signal to the brain that you are moving on.

Other approaches include snapping a rubber band on your wrist following a negative thought, or chasing every negative thought with a positive one either spoken out loud or written down. The trick is to choose an affirmation that is believable. For example, "I could never get out of debt" could be replaced with "I can be a millionaire." Yet, for many, a more believable alternative might be "I can pay off my smallest credit card next month" or "I can create a budget to track my spending." In a transition, more focused propositions can often be more useful in initiating change.

A final approach is to make plans around the negativity. As seen in Behavior 9, <u>Creating a Plan</u>, life plans that outline goals that motivate and inspire have been found to improve optimism and mood.[184] Each of these approaches retrains the brain to avoid unwanted pessimism and embrace positivity and potentiality.

Your inner Monk realizes that life responds to your expectations. Expectations influence what you see, say, and do—attracting their own kind. They permeate one's thoughts, leaking out into every action and affecting the final outcomes. Accomplished people allow for possibility. Their positive attitudes fruitfully influence both their experiences and the results they achieve along their life journey. Every success is preceded by hopeful anticipation.

Your contented Monk knows that to live more successfully, you must expect good things. Consider possibility over limitation. If you are on the right track, positivity will show up in your thoughts, words, and actions. One of the most powerful habits you can have is to expect good things in your life. Optimism enhances relationships, improves happiness, and generates better outcomes in a myriad of ways. It is better to expect something wonderful, and get some of it, than to expect nothing, and get all of it.

BEHAVIOR 19: HAVING FAITH

"Fear knocked at the door. Faith answered. And lo, no one was there."
— *Author Unknown*

The faith-filled life is blessed. To achieve it, you must believe in something greater than yourself. For those who believe, failure is impossible. This kind of confidence is lacking in the world, and yet faith is a powerful thing. To succeed you must trust that you can be anything, do anything, and have anything. Only then will it be yours.

You were not born with a spirit of fear. Fear is not your natural state. It is a learned, human response. People are taught to fear. In contrast, take animals, for example. In nature, animals do not fear, but more accurately, react with alarm that is both brief and purposeful. When faced with an immediate threat they respond, sometimes vigorously. But watch them closely and afterwards you will see them shake off the negative energy and go back to just being. One explanation, is that animals have no ego (Freud, 1923), or self identity, and, as such, do not comprehend that that they are separate from all around them.

You were not born with a spirit of fear.

Psychologists consider fear to be a byproduct of the ego—caused by a perception that you are each a unique, separate, and independent self. Anxiety results from this belief that you are separate from the world around you. This is not the case. The spirit of life from nature, the universe, or God, depending on your preference, resides in each of us. We are all joined through an energy force that provides our consciousness and vigor. The separateness is a lie that seeds fear. It provides a "me" versus "them" mentality where success, plenty, and love become uncertain.

Your mature Monk sees fear as the remnant of a no-longer needed survival mechanism. To endure, primitive man needed to be on constant look-out for things that would bring an abrupt end to his existence. For millennia, fear provided a necessary self-preservation tool. Driving the fight or flight response, fear saved lives.

> To get a handle on fear, shift from reflexive feelings toward your analytical mind.

In the modern world, however, there are few significant risks to life and limb. The practical need for fear has been greatly reduced. Yet the cognitive space is still occupied and busily looks for ways to keep you safe. Consequently, the focus on fear has morphed, and worry has grown to take its place. The difference between them is significant. Fear is a temporary, real-time emotion that drives an immediate physical response, whereas worry is a systemic anticipation about something that might happen in the future. Fear, as a biological response, is healthy; worry is anything but. Expecting bad things, as a matter of course, is counterproductive and problematic. Taken to the extreme, psychologists call the tendency to overinflate negative possibilities catastrophizing (Ellis, 1958). Catastrophizing is an irrational tendency to imagine the worst possible outcome in a given situation. Worry, in all its forms, can alter a person's thinking, driving one to suboptimal decision making and bringing about a lesser life.

While useful long ago, the practical fear mechanism has evolved into a counterproductive process. So how do you wrestle back control from this insidious pattern that will act to stand in the way of your peace, happiness, and joy? To get a handle on fear, shift from reflexive feelings toward your analytical mind. Here's an example.

What is it you worry most about? Write that in the top row of Thought Expander 19.1, Rationalizing Fear. Next, assign a percentage reflecting the likelihood that what you most worry about will actually happen. After that, write down a few other alternative outcomes that could occur instead of your main worry. Place those in the alternate (alt.) rows, assigning a probability for each. Guessing is fine when assigning likelihoods. For example, if you think your main worry is really unlikely from a statistical perspective, you might assign a 5% or 10% probability. After you have completed the three middle rows, fill in the last row detailing what outcome is most likely in light of the situation. Consider how that stacks up to your main worry.

Thought Expander 19.1: Rationalizing Fear

	Outcomes	Probability (%)
Main Worry:		
Alt 1.		
Alt 2.		
Alt 3.		
New View:		

For example, if you were afraid of flying, a review of the research would reveal that dying in a plane crash between the five year period ending 2012 occurred less than once in every 8.5 million departures or 0.00001%.[185] It is much more likely that your flight will be cancelled (0.8%), diverted (0.2%), or arrive late/be delayed (15.7%). Most likely you will arrive on time, whole and unscathed (83.3%).[186] Taking this perspective, a much more productive view can be maintained—one unbiased by irrational fears. By challenging the worry squirreled away in our subconscious, it quickly becomes clear that pervasive fears and phobias are based on exaggerated suspicions that have been left unexamined.

Many worries are inflated. A long-standing study of a woman who suspected worry was ruining her life is telling.[187] By recording her thoughts, it was determined that 40% of what she worried about could never practically happen. Another 30% was anxiety about things that had already happened and were simply replaying in her mind. Opinions and judgements of other people comprised 12% of her concerns, while 10% were health-related (ironically detrimental to the same). The remaining 8% were real problems that needed to be faced. There it is. Less than one in ten things she worried about made sense. The other 90% stood in the way of her well-being and left her feeling miserable.

Long-term worry can become self-fulfilling.

Tongue in cheek, Samuel Clemens said, "I have been through some terrible things in my life, some of which actually happened." The vast majority of what we worry about is a useless waste of emotional energy. People spend far too much time in worry. The average person spends 55 minutes worrying each day, meanwhile ten percent of the population, labeled as chronic worriers, fret more than five hours daily.[188,189] Considering that only 8% or so of our qualms are valid, the average person should reasonably budget about five minutes a day to worry and put the other time toward more productive use. That is because situation specific worries are unlikely to materialize or come to pass in the near-term.

However, long-term worry can become self-fulfilling as it develops into an expectation. Expectations, discussed in exploring Success Behavior 18, Expecting Good Things, do not come to pass overnight, but take time to manifest. As such, if you worry for years over your health, you are more likely to experience stress which is well-documented to increase your chances of eventually getting sick. In all instances, the vast preponderance of worry is wasteful and counterproductive.

Are you feeling drained? Worry may be the culprit. The stressful state of negative anticipation can have adverse consequences in a range of life arenas including our health. Charles Mayo, founder of the world-famous clinic by the same name observed that: "Worry affects the circulation, the heart, the glands, the whole nervous system. I have never known a man who died from overwork, but many who died from doubt." Researchers have found time and again that anxiousness increases stress, worsens health, and reduces overall, psychological well-being.[190]

So what other things do you worry about? In Thought Expander 19.2,

Desired Outcomes, identify a few of the negative situations you fret over and place them in the left-hand column. These might include not having money to retire, losing a job, failing health, or a deteriorating relationship. For each, write the negative possibility regarding the situation in the Worry-Based Column. This would be what you most worry about. Next, step back and consider reality. Based on what you know about the world or other's experiences in general, identify the most likely outcome and enter it into the middle column. After that, determine what you would like to happen and write in the next column. Finally, look at the options before you. What can you do to improve the likelihood your desired outcome will happen?

Take the fear of flying for example. You might really fret over flying in a plane because it might crash, yet you realize it is most likely going to be fine with a quick internet search revealing that you are 15,000 times more likely to die in a car.[191] In fact, you stumble upon the possibility that you are more likely to die from a lighting strike. You desire to enjoy flying more, so one potential action you can take is to consider travel as an adventure where daring pays off with experiences and memories that last a lifetime.

Thought Expander 19.2: Desired Outcomes

Situation	Outcome			Options and Potential Actions
	Worry-Based	Most Likely	Desired	
1.				
2.				
3.				

Worry is often a well-engrained pattern. Dwelling on any worry gives it energy and presence of mind often far beyond its worth. As with any counter-productive habit, the way to deal with it is to first become aware of it and, second, to replace it with a better alternative.

One way to reduce worry is to feed it less. To better manage anxiety, try setting aside 15 minutes per day to fret about anything and everything. Use this time to catastrophize to your heart's content. Write all your fears and concerns down. After 15 minutes, stop. At this point you have used up your daily worry time. Don't permit yourself to worry again until tomorrow during the next designated time.

> One way to reduce worry is to feed it less.

To help you stop once your daily worry time is complete, spend an equal amount of time focusing on what you want in life. Envision the events, situations, and conditions you desire, the goals you wish to achieve. Complement each worry with a visualization of what could go right in your life. Develop a clear image of what you want and envision it coming to pass. Find your answer, and write it down. Feel what it will be like when your wish comes to be. Capture that idea in your mind's eye so you can experience freedom, happiness, and peace a little every day.

The use of emotions to reflect what we want out of life can be powerful. Emotions clarify how our brain should feel as we venture toward our dreams. Through visualization, we override adverse ideations arriving at the place where we can enjoy our desired outcome long before it is accomplished. With practice, this approach counterbalances worry and allows people to get increasingly comfortable with the possibility of success. Focusing on the positives provides a better ability to identify and access the many opportunities that reside around you. The process also provides insight and clarity around what needs to be done to achieve your goals, further placing you in a position to more readily accomplish them.

Regular introspective processes like visualization develop a conscious awareness and mental alertness. Mindfulness, a form of self-attentiveness, is a psychological practice where one becomes more consistently aware of their thoughts and behaviors. According to Buddhism, it is one of the seven factors necessary for enlightenment. Specifically, the detached and compassionate observation of our negative thoughts has been found to mitigate worry.[192] Mindfulness works, in part, because it shifts attention both to and beyond the self toward a more holistic perspective. Doing so takes advantage of the brain's neuroplasticity, acting to rewire access to regions with better coping responses and improved creativity.[193] Over time, improved self-awareness replaces worry with possibility. This is why worriers seldom have success and successful people seldom worry.

Your inner Monk realizes that every fear is ultimately rooted in ideas about death. Every adverse premonition has its roots based in the possibility of your demise. The spider, bee, and snake all represent a perceived threat to your well-being—hence the many phobias that exist around them. Today, the love scorned, job lost, or money gone can do the same. But such fears are misplaced. Such losses do not mean your life.

Average people fear death; successful people seek the death of fear. As Ralph Waldo Emerson famously noted, "Do the thing you fear, and the death of fear is certain." Accomplished people perceive fear as a loud sound lacking physical substance, a troublemaker crying wolf. In managing this emotion, they have learned that a healthy indifference to it is necessary for success.

The Bible supports a fear-free approach. The most frequently uttered command in the Bible is "Fear not." Some version of "Be not afraid," or "Fear not" shows up in the King James version over 100 times, while some form of the

> Average people fear death; successful people seek the death of fear.

original Greek word for fear shows up over 300 times irrespective of translation. The Bible's command to "Fear not!" is an order, not a suggestion. God explicitly, directly, and forcefully tells us to not fear. Fear ends where faith starts.

But why does it matter? First, we are instructed to avoid fear because it is within our control to do so. Fear, like faith, is a choice. We are creatures of free will and are open to pick our thoughts and the lives that result. Second, we are told to avoid fear because it hurts us. Fear is negative faith, confidence of the wrong variety. Fear reflects a weak conviction in a greater power and a distrust regarding the future. Doubt results in worry. As such, the detrimental duo of worry and doubt stand front and center between where we are and where we want to be. When the disciple Peter starts to sink while walking on water, Jesus chides him saying, "Oh you of little faith, why did you doubt?" (Matthew 14:31; ESV). For doubt, a state of diminished faith, and worry, a state of uncertain assurance, partner to limit accomplishments and strangle achievements. Are you doing nothing in fear or something in faith?

Your contented Monk comprehends that living with any negative belief is a lie. Worry causes you to dwell in the very place you wish to leave. It creates a tie that binds. Dwelt upon, negative possibility seems stronger and more daunting. The habitual practice of worry adds strands to an ever-thickening rope.

Fear ends where faith starts.

It is in this very manner that elephants are trained. When young, baby elephants are bound by a thin cord. They yank and pull at it, to no avail. Eventually they come to see the cord as unbreakable and inevitable. As adult elephants, they remain bound by those thin ropes, which, now they could easily break. How many of you do this very thing? Your tethered mind is often the thing holding you back from the success you desire.

Like Plato's *Allegory of the Cave*, you see doubts and worries, as scary shadows, believing them to be real. They are not. Doubt and worry are illusions that appear as impenetrable bars keeping you confined and limiting your view of what is beyond. Every unmet expectation, delay, or challenge acts to reinforce your perceptions, further tempering the bars. Yet, the prison bars that hold you are ones that you, yourself, have crafted. Each piece of metal and slab of concrete has been formed by your thoughts and is cemented further with every doubt and worry.

Are you doing nothing in fear or something in faith?

So, how do you escape the prison of fear? Fighting back isn't the answer. To attack fears directly only acts to give your trepidations credibility and your insecurities a foothold. To overcome fear, face it. Sit with your fear; allow it to be what it is. Spend time with it, study it, get to know and understand it. Like shining light in a dark room, a good look at fear makes its hollowness evident. It is a blowhard, lacking substance. A steady stare reveals that the only power fear has is the power that you give to it. Take your authority back. Moses answered his people, "Do not fear! Stand by (be calm and at peace) and see the salvation of the Lord which He will accomplish for you" (Exodus 14:13; NAS).

Faith in the adverse is ill-placed. True failure is impossible as every outcome contains within it seeds of possibility. Things always work out. For as Franklin D. Roosevelt admonished, "There is nothing to fear but fear itself."

To explore this idea more deeply, consider the proposition that failure doesn't really exist, that it is an illusionary construct. To demonstrate, participants at my seminars are asked to think about and visualize the worst day of their lives. The following question is then posed, "If you could go back and eliminate the worst day of your life, would you?" Typically, about half the audience raises their hands indicating they would forgo a previously awful experience if they could. Sounds pretty reasonable, right? The remaining participants who did not raise their hands are then asked why they wouldn't sign up for removing their most awful day. The most common answer is along the lines of, "If it would make me someone other than who I am today, then it wouldn't be worth it." Finally, those with their hands up are asked to make the assumption that they won't be the same person they currently are and they are again asked, "If you could go back and eliminate the worst day of your life, would you?" Seldom is a hand raised.

Apparently, the vast majority of people don't want to trade off dreadful events for a less tumultuous history. Why? It is through your greatest challenges that the seeds for personal growth and future opportunity are sown. Eliminating these events removes important experiences that make you who you are and position you to more fully become. Most people aren't willing to change their past, even at its worst, because they understand at some fundamental level that each and every experience has yielded a benefit, in some form or another, which has shaped them to become who they are.

Take failure as an example. A deep misconception is perpetuated regarding failure in society today. Failure is not something to fear. It is a fertilizer, not an herbicide, bringing wisdom, not ignorance. In retrospect, even the worst possible outcome in life is surmountable. Think about it, if

> **Living with any negative belief is a lie.**

> **True failure is impossible as every outcome contains within it seeds of possibility.**

you wouldn't trade your worst life event for the benefits it provides, than nothing that happens can be counted a failure. If this is the case, then every fear is misplaced. There is no risk that can't be managed, no challenge that can't be overcome. Failure is a fallacy, it doesn't exist. Only opportunity is real, and it is everywhere.

There is nothing to fear. That is not to say you can't fail on the world's terms—lose money, have the venture go under, break-up a relationship etc.—this can and will happen from time to time. However, by listening to your heart, you give yourself the best opportunity to live fully. Failure is impossible if you honor your spirit. You may fail in the world's eyes, but you will never be a failure. It is only in honoring your spirit, you fully live.

Success is the result of being true to you. Fully embracing the possibility of life, you triumph. Ronald Reagan summed this up nicely stating, "If we make up our mind what we are going to make of our lives…we never lose." Success lies in facing your fear.

So what are you afraid of? To gain clarity, identify two significant fears, major worries, or nagging doubts and write them in the top row of Thought Expander 19.3, Getting in Faith. Now take a minute and ponder what you currently believe. Next, consider what you could believe instead. If you were in complete faith what could you believe? Knowing that everything works out in the end, what alternative, more constructive view could you hold? Write your thoughts in the last row of the Thought Expander. For example, if you are afraid of flying you could believe it is actually quite safe—more so than driving a car.

Thought Expander 19.3: Getting in Faith

My fear is:	Fear A.	Fear B.
What do I believe?		
What could I believe?		

Notice anything? How did it feel to embrace the prospect of being fear-free? Without fear, one is better able to embrace life's potential. Free of fear, worry morphs into confidence, doubt gives way to faith. The fearless life is faithful, convinced of good things to come. Nothing is off limits to a person with faith. For a light-hearted, peaceful, and happy life can only happen in the presence of faith.

"Don't ever let fear turn you against your playful heart" (Jim Carrey).

Failure is impossible if you honor your spirit.

Faith is trust in something greater, and it determines the amount of success that shows up in life. Believe, and it shall be done for you. Jesus said, "I tell you the truth, if you had faith even as small as a mustard seed, you could say to this mountain, 'Move from here to there,' and it would move. Nothing would be impossible... You can pray for anything, and if you have faith, you will receive it" (Matthew 17:20-22; NLT). According to scripture, the power of faith is unbounded.

Faith is fearless trust. Faith provides a confidence to call that which is not as though it were. Society tells you to see and then believe, faith allows you to believe before you see.

But where does faith come from, and how do you get it? According to the Bible, "Faith comes from hearing, and hearing through the Word" (Romans 10:17; ESV). Seeing isn't believing, for faith requires that believing come first. Faith comes from cultivating a relationship with something beyond you. To grow in faith, you need to feed your spirit; to become more confident, you need to enter into a relationship with a greater power.

One way to do this is to ask, "What is life all about?" Something amazing resides in the answer. Pray, reflect, and study on it. Develop your spirit until you gain a deeper understanding and kindle a sense of trust. Faith is the end result of spiritual exploration and effort. It comes no other way. To grow in faith, pursue it until you know that you are blessed, worthy and loved. Work at it until you are certain the universe is infinitely abundant and will supply whatever you need. Belief results in feeling spiritually connected with life and feeling greater life satisfaction and happiness.[194]

Living in faith is pleasing to God. In fact, it is impossible to please Him without it. Weak economic growth, high unemployment, terrorism, corruption, crime, and depravity comprise the diet of news we digest daily. For a person who has placed his or her trust in themselves or others around them, the world's problems are reason for concern. But for the person in faith, these circumstances are already overcome. In the end, "You will decide on a matter, and it will be established for you, and light will shine on your ways" (Job 22:28; ESV). Let me give you a personal example of such divine guidance.

Faith has served me well in my life. When I started my advisory services business, my customers were primarily short-term and one-and-done opportunities. This made it impractical for me to go back to school and pursue my Ph.D. in psychology, since I was spending an inordinate amount of time looking for new business. Yet, I was confident the time was right to honor my lifelong dream of getting an advanced degree and working for myself.

So, I entered a Ph.D. program as an act of faith. Less than a year after I started school, a unique opportunity arose. A client wanted me to partner with them to help ready their company for sale. It was the perfect job. The best part was the arrangement included a monthly retainer that covered my income needs allowing me to pursue my Ph.D. full-time, unencumbered by the constant need to develop new business. It also offered equity to generate a handsome payout upon successful completion. I know it was an answer to my prayers.

Faith comes from a knowing and having a relationship with something beyond you.

I loved this job and poured my heart into it. After almost a year of work, hundreds of interested buyers had been contacted and interested parties narrowed down to a select few. With final bids in, a major customer unexpectedly cancelled their contract eliminating more than half of the company sales and all its profits. Not surprisingly, all potential buyers pulled out.

I thought my dream was lost. How could God do this, give me the answer to my prayers, and then take it away? I spent months reflecting and praying on the situation. One day, while studying the Word it came to me that the final outcome was up to me. It was mine to choose, the only missing ingredient was faith. "Whatever you ask in prayer, you will receive, if you have faith" (Matthew 21:22; ESV). The opportunity wasn't lost, my conviction was misplaced. For, "Nothing is impossible with God" (Luke 1:37; NLT).

I chose to stand firm. I refused to believe that the opportunity was gone. I chose to believe God was good and He would honor the promise of his Word, while having no idea of how this situation could possibly work out. After the sale process fell apart, the company offered to keep me on as an employee at a salary that allowed me to continue my graduate work. The lost sales did not immediately return, and several years passed as the company struggled to reposition and reinvent itself. All I could do was work to serve the owners to the best of my ability. Waiting, expecting, hoping, I claimed God's promise believing that I had not been brought such an amazing, once-in-a-lifetime opportunity only to have it fall fallow. God honored that faith.

> When you've done all you know how to do, relax, believe, and stand firm.

Then one day, without notice, one of the owners offered to buy me out. They said it was because they felt bad a deal never materialized. To rectify this, they wanted to fulfill the original agreement.

That outcome was as unlikely as it was extraordinary. It turned out that I was able to achieve the benefit of a sale that never happened. From "nowhere" to "now-here," that is the power of faith.

Your contented Monk understands that success results from faith in something greater. Fear, worry, and doubt destroy, while faith, trust, and belief build up. Choose faith. "All who call on God in true faith, earnestly from the heart, will certainly be heard, and will receive what they have asked and desired" (Martin Luther). Stop making decisions based on fear, and start making choices based on faith. Fear, worry, and doubt have no value, face them and they will flee from you. Focus on opportunity instead of lack, and your dream will manifest. Jesus said, "All things are possible for one who believes" (Mark 9:23; ESV). When you've done all you know how to do, relax, believe, and stand firm.

BEHAVIOR 20: ENJOYING THE JOURNEY

"When you have completed 95% of your journey, you are only halfway there."
— Japanese Proverb

Live well. You are immensely blessed and profoundly loved. The miracle of life is yours to enjoy. Take time to appreciate life and embrace it fully, remembering that a well-lived life is a journey not a destination.

Happiness is essential to a good life. The only thing that gets in the way of your contentment is suboptimal thinking. Worry, doubt, and desire all act to diminish joy. Like New England clam chowder, if low-quality ingredients go in, a mediocre soup results. Life is no different. If inferior thoughts fill your mind, subpar outcomes result. Life is a direct reflection of thoughts applied. Dysfunctional thoughts provide adverse experiences, while productive ideas generate beneficial outcomes. Since you control your thoughts, your life experience is up to you. Every situation is a reflection of yourself—introducing you to your own nature.

> Happiness is essential to a good life. The only thing that gets in the way is suboptimal thinking.

The truth is that you are talented, beautiful, and able beyond your imagination. You are a sliver of the divine and the result of love incarnate. As a spirit having a human experience, you are part of an existence that is infinite and enduring. Yet, your thinking can stand in the way of your magnificence.

The thoughts you hold about yourself and life are probably incomplete, or worse yet, invalid. This point is critically important. What you think is not what really is. Thoughts are *not* reality. Thoughts are only mirages that reflect the level of consciousness from which they were created. Since we are all imperfect, we cannot rely solely on our impressions and ideas as they can be woefully inadequate.

The truth of anything can never be found in thoughts about it. Reality can only be understood when uncloaked by preconceived notions. To live fully and completely, it is necessary that you rise above suboptimal states of mind. Dropping the adverse is essential to living successfully.

But how is that accomplished? How do we start to think better and become more enthusiastic about life? Understand that standing against any negative state is not the answer. Focusing on what you don't want only brings more of it into your life. That is why Mother Theresa wisely noted: "I will never attend an anti-war rally; if you have a peace rally, invite me." Instead, of railing against what you don't want, you need to focus on what you do want. The universe answers "Yes" to whatever you ask of it. Therefore, a shift toward a more positive, thankful existence is true success.

> **The truth is that you are talented, beautiful, and able beyond your imagination. You are a sliver of the divine and the result of love incarnate. Yet, your thinking can stand in the way of your magnificence.**

According to researchers, there are two primary states of being: apprehension and appreciation. It is physically impossible for them to co-exist simultaneously. The brain cannot process the opposing emotions of worry and gratitude at the same time.[195] Herein lies the key to enjoying life.

Psychological science uses what is known as the Big Five personality traits to differentiate key dimensions of individual personalities. These five dimensions are openness, conscientiousness, extraversion, agreeableness, and neuroticism. Collectively, these traits are thought to broadly delineate a person's uniqueness. More recently, however, researchers have identified gratitude as another important trait, since it explains a significant amount of individual personality variance not captured by the Big Five measures.[196] Known as the "parent of all virtues," gratitude is integral to mental health and personal well-being.[197] This "sixth dimension" of gratitude also correlates with life satisfaction; as appreciation increases so does happiness.[198] Fortunately, both gratitude and worry are choices—and where one is the other is not.

Zig Ziglar encouraged people to, "Have an attitude of gratitude." There are two pathways to cultivate greater levels of gratitude or develop an enhanced appreciation for life. Similar in outcome, they are different in focus. Appreciation exercises tend to focus inward, working to generate a more positive view of yourself relative to your situation and ability, while gratitude exercises tend to focus outward, encouraging you to extend thankful feelings to others, build social value and engender perceptions of support.[199,200] Both types help you better realize, reflect, and share the many good things in life and ultimately lead to a wide range of personal benefits such as happiness, joy and peace.

A shift toward a more positive, thankful existence is true success.

So how do you develop a more appreciative perspective and grateful persona? One way is to expand your realization. People who spent five minutes before bed, for 21 nights, writing down what they appreciated in their lives, experienced marked increases in positive feelings versus those who simply journaled about life's burdens or nothing in particular.[201] This three-week appreciation exercise was found to increase happiness for six months or longer. Such practices help you realize how much there is to appreciate and how blessed you really are. Further, they have a cumulative effect. Once expanded perspectives of appreciation are engrained into your life, they build upon themselves and grow over time.[202]

To start enhancing your appreciation levels, complete Thought Expander 20.1, Appreciation. Address each column phrase by writing down five answers that complete the top row statements. Consider getting a journal and repeating this process daily, before bed, over the next several weeks. Feel free to include everything and anything, irrespective of how big or small, that expresses your gratefulness. There are no wrong answers.

Thought Expander 20.1: Appreciation

I am blessed because...	I am grateful for...	I take pride in...	...makes me happy.
1)	1)	1)	1)
2)	2)	2)	2)
3)	3)	3)	3)
4)	4)	4)	4)
5)	5)	5)	5)

In addition to cultivating appreciation, gratitude-based exercises can also be used to generate increased positive feelings and life satisfaction.[203] Three ways this can be accomplished are assessing, projecting, and sharing. First, a sense of gratitude can be generated by consciously counting the good that comes to us from others. No one lives in a vacuum. As such, the people around us are a source of a great many of our blessings. To increase gratitude using this method, you can count the kindnesses experienced each day, noting these in a journal, or by writing letters of gratitude to others.[204,205] Such practices have been shown to significantly increase joy and happiness.

Only matters of the heart and spirit are indelible.

Second, a sense of gratitude can be enhanced by intentionally projecting what is good. Using a form of meditation that projects positive feelings toward others, researchers found substantially higher levels of positive feelings resulted for the sender.[206] Known as loving kindness meditation (LKM), this practice has been found to significantly improve positive feelings even during short, nine-week training sessions, while also receiving other social and physical advantages.[207] An impressive example, LKM benefits have been observed in the brains of Tibetan monks. Practicing a form of LKM, they spend thousands of hours projecting compassion. This activity has been found to fundamentally alter the areas of the brain responsible for cognition and emotion, taking advantage of brain plasticity—the mind's ability to change.[208] While detailed training in LKM is beyond the scope of this book, the technique consists of sitting in a quiet place and projecting positive feelings first to yourself, and then beyond yourself to your surroundings, other people, and the world as a whole. This process could, for example, include visualizing people who are suffering and then either wishing or imagining their hardships relieved. There are many other ways to practice LKM. Through a regular practice of projecting tranquility, compassion, and harmony, you grow in peace and joy.

Third, a sense of gratitude can be cultivated through sharing. Using your tools, talents, and time to benefit others creates seeding points that precipitate positive outcomes. "Paying it forward" and "random acts of kindness" are good examples. Both generate feelings of gratitude by creating positive events that can become self-perpetuating in a cycle of goodwill. The advantage of such intentional generosity is that it benefits others while also engendering positive feelings for you.[209] Collectively, doing things to improve your sense of appreciation and gratitude works to expand your perspective on what is good, generating greater joy, happiness, and well-being in life—key barometers of success.

The things you own also appear to play a role in your level of gratitude.

Gratitude, it turns out, is inversely related to the importance placed on your possessions. In general, psychologists have found that people with the highest levels of gratitude tend to have the lowest levels of materialism.[210] The cause of the relationship is unclear. It could be that people have less need to secure positive feelings from acquiring and owning things when they have grateful lives.

To take advantage of this finding and increase your joy, one option is to spend money on experiences rather than on purchasing more stuff. Researchers have found that people garner significantly more happiness from events then they do from things.[211] This may occur because people create lasting memories with experiences to enjoy over and over again, while the impact of, and appreciation for, new things wanes quickly.

People, it turns out, quickly get used to novel external improvements. Known as adaptation (Piaget, 1952), this psychological process explains that which was novel and new yesterday becomes less novel and more normal as time goes on. The raise received yesterday is all spent tomorrow, the promotion earned results in even bigger work challenges, and the new car eventually morphs into only a mode of transportation.

> To change your life, you must change how you see it.

Material things are especially problematic. Not only is the pleasure of the acquisition fleeting, but things eventually rot, rust or decay. Their maintenance and preservation requires a portion of valuable mental energy along with time, physical energy, and money. By seeking experiences, we position ourselves to partake in more lasting joy, not just for one day, but throughout a lifetime. Only matters of the heart and spirit are indelible.

Moving away from materialism is the impetus behind the voluntary simplicity movement (Gregg, 1936). Voluntary simplicity is a way of living where consumption is minimized, and you strive to use only that which is necessary to sustain life. All forms of waste and excess are eschewed. The practice of voluntary simplicity focuses your efforts on living rather than amassing. As such, it is another path to achieve a more gratifying way of life than the pursuit of tangibles proffered by a materialistic society.

Possessions not only provide inferior joy, but they tend to clutter our lives and consume our time. Every acquisition must be stored and maintained. More stuff leads to bigger houses, while bigger houses lead to more stuff. Materialism results in a custody treadmill that increases in slope over time—requiring ever increasing effort. Take home ownership, for example. Consider the time spent maintaining this major asset. In the yard, raking leaves, fertilizing, cutting the grass, and trimming the hedges are all required duties. Inside, cleaning, repairing, painting, and making regular improvements to replace normal wear are all ongoing endeavors. In addition, a mortgage, interest, taxes, and insurance must be paid. All these things consume enormous time and energy. Materialism is an unknown debt and a drain on joy.

Employing a smaller footprint, or impact on the environment, can work to dramatically free up an individual's life. Fewer possessions require less money, time, and attention. Americans have been found to spend between 8 and 28 hours every week on chores of which a significant portion is, presumably, related to maintaining their things.[212] Too many possessions can distract and dilute what is really important in life. Amassing wealth, in particular, can become a pattern that coaxes us into excessive work to the point where we would be better off using money to buy enjoyable time.[213] Not surprisingly, having more time has been found to equate to greater happiness.[214] Researchers conclude that individuals would be happier if they shifted from extrinsic goals with tangible rewards toward intrinsic goals where growth, relationships, and satisfaction result.[215] "A person's life doesn't consist of the amount of possessions he has" (Luke 12:15; ISV). When it comes to enjoying life, it appears that less stuff equates to more happiness.

> Cons and downsides are a part of life; they make pros and upsides possible.

Joy can also be enhanced by appreciating yourself and not engaging in comparisons with those around you. In a recent study, researchers found that almost a third of the people using a popular social media networking site had a negative experience.[216] This was not attributable to the website itself; rather it was the result of excessive self-comparison. Undue self-judgment left users feeling lonely, frustrated, and jealous. As a result, many participants found the online environment to be stressful. Frequent social comparison has been found to reduce a person's well-being in other studies as well.[217] To maintain our joy, we must appreciate who we are.

In addition to unproductive assessment against others, people also inappropriately judge their own status. The standard of comparison used is often some form of magical thinking or a Hollywood-based dream life resulting in a belief that the grass on the other side of the fence is greener. People tell themselves that they would be much happier if only they (fill in the blank). It is unlikely. The grass isn't greener on the other side of the fence; it is greenest where you water it.

External circumstances are simply reflections of internal choices. Robert Frost's journey down the road less traveled found that: "Though as for that the passing there, had worn them really about the same." Every field has weeds, rocks, and road apples in it. To change your life, you must change how you see it.

Comparison is an illusionary act. Almost everything we think we want or desire is a mirage on some level. Idealism loses out when imagination breaks against the rocks of reality. That doesn't mean dreams, desires, and wishes aren't important—they are essential. However, every situation, improvement, acquisition, or advantage, no matter how improved it looks, has negatives. Cons and downsides are a part of life; they make pros and upsides possible. Irrespective of the stories you tell yourself, everyone has problems, challenges, and issues. It is the human condition. There is no perfect life.

> **By waiting for someday, happiness becomes unattainable in the present.**

So, you might be asking, "Russ, are you saying that if I make changes in my life and strive for something new or bigger, I won't necessarily be happier?" Yes. Clearly, this book is all about growth and change. They are critically important to achieving success, and I encourage them wholeheartedly. Joy definitely comes from achieving important goals, becoming all you can be, and living fully. The challenge is that no matter how much you accomplish, if you can't be happy now, you won't be happy in the future.

Many people live in a state of what I call contemporaneous anhedonia where they don't derive pleasure from their current life because they are always fantasizing about what it could be. They are chronically wanting, always seeking satisfaction outside themselves. They tell themselves, "If I only did this," "If I only had that," or "When that happens...then I'll be happy." They won't. If you can't enjoy life now, it is unlikely you will be any happier when the future arrives. Said another way, if your life is an ongoing, continuous state of longing and dissatisfaction, it will likely remain that way.

I know this firsthand. I have a strong tendency to strive toward a better future at the expense of my current joy. My King, Wizard, and Warrior are well-exercised and relatively buff, but this part of my Monk is a bit scrawny. My wife has pointed this out many times noting that, "You're never satisfied." That is because I have a tendency to work so hard that I don't enjoy the journey, moving immediately from one challenge to the next without savoring the win or appreciating the space in-between. I have been referred to as intense, and this future focus all too often costs me my joy in the current day.

Your mature Monk realizes that to live more successfully, you must be able to enjoy life now. "Life is made up, not of great sacrifices or duties, but of little things, in which smiles and kindness and small obligations, given habitually, are what win and preserve the heart and secure comfort" (Humphry Davy).

Together, the past and future detract from the joy that is possible now.

That doesn't mean you can't and shouldn't strive to accomplish important goals or work to achieve a better future—you should, because great satisfaction lies in living life on purpose. It does mean, however, that joy can only be cultivated and exist in the current moment. Once joy becomes a regular staple in your life, enthusiasm and excitement become standard. Finding joy the common day, you successfully position yourself to flourish throughout the whole of life.

To accomplish this, be aware of the "someday" trap. It is not uncommon for people to spend their lives waiting. In the someday trap, people wait for their children to grow up, the next promotion, a spouse to change, enough money in the bank, the right time, a streak of good luck, retirement, etc. before they do what they really want to do. They tell themselves once these things happen, then they can start to live as they wish. By waiting for someday, happiness becomes unattainable in the present moment. To be successful, it is important that you find a way to pursue and enjoy some part of your dreams now.

Heaven and Hell exist on earth—you decide which one you experience. A better future starts with joy today. To explore this idea further, complete Thought Expander 20.2, The Good Life. Write a few sentences in the first row that describe the "good life" you hope to achieve.

Thought Expander 20.2: The Good Life

My longing for the "good life"...

Next, consider the possibility that you are already living some version of the good life. When doing so, it might be useful to consider that one third of all people on the planet live in abject poverty, and that earning $34,000 a year would place you in the top 1% of income in the world.[218] Considering that broader perspective, write a description of how your current life already qualifies as the good life. Although, often clearest after a major life shock, think about your life, holistically. Consider, for example, how the bottom two billion people, who barely subsist, might see your blessings. What do you really have to be thankful about? Capture your thoughts in Thought Expander 20.3, My Great Life, below.

Thought Expander 20.3: My Great Life

My current life as the "great life"...

Perspective matters. Appreciating what you have paves the way for more. Every future is crafted from the present. Therefore, it is helpful to learn to live more readily in the moment and less in the past or future. Life is a series of moments all culminating to this one.

In many respects, the past and future are make-believe, comprised of questionable memories and unrealistic ideas. The ideas you hold regarding the past are no more fundamentally true, being just one version of an infinite number of possibilities that seem better or not good enough. The ideas you hold regarding the future are fantasies, seldom realized as imagined. Together, the past and future detract from the joy that is possible now.

Perfect joy is being fully-present.

A life out of balance with the present moment is evidenced by feelings of angst, frustration, and unhappiness. "Learn from the past, set vivid, detailed goals for the future, and live in the only moment of time of which you have any control: now" (Denis Waitley). A life spent worrying about the future or dwelling on the past is both painful and wasted.

Life is lived in the present moment. Everything happens and reality only takes place in the current instant, the now. It is such a gift that we even call it the "present." However, many people are so preoccupied with daydreams, busyness, and worry they often aren't awake to the occurrences of the moment. Don't let such distractions or an overemphasis on the past or the future stand in the way of the gift of now. Perfect joy is the result of being fully-present. This bliss disappears when we bring something into the current moment that does not belong.

You need to be cautious that your ambitions don't strangle your joy.

Of course, for those in constant pain or continuous suffering, the present moment may not seem like much of a blessing. It may feel like something better escaped and avoided. While evasion may be a fine coping strategy for a period, it is not a beneficial long-term approach. To step back in the present, you only need to reach for the next best feeling, as there is always something to be grateful for and appreciate; there is always some joy. Living successfully requires that you find it. Since you cannot hold two opposing concepts at once, even grasping the thought of gratitude for only a few seconds can bring much needed relief to your body and mind.

To enjoy life more, take steps to become more conscious in the present. One way to do this is to get quiet. Methods such as prayer, meditation, and awareness exercises can help reign in extraneous thoughts allowing you to experience the joy of simply being.

By calming and gaining control over your thoughts, you release assumptions, and limitations leaving more joy, peace, and love.

Freedom is the result of letting go. After you have done all you can to change your world, release your expectations, hold outcomes loosely, and let life be what it will. Accomplished people know that sometimes they need to accept and

> # Allow life to surprise you. The universe has more alternatives, options, possibilities, and opportunities than you could ever imagine.

allow in order to fully live. It is in transcending your wants and needs that your mind is freed to enjoy life's unfolding adventure.

Research supports this idea. Psychologists have noticed that the act of accepting an outcome as good enough, or "satisficing" (Simon, 1956), is an effective life strategy that results in happiness and contentment. Conversely, "maximizers", people who strive to optimize their outcome or seek perfection, sacrifice their happiness.[219] Maybe that is why individuals with fewer choices available are found to be more satisfied with their decisions than those who have more options.[220] Equilibrium must be struck between pursuing your dreams and allowing them to come to you.

> # Expect life to be better than planned.

Contrasting your inner Warrior and Monk, there is a time to strive and another to let go, a time to do and another to be. The accomplished person maintains a healthy balance between them. Creating, dreaming, and ideating can become all-consuming. You need to be cautious that your ambitions don't strangle your joy. At times, it is necessary to go with the flow and leverage what comes. Adept martial artists know not to fight energy but to redirect it, move with it, and use it to their advantage. To be successful, you must do the same.

Remember in the prior chapter, the family business sale that fell through? Very little about that project went as planned. However, in rolling with the punches and keeping the faith, it turned out to be an opportunity that exceeded my original expectations by providing years of additional income, and that was in addition to the original equity value.

Avoid living life too seriously.

Each of us is born with our fists clenched, clutching at life, yet we die with our hands open. Don't wait until the end to let go. Allow life to surprise you. The universe has more alternatives, options, possibilities, and opportunities than you could ever imagine. Things won't happen as expected. Life typically presents superior options, offering a better path. In addition to striving, success is the art of getting out of the way. If you want more from life, allow life to give it to you. Avoid being rigid. Go forward on your quest, seek your dreams, but hold your requirements and demands loosely. Provide room for possibility. "Enjoy the journey, enjoy every moment, and quit worrying about winning and losing" (Matt Biondi). Whatever happens will be great.

Your inner Monk enthusiastically expects life to be better than planned. Let your life be wonderful; influence what you can, and make peace with the rest. Life is a process not an outcome, a voyage not a port. "Focus on the journey, not the destination. Joy is found not in finishing an activity but in doing it" (Greg Anderson). See yourself as an integral part of the process. Love, play, strive, enjoy. Avoid living life too seriously. Unattached to outcome, you have already won.

Appreciation is fundamental to a feeling of success. Joy and happiness are your natural state. The good life is taking place all around you right at this very moment. Embrace the wonder of life and make your journey enjoyable, successful, and incredible.

THE MONK

Your contented Monk appreciates that fulfillment comes from renewing yourself, serving others, expecting good things, having faith, and enjoying the journey. Developing a contented Monk is pivotal to fully experiencing and getting the most out of life. By embracing the wonder of it all, you will come to grow in happiness, peace, and satisfaction. You will learn more about yourself and the world, finding that you have additional questions to ask and decisions to make. This will bring you full circle, requiring the input of your King...

KING

WIZARD   # MONK

WARRIOR

CONCLUSION

Success is yours for the taking. To live well, you need a wise King, an inspired Wizard, a strong Warrior, and a contented Monk. Collectively, these four aspects work together to ensure abundance, well-being, and victory in life.

To recap, your King is the part of you that guides. Understanding and clarity are strong when your King is wise. It is the part of you that demonstrates wisdom and makes good decisions. This is accomplished through developing personal awareness, creating healthy beliefs, thinking healthy thoughts, and making good choices. Knowledge leads to more effective navigation in all other areas of life. However, learning is never complete and requires a strong innovative energy to test the world around you, so it can continue to develop and grow. That is where the King's valuable counterpart, the Wizard, comes in.

Your Wizard is the part of you that creates. It imagines and invents, setting inspiring goals and charting ways to secure them. This is accomplished by following the heart, looking far ahead, dreaming big, planning the future, and visualizing success. The Wizard manifests things into existence, transmuting dreams into reality. However, the best ideas in the world remain nothing unless they are implemented. That is the role of the Warrior.

Your Warrior is the part of you that "does." It takes action. The Warrior exhibits courage, vigor, and valor while getting things done. This is achieved by taking action, working smart, and continually pursuing the next best thing. Doing the right thing in the right way is a powerful driver of outcome. The strong Warrior is a master of execution. Yet, without contentment, achievement remains unsatisfying. It is in a state of being where the Warrior's spiritual complement, the Monk, resides. The Monk is the "be" to the Warrior's "do."

Your Monk is that part of you cognizant of the meaning inherent in life. It appreciates, values, and enjoys while fully embracing the present moment. The Monk maximizes life's possibilities by serving others, pursuing personal development, and seeking spiritual growth. Faith, combined with a positive attitude and a focus beyond the self, provides a way to a deeply authentic sense of aliveness, happiness, and peace.

The King represents the mind which thinks and knows, the Wizard symbolizes the spirit which creates and plans, the Warrior signifies the heart which acts and does, and the Monk characterizes the soul which believes and values. All four aspects of success are essential elements to achieve a successful life. Living well is a result of developing a mature composite of these four core aspects. Mastering each aspect of success will result in a more accomplished, satisfied, and joyous life.

So, where is your next best opportunity to progress? As a closing reflection, review the four aspects of success summaries in the table titled My Best Opportunity that follows. Check the boxes next to the statements that most resonate with you. Chances are a greater personal opportunity still awaits you within these chapters. I encourage you to spend time working these aspects and revisiting their success behaviors.

Reflection: My Best Opportunity

The Wise King understands:

☐ You are the seed to every success; start there. [Behavior 1]

☐ Healthy beliefs drive accomplishment, enhance yours. [Behavior 2]

☐ If you don't get what you want, change what you are thinking. [Behavior 3]

☐ Your life story is written by you; craft it to your benefit. [Behavior 4]

☐ No matter what is going on in your life, you have a choice. [Behavior 5]

The Strong Warrior knows:

☐ Much can be accomplished with effort; take action now. [Behavior 11]

☐ The person that masters time wins. [Behavior 12]

☐ Focus your energies and hold one clear goal at a time. [Behavior 13]

☐ Don't worry about how it will happen, just do the next best thing. [Behavior 14]

☐ Success is inevitable if you keep trying. [Behavior 15]

The Inspired Wizard realizes:

☐ Do what you love and the money will follow. [Behavior 6]

☐ Take the long-term view to make better decisions. [Behavior 7]

☐ Work toward something bigger than yourself. [Behavior 8]

☐ To achieve your goals, you need a plan. [Behavior 9]

☐ Envision your success in order to attain it. [Behavior 10]

The Contented Monk values:

☐ Living to serve others is a mark of a successful life. [Behavior 16]

☐ Lifelong returns result from a focus on personal growth. [Behavior 17]

☐ A positive attitude is the number one predictor of success. [Behavior 18]

☐ Have faith, for everything is possible. [Behavior 19]

☐ Life is more a journey than a destination, enjoy the trip. [Behavior 20]

Congratulations, you are headed toward a better life. There is no right or wrong way to pursue your personal journey. To move forward, identify an area of opportunity and spend time with it. Study the material, do additional research, and create meaningful goals around it. Define what you want to accomplish because, "A problem well-stated is a problem half-solved" (Charles Kettering). Then, take steps toward your dreams.

As you embark, strive for balance. Each aspect of success is both complementary and opposing. While one cannot exist without the other, sometimes they are not readily compatible. For example, the King's knowledge of what "is" is often challenged by the Wizard's need to create what "could be." Collectively, the Wizard and King reflect the governance functions where knowledge-based decisions are made and creative options formulated. Alternatively, the Warrior and Monk reflect ways of living where the age-old balance between doing and being must continuously be struck.

If one aspect is particularly weak and ineffective, or another overemphasized and domineering, your well-being will be impaired. For example, a weak Monk is problematic with a strong Warrior in that much may be accomplished but little enjoyed. Likewise, a strong Wizard and weak Warrior will result in many great ideas that are never attempted. Weak aspects leave important areas of life underdeveloped while overbearing aspects monopolize, both act to impede the development of an integrated, whole person.

Success results from a situational-effective balance between each aspect. To live well, all four energies must be healthy, mature, and in equilibrium. Developed fully and in alignment with your goals, success becomes inevitable.

You have come this far in the book because you are committed to living well. Most people don't make the effort, preferring the known to what could be. But, it is your life, and you only get one shot at it. You owe it to yourself to aim high, and shoot for the stars.

Great wisdom resides in taking steps to live a superior existence. Those who have mastered themselves live different lives than everyone else. They are kind, wise, and calm. Perceiving their success from the onset, they are genuinely content, deeply peaceful, and profoundly happy. Good things happen in their lives.

Of course, just like today's food doesn't satisfy tomorrow's hunger, the journey to success is never really done. "Success is not a place at which one arrives, but rather the spirit with which one undertakes and continues the journey" (Alex Noble). Transformation is the cornerstone of an accomplished life. It is the essential, fundamental, and unstoppable part of life. If you aren't actively pressing forward, you are falling behind. If you aren't managing your life, it is managing you. To succeed, you regularly must listen to what life is telling you. Sometimes life asks you to change your situations, other times it asks you to change yourself.

Needs and perspectives transform as you age and grow, and different life stages arise. Situations will change, your environment will evolve, and the world will move forward. Life is constantly pushing and pulling you. You must be ever vigilant to manage this constant stream of variation in a conscious and deliberate way, making small changes in your direction to stay on course.

It is essential for you to learn to more effectively think, plan, act, and embrace life, not for a time, but as a way of being for success is born in this ebb and flow between these aspects. Success comes from navigating the yin and yang between your King, Wizard, Warrior, and Monk. It is natural and healthy to move between them. In fact, an accomplished, fully satisfied life, results from effectively navigating the circadian rhythms among these four aspects of success.

Life is an amazing adventure. Thrill at the infinite possibilities, for opportunity is everywhere and unlimited prospects abound. Pursue each day with gusto, as success is yours for the taking. The Native American Sioux Indians have a saying, "Nake nula waun welo!" Cried out in battle, it means, "Today is a good day to die." These are powerful, telling words that indicate a full commitment to life. It suggests that you strive to live life so fully that you could have not have used it better. What is the point of being alive if you are not going to live? Make every day a good day to die.

Too many people live a nominal existence. Not you. You can be one of the rare few who know the real exhilaration and wondrous adventure of life—living in a state of constant amazement and awe. To live fully you must move beyond your fears and transcend your limitations. "The tragedy of life is not death…but what we let die inside of us while we live" (Norman Cousins). Fearless, we become free. Liberated without constraint, we can pour ourselves into living fully, where everything becomes possible.

To be all you can be, that above all else, is success. Grab a hold of your life—mind, spirit, heart, and soul, and embark on a pilgrimage that makes you come alive. Embrace your King and Warrior; commune with your Wizard and Monk. Meditate upon them, wrestle with them, and grow in them. Dream, strive, achieve, and enjoy. Each day is an unbounded prospect.

My wish is that you will enter wholeheartedly into life's vastness, embracing its infinite potential, possibility, and wonder. Success is impossible to miss if you choose wisdom, plan for possibility, seek that which is important, and value what is good. As you walk in these divine truths, not only are you destined to live a rich, full life, but you will also come to know the heart of God.

APPENDIX A:
BIBLE TRANSLATION KEY

AMP   Amplified Bible (1987)

ESV   English Standard Version (1971)

GNT   Good News Translation (1992)

KJV   New King James Version (1979)

NAS   New American Standard (1971; update 1995)

NCV   New Century Version (1991)

NIV   The New International Version (NT, 1973; OT, 1978)

NLT   New Living Translation (1996)

APPENDIX B:
THEORY REFERENCES

Ajzen, I. (1985). From intentions to actions: A theory of planned behavior. In J. Kuhl & J. Beckmann (Eds.), *Action-control: From cognition to behavior,* 11-39). Heidelberg: Springer.

Bandura, A. (1977). Self-efficacy: Toward a unifying theory of behavioral change. *Psychological Review, 84*(2), 191-215. doi:10.1037/0033-295X.84.2.191

Beck, A. T., Rush, A. J., Shaw, B. F., & Emery, G. (1979). *Cognitive Therapy of Depression.* New York, NY: Guilford Press.

Braid, J. (1843). *Neurypnology.* London: J. Churchill. Retrieved from http://www.hypno1.co.uk/BookNeurypnology.htm

Buss, D. M. (2000). The evolution of happiness. *American Psychologist, 55*(1), 15-23. doi:10.1037/0003-066X.55.1.15

Chung, S. H., & Herrnstein, R. J. (1967). "Choice and delay of Reinforcement." *Journal of the Experimental Analysis of Behavior, 10*(1): 67–74. doi:10.1901/jeab.1967.10-67.

Cooperrider, D. L., & Srivastva, S. (1987). Appreciative inquiry in organizational life. In R. W. Woodman, W. A. Pasmore (Eds.), *Research in organizational change and development: An annual series featuring advances in theory, methodology and research, 1,* 129-169. US: Elsevier Science/JAI Press.

Covey, S. R. (1989). *The 7 habits of highly effective people: Powerful lessons in personal change.* New York, NY: Fireside of Simon & Schuster.

Covey, S., Merrill, A. R., & Merrill, R. R. (1994). First things first: To live, to love, to learn, to leave a legacy. New York: Simon and Schuster.

Crocker, J., Olivier, M., & Nuer, N. (2009). Self-image goals and compassionate goals: Costs and benefits. *Self and Identity, 8*(2), 251–269. doi:10.1080/15298860802505160

DeCicco, T. L., & Stroink, M. L. (2007). A third model of self-construal: The metapersonal self. *The International Journal of Transpersonal Studies, 26*(1), 82-104. Retrieved from http://www.transpersonalstudies.org/ImagesRepository/ijts/Downloads/A%20Third%20Model%20of%20Self-Construal%20The%20Metapersonal%20Self.pdf

Diener, E., & Diener, C. (1996). Most people are happy. *Psychological Science, 7*(3), 181-185. doi:10.1111/j.1467-9280.1996.tb00354.x

Ellis, A. (1958). Hypnotherapy with Borderline Schizophrenics. *Journal Of General Psychology, 59*(2), 245. doi:10.1080/00221309.1958.9710193

Erikson, E. H. (1950). Growth and crises of the "healthy personality." In M. E. Senn (Ed.), *Symposium on the healthy personality* (pp. 91-146). Oxford England: Josiah Macy, Jr. Foundation.

Festinger, L. (1957). *A theory of cognitive dissonance.* Stanford, CA: Stanford University Press.

Fishbein, M., & Ajzen, I. (1975). *Belief, attitude, intention, and behavior: An introduction to theory and research.* Reading, MA: Addison-Wesley.

Fredrickson, B. L. (1998). What good are positive emotions? *Review of General Psychology, 2*(3), 300-319. doi:10.1037/1089-2680.2.3.300

Fredrickson, B. L. (2010). *Positivity: Groundbreaking research to release your inner optimist and thrive.* Oxford, England: One World Publications.

Freud, S. (1923). The Ego and the Id. *The Standard Edition of the Complete Psychological Works of Sigmund Freud, Volume XIX (1923-1925): The Ego and the Id and Other Works,* 1-66. London: The Hogarth Press and the Institute of Psychoanalysis.

Gillham, J., & Seligman, M. (1999). Footsteps on the road to a positive psychology. *Behaviour Research and Therapy, 37*(1), S163-S173. Retrieved from http://www.journals.elsevier.com/behaviour-research-and-therapy/

Greg, R. (1936*). The value of voluntary simplicity.* US: Pendle Hill.

Hill, N. (1937). *Think and grow rich.* US: Napoleon Hill Foundation.

Jung, C. (1959). *Collected works. Vol. IX, Pt. I. The archetypes and the collective unconscious.* Oxford England: Patheon.

Jung, C. G. (1960). Good and evil in analytical psychology. *Journal of Analytical Psychology, 5*(2), 91. doi:10.1111/j.1465-5922.1960.00091.x

Kahneman, D., & Tversky, A. (1984). Choices, values, and frames. *American Psychologist, 39*(4), 341-350. doi:10.1037/0003-066X.39.4.341

Locke, E. A. (1968) Toward a Theory of Task Motivation and Incentives. *Organizational Behavior and Human Performance, (3)*2: 157-189. doi:10.1016/0030-5073(68)90004-4

Mack, A., & Rock, I. (1998). Inattentional Blindness. Cambridge, MA: MIT Press.

Maslow, A. H. (1943). A theory of human motivation. *Psychological Review, 50*(4), 370-396. doi:10.1037/h0054346

Mazur, J. E., Snyderman, M., & Coe, D. (1985). Influences of delay and rate of reinforcement on discrete-trial choice. *Journal of Experimental Psychology: Animal Behavior Processes, 11*(4), 565-575. doi:10.1037/0097-7403.11.4.565

Moore, R., & Gillette, D. (1990). *King, Warrior, Magician, Lover.* New York, NY: HarperCollins.

Nakamura, J., & Csikszentmihalyi, M. (2002). The concept of flow. In C. R. Snyder, S. J. Lopez (Eds.), *Handbook of Positive Psychology* (pp. 89-105). New York, NY: Oxford University Press.

Pareto, V. (1896). Cours d'economie politique. Droz, Geneva.

Peterson, C., & Seligman, M. E. P. (2004). *Character strengths and virtues: A handbook and classification.* Washington, DC: APA Press.

Piaget, J. (1952). *The origins of intelligence in children.* New York: International Universities Press.

Porter, M. E. (1980). *Competitive Strategy: Techniques for analyzing industries and competitors.* New York, NY: The Free Press.

Quoidbach, J., Gilbert, D. T., & Wilson, T. D. (2013). The End of History Illusion. *Science, 339*(6115), 96-98. doi:10.1126/science.1229294

Ryan, R. M., & Deci, E. L. (2000). Self-determination theory and the facilitation of intrinsic motivation, social development, and well-being. *American Psychologist, 55*(1), 68-78. doi:10.1037/0003-066X.55.1.68

Ryan, R. M., Huta, V., & Deci, E. L. (2008). Living well: A self-determination theory perspective on eudaimonia. *Journal of Happiness Studies, 9*(1), 139-170. doi:10.1007/s10902-006-9023-4

Seligman, M. E. P. (1975). *Helplessness: On depression, development, and death.* San Francisco: Freeman.

Simon, H. (1956). Rational choice and the structure of the environment. *Psychological Review, 63*(2), 129-138. doi:10.1037/h0042769

Thompson, S. C. (1981). A complex answer to a simple question: Will it hurt less if I can control it? *Psychological Bulletin, 90,* 89-101. Retrieved from http://psycnet.apa.org/index.cfm?fa=buy.optionToBuy&id=1981-27280-001

Treisman, A. M. (1960). "Contextual cues in selective listening". *Quarterly Journal of Experimental Psychology, 12*(4), 242–248. doi:10.1080/17470216008416732.

Wason, Peter C. (1960). On the failure to eliminate hypotheses in a conceptual task. *Quarterly Journal of Experimental Psychology* (Psychology Press) *12*(3), 129–140. doi:10.1080/17470216008416717

APPENDIX C:
RESEARCH REFERENCES

[1] Diener, E., Emmons, R. A., Larsen, R. J., & Griffin, S. (1985). The Satisfaction With Life Scale. *Journal of Personality Assessment, 49*(1), 71-75. doi:10.1207/s15327752jpa4901_13

[2] Diener E., & Biswas-Diener, R. (2008). *Happiness: Unlocking the mysteries of psychological wealth.* Malden, MA: Blackwell Publishing.

[3] Baumeister, R. F., Bratslavsky, E., Finkenauer, C., & Vohs, K. D. (2001). Bad is stronger than good. *Review of General Psychology, 5*(4), 323-370. doi:10.1037/1089-2680.5.4.323

[4] Keyes, C. M., & Annas, J. (2009). Feeling good and functioning well: Distinctive concepts in ancient philosophy and contemporary science. *The Journal of Positive Psychology, 4*(3), 197-201. doi:10.1080/17439760902844228

[5] Warner, J. (2002). *Aspirations of greatness: Mapping the midlife leader's reconnection to the self and soul.* Wiley & Sons, Inc. New York, NY: John Wiley & Sons.

[6] Shadow Work® Seminars Inc., created by Cliff Barry and Mary Blandford. Retrieved from www.shadowwork.com.

[7] Copley, D. (2008). Four energies model. Unpublished retreat material from breakthroughretreats.com.

[8] Iveson, C. (2002). Solution-focused brief therapy. *Advances in Psychiatric Treatment, 8*, 149-156. doi:10.1192/apt.8.2.149

[9] Pajares, F. (1996). Self-efficacy beliefs in academic settings. *Review of Educational Research, 66*(4), 543-578. Retrieved from http://rer.sagepub.com/content/66/4/543.short.

[10] Buss, D. M. (2005). *The Handbook of Evolutionary Psychology.* Hoboken, NJ: John Wiley & Sons.

[11] Cohn, M. A., Fredrickson, B. L., Brown, S. L., Mikels, J. A., & Conway, A. M. (2009). Happiness unpacked: Positive emotions increase life satisfaction by building resilience. *Emotion, 9*(3), 361- 368. doi:10.1037/a0015952

[12] The moon-walking bear video can be viewed at http://www.youtube.com/watch?v=47LCLoidJh4

[13] Bauer, J. J., McAdams, D. P., & Pals, J. L. (2008). Narrative identity and eudaimonic well-being. *Journal of Happiness Studies, 9*(1), 81-104. doi:10.1007/s10902-006-9021-6

[14] Sheldon, K. M., & Lyubomirsky, S. (2006). How to increase and sustain positive emotion: The effects of expressing gratitude and visualizing best possible selves. *The Journal of Positive Psychology, 1*(2), 73-82. doi:10.1080/17439760500510676

[15] Meevissen, Y., Peters, M., & Alberts, H. (2011). Become more optimistic by imagining a best possible self: Effects of a two week intervention. *Journal of Behavior Therapy And Experimental Psychiatry, 42*(3), 371-378. doi:10.1016/j.jbtep.2011.02.012

[16] Trafton, A. (2012). How the brain controls our habits: MIT neuroscientists identify a brain region that can switch between new and old habits. Retrieved from Massachusetts Institute of Technology website http://web.mit.edu/press/2012/understanding-how-brains-control-our-habits.html.

[17] Buss, D. M. (2005). *The Handbook of Evolutionary Psychology.* Hoboken, NJ: John Wiley & Sons.

[18] Garland, E. L., Fredrickson, B., Kring, A. M., Johnson, D. P., Meyer, P. S., & Penn, D. L. (2010). Upward spirals of positive emotions counter downward spirals of negativity: Insights from the broaden-and-build theory and affective neuroscience on the treatment of emotion dysfunctions and deficits in psychopathology. *Clinical Psychology Review, 30*(7),849-86. doi:10.1016/j.cpr.2010.03.002

[19] Bye, D., & Pushkar, D. (2009). How need for cognition and perceived control are differentially linked to emotional outcomes in the transition to retirement. *Motivation and Emotion 33*(3), 320-332. doi:10.1007/s11031-009-9135-3

[20] Kitayama, S., Karasawa, M., Curhan, K. B., Ryff, C. D., & Markus, H. R. (2010). Independence and interdependence predict health and wellbeing: Divergent patterns in the United States and Japan. *Frontiers in Psychology, 1*(163). doi:10.3389/fpsyg.2010.00163

[21] Ruthig, J. C., Perry, R. P., Hladkyj, S., Hall, N. C., Pekrun, R., & Chipperfield, J. G. (2008). Perceived control and emotions: Interactive effects on performance in achievement settings. *Social Psychology of Education, 11*(2), 161-180. doi:10.1007/s11218-007-9040-0

[22] Adapted from James, W. H. (1957). Internal versus external control of reinforcement as a basic variable in learning theory. Unpublished Doctoral Dissertation, Ohio State University.

[23] Ruthig, J. C., Haynes, T. L., Perry, R. P., & Chipperfield, J. G. (2007). Academic optimistic bias: Implications for college student performance and well-being. *Social Psychology of Education, 10*(1), 115-137. doi:10.1007/s11218-006-9002-y

[24] Seligman, M. E. P. (1975). *Helplessness: On depression, development, and death.* San Francisco: Freeman.

[25] Stephen L. S., Rahul, D., & Helen P. H. (2009). Helplessness predicts the development of hypertension in older Mexican and European Americans. *Journal of Psychosomatic Research, 67*(4), 333-337. doi:10.1016/j.jpsychores.2009.04.007

[26] Visintainer, M. A., Volpicelli, J. R., & Seligman, M. P. (1982). Tumor rejection in rats after inescapable or escapable shock. *Science, 216* (4544), 437-439. Retrieved from http://meagherlab.tamu.edu/M-Meagher/Health%20360/Psyc%20360%20 articles/seligman.pdf

[27] Patrick, V. M., & Hagtvedt, H. (2012). "I don't" versus "I can't": When empowered refusal motivates goal-directed behavior. Journal of Consumer Research, 39(2), 371-381. doi:10.1086/663212

[28] Tkach, C., & Lyubomirsky, S. (2006). How do people pursue happiness?: Relating personality, happiness-increasing strategies, and well-being. *Journal of Happiness Studies, 7*(2), 183-183-225. doi:10.1007/s10902-005-4754-1

[29] Oishi, S., Diener, E., & Lucas, R. E. (2007). The optimum level of well-being: Can people be too happy? *Perspectives on Psychological Science, 2,* 346–360. doi: 10.1111/j.1745-6916.2007.00048.x

[30] Boehm, J. K., & Lyubomirsky, S. (2009). The promise of sustainable happiness. In S. J. Lopez, C. R. Snyder, S. J. Lopez, C. R. Snyder (Eds.), *Oxford handbook of positive psychology (2nd Ed.)* (pp. 667-677). New York, NY: Oxford University Press.

[31] Dunning, D., Heath, C., & Suls, J. M. (2004). Flawed self-assessment. *Psychological Science in The Public Interest (Wiley-Blackwell), 5*(3), 69-106. doi:10.1111/j.1529-1006.2004.00018.x

[32] College Board. (1976–1977). *Student Descriptive Questionnaire.* Princeton, NJ: Educational Testing Service.

[33] Women spend nearly one year deciding what to wear. (July 7, 2009). *The Telegraph.* Retrieved from http://www.telegraph.co.uk/news/uknews/5783991/ Women-spend-nearly-one-year-decidingwhat-to-wear.html

[34] Figlio, D. (2005). Why Barbie says "math is hard." Unpublished manuscript, Department of Economics, University of Florida, US.

[35] Pelham, B. W., Mirenberg, M. C., & Jones, J. T. (2002). Why Susie sells seashells by the seashore: Implicit egotism and major life decisions. *Journal of Personality and Social Psychology, 82*(4), 469-487. doi:10.1037//0022-3514.82.4.469

[36] Bureau of Labor Statistics, U.S. Department of Labor. (2012). *Number of jobs held, labor market activity, and earnings growth among the youngest baby boomers: Results from a longitudinal survey* (USDL Publication No. 12-1489). Retrieved from http://www.bls.gov/news.release/pdf/nlsoy.pdf

[37] Himmelstein, D., Thorne, D., Warren, E., & Woolhandler, S. (2007). Medical Bankruptcy in the United States, 2007: Results of a National Study. *American Journal of Medicine, 122*(8), 741-746. doi:10.1016/j.amjmed.2009.04.012

[38] Kifer, Y., Heller, D., Perunovic, W. Q. E., & Galinsky, A. D. (2013). The good life of the powerful: The experience of power and authenticity enhances subjective well-being. *Psychological Science, 24*(3), 280-288. doi:10.1177/0956797612450891

[39] Biswas-Diener, R., Kashdan, T. B., & King, L. A. (2009). Two traditions of happiness research, not two distinct types of happiness. *The Journal of Positive Psychology, 4*(3), 208-211. doi:10.1080/17439760902844400

[40] Deci, E. L., & Ryan, R. M. (2008). Hedonia, eudaimonia, and well-being: An introduction. *Journal of Happiness Studies, 9*(1), 1-11. doi:10.1007/s10902-006-9018-1

[41] Nussbaum, M. C. (2008). Who is the happy warrior? Philosophy poses questions to psychology. *Journal of Legal Studies, 37*, 81–113. Retrieved from http://mfs. uchicago.edu/institutes/happiness/prereadings/nussbaum_happy_warrior.pdf

[42] Ryff, C. D., & Singer, B. H. (2008). Know thyself and become what you are: A eudaimonic approach to psychological well-being. *Journal of Happiness Studies, 9*(1), 13-39. doi:10.1007/s10902-006-9019-0

[43] Lyubomirsky, S., Sheldon, K. M., & Schkade, D. (2005). Pursuing happiness: The architecture of sustainable change. *Review of General Psychology, 9*(2), 111-131. doi:10.1037/1089-2680.9.2.111

[44] Ryan, R. M., Huta, V., & Deci, E. L. (2008). Living well: A self-determination theory perspective on eudaimonia. *Journal of Happiness Studies, 9*(1), 139-170. doi:10.1007/s10902-006-9023-4

[45] Ryff, C. D., & Singer, B. H. (2008). Know thyself and become what you are: A eudaimonic approach to psychological well-being. *Journal of Happiness Studies, 9*(1), 13-39. doi:10.1007/s10902-006-9019-0

[46] König, C., & Kleinmann, M. (2007). Time management problems and discounted utility. *The Journal of Psychology, 141*(3), 321-334. Retrieved from http://www.tandfonline.com/toc/vjrl20/current

[47] McCormack, M. (1984). What they don't teach you at Harvard Business School. US: Bantam Books.

[48] Matthews, G. (2013). *Goals Research Summary.* Unpublished manuscript, Department of Psychology, Dominican University, US. Retrieved from http://www.dominican.edu/academics/ahss/undergraduate-programs-1/psych/faculty/fulltime/gailmatthews/researchsummary2.pdf

[49] Canevello, A., & Crocker, J. (2010). Creating good relationships: Responsiveness, relationship quality, and interpersonal goals. *Journal of Personality and Social Psychology, 99*(1), 78-106. doi:10.1037/a0018186

[50] Bauer, J. J., & McAdams, D. P. (2010). Eudaimonic growth: Narrative growth goals predict increases in ego development and subjective well-being 3 years later. *Developmental Psychology, 46*(4), 761-772. doi:10.1037/a0019654

[51] Brinckmann, J., Grichnik, D., & Kapsadoi, D. (2010). Should entrepreneurs plan or just storm the castle? A meta-analysis on contextual factors impacting the business planning–performance relationship in small firms. *Journal of Business Venturing, 25*, 24-40. doi:10.1016/j.jbusvent.2008.10.007

[52] Bauer, J. J., McAdams, D. P., & Pals, J. L. (2008). Narrative identity and eudaimonic well-being. *Journal of Happiness Studies, 9*(1), 81-104. doi:10.1007/s10902-006-9021-6

[53] Walker, C. O., Winn, T. D., & Lutjens, R. M. (2012). Examining relationships between academic and social achievement goals and routes to happiness. *Education Research International, 2012,* 1-7. doi:10.1155/2012/643438

[54] MacLeod, A. K., Coates, E., & Hetherton, J. (2008). Increasing well-being through teaching goal setting and planning skills: Results of a brief intervention. *Journal of Happiness Studies, 9*(2), 185-196. doi:10.1007/s10902-007-9057-2

[55] Deci, E. L., & Ryan, R. M. (2000). The 'what' and 'why' of goal pursuits: Human needs and the self determination of behavior. *Psychological Inquiry, 11*(4), 227-268. doi:10.1207/S15327965PLI1104_01

[56] Conrad, N., Doering, B. K., Rief, W., & Exner, C. (2010). Looking beyond the importance of life goals. The personal goal model of subjective well-being in neuropsychological rehabilitation. *Clinical Rehabilitation, 24*(5), 431-443. doi:10.1177/0269215509358930

[57] Deci, E. L., & Ryan, R. M. (2000). The 'what' and 'why' of goal pursuits: Human needs and the self determination of behavior. *Psychological Inquiry, 11*(4), 227-268. doi:10.1207/S15327965PLI1104_01

[58] Linley, P., Nielsen, K. M., Gillett, R., & Biswas-Diener, R. (2010). Using signature strengths in pursuit of goals: Effects on goal progress, need satisfaction, and well-being, and implications for coaching psychologists. *International Coaching Psychology Review, 5*(1), 6-15. Retrieved from http://www.intentionalhappiness.com/IH-pdf/Strengths_Goals.pdf

[59] McKnight, P. E., & Kashdan, T. B. (2009). Purpose in life as a system that creates and sustains health and well-being: An integrative, testable theory. *Review of General Psychology, 13*(3), 242-251. doi:10.1037/a0017152

[60] Eryilmaz, A. (2011). Investigating adolescents' subjective well-being with respect to using subjective well-being increasing strategies and determining life goals. *Journal of Psychiatry and Neurological Sciences, 24*(1), 44-51. doi:10.5350/DAJPN2011240106

[61] Haidt, J. (2006). *The happiness hypothesis: Finding modern truth in ancient wisdom.* New York, NY: Basic Books.

[62] Lyubomirsky, S. (2008). *The how of happiness: A scientific approach to getting the life you want.* New York, NY: Penguin Press.

[63] Creswell, J. D., Dutcher, J. M., Klein, W. M. P., Harris, P. R., Levine, J. M. (2013). Self-affirmation improves problem-solving under stress. *PLoS ONE 8*(5): e62593. doi:10.1371/journal.pone.0062593

[64] Sherman, D. K., Hartson, K. A., Binning, K. R., Purdie-Vaughns, V., Garcia, J., Taborsky-Barba, S., & ... Cohen, G. L. (2013). Deflecting the trajectory and changing the narrative: How self-affirmation affects academic performance and motivation under identity threat. *Journal of Personality and Social Psychology, 104*(4), 591-618. doi:10.1037/a0031495

[65] King, L. A., & Hicks, J. A. (2007). Whatever happened to "What might have been"? Regrets, happiness, and maturity. *American Psychologist, 62*(7), 625-636. doi:10.1037/0003-066X.62.7.625

[66] Marcel, Z., & Rik, P. (2007). Research Dialogues: Theory of Regret Regulation 1.0. *Journal of Consumer Psychology, 17,* 3-18. doi:10.1207/s15327663jcp1701_3

[67] Ware, B. (2009). *Inspiration and Chai: Warmth for the soul and the body.* Retrieved from http://www.inspirationandchai.com/Regrets-of-the-Dying.html

[68] Feldman, J., Miyamoto, J., & Loftus, E. F. (1999). Are actions regretted more than inactions? *Organizational Behavior and Human Decision Processes, 78*(3), 232-255. doi:10.1006/obhd.1999.2833

[69] Gilovich, T., & Medvec, V. H. (1994). The temporal pattern to the experience of regret. *Journal of Personality and Social Psychology, 67*(3), 357-365. Retrieved from http://www.apa.org/pubs/journals/psp/index.aspx

[70] Wiseman, R. (2009). *59 Seconds: Change your life in under a minute.* New York, NY: Random House.

[71] Beike, D. R., & Crone, T. S. (2008). When experienced regret refuses to fade: Regrets of action and attempting to forget open life regrets. *Journal of Experimental Social Psychology, 44*1545-1550. doi:10.1016/j.jesp.2008.06.008

[72] Morrison, M., & Roese, N. J. (2011). Regrets of the typical American: Findings from a nationally representative sample. *Social Psychological and Personality Science, 2*(6), 576-583. doi:10.1177/1948550611401756

[73] Rosenwid, E., & Gilovich, T. (2012). Buyer's remorse or missed opportunity? Differential regrets for material and experiential purchases. *Journal of Personality and Social Psychology, 102*(2), 215-223. doi:10.1037/a0024999

[74] Mausbach, B. T., Roepke, S. K., Depp, C. A., Patterson, T. L., & Grant, I. (2009). Specificity of cognitive and behavioral variables to positive and negative affect. *Behavioral Research and Therapy, 47*(7), 608–615. doi:10.1016/j.brat.2009.04.006

[75] Schimelpfening, N. (2011). *Why is depression more common in women than in men?* Retrieved from http://depression.about.com/od/forwomen/f/prevalence.htm

[76] Moberly, N. J., & Watkins, E. R. (2008). Ruminative self-focus, negative life events, and negative affect. *Behaviour Research and Therapy, 46*(9), 1034-1039. doi:10.1016/j.brat.2008.06.004

[77] Smith, J., & Alloy, L. (2009). A roadmap to rumination: a review of the definition, assessment, and conceptualization of this multifaceted construct. *Clinical Psychology Review, 29*(2), 116-128. doi:10.1016/j.cpr.2008.10.003

[78] Nolen-Hoeksema, S., Wisco, B., & Lyubomirsky, S. (2008). Rethinking Rumination. *Perspectives on Psychological Science, 3*(5), 400-424. Retrieved from http://www.cragman.com/dox/Rethinking%20Rumination.pdf

[79] Roelofs, J., Rood, L., Meesters, C., te Dorsthorst, V., Bögels, S., Alloy, L., & Nolen-Hoeksema, S. (2009). The influence of rumination and distraction on depressed and anxious mood: a prospective examination of the response styles theory in children and adolescents. *European Child & Adolescent Psychiatry, 18*(10), 635-642. doi:10.1007/s00787-009-0026-7

[80] Martin, L.L., & Tesser, A. (1996). Some ruminative thoughts. In R.S. Wyer Jr. (Ed.), Ruminative thoughts (pp. 1–47). Mahwah, NJ: Erlbaum.

[81] Nesse, R. M. (2000). Is depression an adaptation? *Archives of General Psychiatry, 57*(1), 14-20. Retrieved from http://archpsyc.jamanetwork.com/issues.aspx

[82] Lambert, K. G. (2005). Rising rates of depression in today's society: Consideration of the roles of effort-based rewards and enhanced resilience in day-to-day functioning. *Neuroscience & Biobehavioral Reviews, 30*(4), 497-510. doi:10.1016/j.neubiorev.2005.09.002

[83] Kumashiro, M., Rusbult, C. E., Finkenauer, C., & Stocker, S. L. (2007). To think or to do: The impact of assessment and locomotion orientation on the Michelangelo phenomenon. *Journal of Social and Personal Relationships, 24*(4), 591-611. doi:10.1177/0265407507079261

[84] Wegge, J., van Dick, R., Fisher, G. K., Wecking, C., & Moltzen, K. (2006). Work motivation, organisational identification, and well-being in call centre work. *Work & Stress, 20*(1), 60-83. doi:10.1080/02678370600655553

[85] Mischel, W., Ebbesen, E. B., & Zeiss, A. R. (1972). Cognitive and attentional mechanisms in delay of gratification. *Journal of Personality and Social Psychology, 21*(2): 204–218. doi:10.1037/h0032198

[86] Ayduk, O. N., Mendoa-Denton, R., Mischel, W., Downey, G., Peake, P. K., & Rodriguez, M. L. (2000). Regulating the interpersonal self: Strategic self-regulation for coping with rejection sensitivity. *Journal of Personality and Social Psychology, 79*(5): 776–792. doi:10.1037//0022-3514.79.5.776

[87] Yuichi, S., Mischel, W., & Peake, P. K. (1990). Predicting adolescent cognitive and self-regulatory competencies from preschool delay of gratification: Identifying diagnostic conditions. *Developmental Psychology, 26*(6), 978–986. doi:10.1037/0012-1649.26.6.978

[88] Freedman, D. H. (2013). Time-Warping Temptations. *Scientific American Mind, 24*(1), 45-49. Retrieved from http://www.scientificamerican.com/article.cfm?id=time-warping-temptations

[89] Good, C., Aronson, J., & Inzlicht, M. (2003). Improving adolescents' standardized test performance: An intervention to reduce the effects of stereotype threat. *Journal of Applied Developmental Psychology* 24(6):645-662. doi:10.1016/j.appdev.2003.09.002

[90] Blackwell, L. S., Trzesniewski, K. H., & Dweck, C. (2007). Implicit theories of intelligence predict achievement across an adolescent transition: A longitudinal study and an intervention. *Child Development, 78*(1), 246-263. doi:10.1111/j.1467-8624.2007.00995.x

[91] Garcia, D. (2011). Two models of personality and well-being among adolescents. *Personality and Individual Differences, 50*(8), 1208-1212. doi:10.1016/j.paid.2011.02.009

[92] Gillham, J., Adams-Deutsch, Z., Werner, J., Reivich, K., Coulter-Heindl, V., Linkins, M., & ...Seligman, M. P. (2011). Character strengths predict subjective well-being during adolescence. *The Journal of Positive Psychology, 6*(1), 31-44. doi: 10.1080/17439760.2010.536773

[93] Seligman, M. E. P., & Maier, S. F. (1967). Failure to escape traumatic shock. *Journal of Experimental Psychology, 74*: 1–9. doi:10.1037/h0024514

[94] Overmier, J. B., & Seligman, M.E.P. (1967). Effects of inescapable shock upon subsequent escape and avoidance responding. *Journal of Comparative and Physiological Psychology, 63*: 28–33. doi:10.1037/h0024166

[95] Mikulincer, M. (1996). Mental rumination and learned helplessness: Cognitive shifts during helplessness training and their behavioral consequences. In I. G. Sarason, G. R. Pierce, B. R. Sarason (Eds.), *Cognitive interference: Theories, methods, and findings* (pp. 191-209). Hillsdale, NJ England: Lawrence Erlbaum Associates, Inc.

[96] Durkin, J., & Joseph, S. (2009). Growth following adversity and its relation with subjective well-being and psychological well-being. *Journal of Loss and Trauma, 14*(3), 228-234. doi:10.1080/15325020802540561

[97] Kelly, R. E., Wood, A. M., & Mansell, W. (2013). Flexible and tenacious goal pursuit lead to improving well-being in an aging population: A ten-year cohort study. *International Psychogeriatrics, 25*(1), 16-24. doi:http://dx.doi.org/10.1017/S1041610212001391

[98] The Sourcebook for Teaching Science. (2007). *Television & Health.* Retrieved from http://www.csun.edu/science/health/docs/tv&health.html

[99] Council for Research Excellence. (2010). *Ground-breaking study of video viewing finds younger boomers consume more video media than any other group.* Retrieved from http://www.researchexcellence.com/news/032609_vcm.php

[100] Lally, P., Van Jaarsveld, C., Potts, H., & Wardle, J. (2010). How are habits formed: Modeling habit formation in the real world. *European Journal of Social Psychology, 40*(6), 998-1009. doi:10.1038/sj.ijo.0803771

[101] Newby-Clark, I. (2009). *Creatures of habit: Expert advice for lasting habit change.* Retrieved from Psychology Today at http://www.psychologytoday.com/blog/creatures-habit/200912/how-long

[102] Kraus, S. J. (2002). *Psychological foundations of success: A Harvard-trained scientist separates the science of success from self-help snake oil.* US: Change Planet Press.

[103] Lally, P., Van Jaarsveld, C., Potts, H., & Wardle, J. (2010). How are habits formed: Modeling habit formation in the real world. *European Journal of Social Psychology, 40*(6), 998-1009. doi:10.1038/sj.ijo.0803771

[104] Duhigg, C. (2012). The power of habit: Why we do what we do in life and business. New York, NY: Random House.

[105] Lyubomirsky, S. (2008). *The how of happiness: A scientific approach to getting the life you want.* New York, NY: Penguin Press.

[106] Ryff, C. D., & Keyes, C. M. (1995). The structure of psychological well-being revisited. *Journal of Personality and Social Psychology, 69*(4), 719-727. doi:10.1037/0022-3514.69.4.719

[107] Humphrey, P. (2010). An exploratory study of the effect of rewards and deadlines on academic procrastination in web-based classes. *Academy of Educational Leadership Journal, 14*(4): 91-99. Retrieved from http://www.alliedacademies.org/public/journals/journaldetails.aspx?jid=5

[108] Farrington, J. (2012). Procrastination-not all it's put off to be. *Performance Improvement Quarterly, 24*(4), 11-16. doi:10.1002/piq.20121

[109] Steel, P., & Ferrari, J. (2013). Sex, education and procrastination: An epidemiological study of procrastinators' characteristics from a global sample. *European Journal of Personality, 27*(1), 51. Retrieved from http://onlinelibrary.wiley.com/journal/10.1002/(ISSN)1099-0984

[110] Knipe, J. (2010). Dysfunctional positive affect: Procrastination. *Eye movement desensitization and reprocessing (EMDR) scripted protocols: Special populations,* 453-458. New York: Springer Publishing Co.

[111] Woolsey, B., & Schulz, M. (2012). Credit card statistics, industry facts, debt statistics. *Creditcard.com.* Retrieved from http://www.creditcards.com/credit-card-news/credit-card-industry-facts-personal-debt-statistics-1276.php

[112] US National Debt Clock retrieved from http://www.brillig.com/debt_clock/ on March 8, 2013.

[113] US Department of Commerce, US Census Bureau. (2103). *State & County Quick Facts.* Retrieved from http://quickfacts.census.gov/qfd/states/00000.html. Note: While these 2011 numbers represent the latest estimate published by the US government, it is unlikely they have increased much, if any at all due to the lingering recession.

[114] US Department of Commerce, US Census Bureau. (2013). Retrieved from http://search.census.gov/search?utf8=%E2%9C%93&affiliate=census&query=people+per+household

[115] Organization for Economic Cooperation and Development. (2010). *Obesity and the economics of prevention: Fit not fat - united states key facts.* Retrieved from http://www.oecd.org/unitedstates/obesityandtheeconomicsofpreventionfitnotfat-unitedstateskeyfacts.htm

[116] Just, M., Keller, T. A., & Cynkar, J. (2008). A decrease in brain activation associated with driving when listening to someone speak. *Brain Research, 1205*70-80. doi:10.1016/j.brainres.2007.12.075

[117] Hamilton, J. (2008). *Multitasking in the car: Just like drunken driving.* Retrieved from National Public Radio. http://www.npr.org/templates/story/story.php?storyId=95702512.

[118] Ellis, Y., Daniels, B., & Jauregui, A. (2010). The effect of multitasking on the grade performance of business students. *Research In Higher Education Journal, 8*1-10. Retrieved from http://www.aabri.com/manuscripts/10498.pdf

[119] Shao, D. H., & Shao, L. P. (2012). The effects of multitasking on individual's task performance. *International Journal of Business Strategy, 12*(1), 75-80. Retrieved from http://www.iabe.org/domains/iabe/journal.aspx?journalid=7

[120] Rubinstein, Joshua S., Meyer, David E., &Evans, Jeffrey E. (2001). Executive control of cognitive processes in task switching. *Journal of Experimental Psychology: Human Perception and Performance, 27*(4), 763-797. doi:10.1037//0096-1523.27.4.763

[121] Schute, N. (2013). *If you think you're good at multitasking, you probably aren't.* Retrieved from National Public Radio. http://www.npr.org/blogs/health/2013/01/24/170160105/if-you-thinkyoure-good-at-multitasking-you-probably-arent

[122] Strayer, D. L., Watson, J. M., & Drews, F. A. (2011). Cognitive Distraction While Multitasking in the Automobile. *The Psychology of Learning and Motivation, 54,* 29-58. doi: 10.1016/B978-0-12-385527-5.00002-4. Retrieved from http://www.psych.utah.edu/lab/appliedcognition/publications.html

[123] Sullivan, B., & Thompson, H. (2013, May 03). Brain, interrupted. *The New York Times.* Retrieved from http://finance.yahoo.com/news/brain--interrupted-173621758.html

[124] Rubinstein, Joshua S., Meyer, David E., & Evans, Jeffrey E. (2001). Executive control of cognitive processes in task switching. *Journal of Experimental Psychology: Human Perception and Performance, 27*(4), 763-797. doi:10.1037//0096-1523.27.4.763

[125] Carus, R. (2007). Why does it take so long for our vision to adjust to a darkened theater after we come in from bright sunlight? *Scientific American.* Retrieved from http://www.scientificamerican.com/article.cfm?id=experts-eyes-adjust-to-darkness

[126] Mark, G., Gonzalez, V. M., & Harris, J. (2005). No task left behind? *Conference on Human Factors In Computing Systems Proceedings,* 321. doi:10.1145/1054972.1055017

[127] Rosen, L. D., Mark Carrier, L. L., & Cheever, N. A. (2013). Facebook and texting made me do it: Media-induced task-switching while studying. *Computers In Human Behavior, 29*(3), 948-958. doi:10.1016/j.chb.2012.12.001

[128] Most, S. B., Simons, D. J., Scholl, B. J., Jimenez, R., Clifford, E., & Chabris, C. F. (2001). How not to be seen: The contribution of similarity and selective ignoring to sustained inattentional blindness. *Psychological Science, 12*(1), 9–17. doi:10.1111/1467-9280.00303.

[129] Rubinstein, Joshua S.; Meyer, David E.; Evans, Jeffrey E. (2001). Executive control of cognitive processes in task switching. *Journal of Experimental Psychology: Human Perception and Performance, 27*(4), 763-797. doi:10.1037//0096-1523.27.4.763

[130] Caplan, R. D., & Jones, K. W. (1975). Effects of work load, role ambiguity, and Type A personality on anxiety, depression, and heart rate. *Journal of Applied Psychology, 60*(6), 713-719. doi:10.1037/0021-9010.60.6.713

[131] McCleary, K. (n.d.) Which Home Improvements Pay Off? Retrieved from HGTV website http://www.hgtv.com/home-improvement/which-home-improvements-pay-off/index.html

[132] Mullins, L. (2010). *The 5 Best—and 5 Worst—Home Improvement Projects for Your Money.* Retrieved from U.S. News website http://money.usnews.com/money/personalfinance/articles/2010/01/27/the-5-bestand-5-worsthome-improvement-projects-for-your-money

[133] Broman-Fulks, J. J., & Urbaniak, A. (2012). Review of 'Exercise for mood and anxiety: Proven strategies for overcoming depression and enhancing well-being'. *Cognitive Behaviour Therapy, 41*(4), 345-346. doi:10.1080/16506073.2012.715670

[134] Windle, G., Hughes, D., Linck, P., Russell, I., & Woods, B. (2010). Is exercise effective in promoting mental well-being in older age? A systematic review. *Aging & Mental Health, 14*(6), 652-669. doi:10.1080/13607861003713232

[135] Maslow, A. (1954). *Motivation and personality.* New York, NY: Harper.

[136] Derived from Maslow, A. (1968). Toward a psychology of being. New York, NY: John Wiley & Sons.

[137] Grant, H., & Dweck, C. S. (2003). Clarifying achievement goals and their impact. *Journal of Personality and Social Psychology, 85*(3), 541-553. doi:10.1037/0022-3514.85.3.541

[138] Halvorson, H., & Higgins, E. (2013). Know what really motivates you. *Harvard Business Review, 91*(3), 117-120. Retrieved from http://hbr.org/magazine

[139] Morrison, M., & Roese, N. J. (2011). Regrets of the typical American: Findings from a nationally representative sample. *Social Psychological and Personality Science, 2*(6), 576-583. doi:10.1177/1948550611401756

[140] Gilbert, P., & Procter, S. (2006). Compassionate mind training for people with high shame and self criticism: Overview and pilot study of a group therapy approach. *Clinical Psychology & Psychotherapy, 13*(6), 353. doi:10.1002/cpp.507

[141] McCracken, L. M., & Yang, S. (2008). A contextual cognitive-behavioral analysis of rehabilitation workers' health and well-being: Influences of acceptance, mindfulness, and values-based action. *Rehabilitation Psychology, 53*(4), 479-485. doi:10.1037/a0012854

[142] Ryan, R. M., & Deci, E. L. (2000). Self-determination theory and the facilitation of intrinsic motivation, social development, and well-being. *American Psychologist, 55*(1), 68-78. doi:10.1037/0003-066X.55.1.68

[143] Seligman, M. E. P. (2011). *Flourish: A visionary new understanding of happiness and well-being.* New York, NY: Free Press.

[144] Caldwell Banker (2014). *Planning for home maintenance.* Retrieved from http://www.coldwellbankertec.com/learn/home_maintenance.cfm

[145] Environmental Protection Agency (2006). *What is the value of a statistical life?* National Center for Environmental Economics. Retrieved from http://yosemite.epa.gov/ee/epa/eed.nsf/pages/MortalityRiskValuation.html#whatisvsl

[146] Mara, C. A., DeCicco, T. L., & Stroink, M. L. (2010). An investigation of the relationships among self-construal, emotional intelligence, and well-being. *The International Journal of Transpersonal Studies, 29*(1), 1-11. Retrieved from http://www.transpersonalstudies.org/

[147] Kamis, R. P. (2013). The relationship between expanded concepts of self and well-being (Doctoral dissertation, Northcentral University). Retrieved from http://pqdtopen.proquest.com/pqdtopen/doc/1476938871.html?FMT=AI

[148] Steger, M. F., Kashdan, T. B., & Oishi, S. (2008). Being good by doing good: Daily eudaimonic activity and well-being. *Journal of Research in Personality, 42*(1), 22-42. doi:10.1016/j.jrp.2007.03.004

[149] Canevello, A., & Crocker, J. (2010). Creating good relationships: Responsiveness, relationship quality, and interpersonal goals. *Journal of Personality and Social Psychology, 99*(1), 78-106. doi:10.1037/a0018186

[150] Gillham, J., Adams-Deutsch, Z., Werner, J., Reivich, K., Coulter-Heindl, V., Linkins, M., & ...Seligman, M. P. (2011). Character strengths predict subjective well-being during adolescence. *The Journal of Positive Psychology, 6*(1), 31-44. doi:10.1080/17439760.2010.536773

[151] Vella-Brodrick, D., Park, N., & Peterson, C. (2009). Three ways to be happy: Pleasure, engagement, and meaning--findings from Australian and US samples. *Social Indicators Research, 90*(2), 165-165-179. doi:10.1007/s11205-008-9251-6

[152] Crocker, J., & Canevello, A. (2008). Creating and undermining social support in communal relationships: The role of compassionate and self-image goals. *Journal of Personality and Social Psychology, 95*(3), 555-575. doi:10.1037/0022-3514.95.3.555

[153] Crocker, J., Canevello, A., Breines, J. G., & Flynn, H. (2010). Interpersonal goals and change in anxiety and dysphoria in first-semester college students. *Journal of Personality and Social Psychology, 98*(6), 1009-1024. doi:10.1037/a0019400

[154] Thanakwang, K., & Isaramalai, S. (2013). Productive engagement in older adults: A concept analysis. *Nursing and Health Sciences, 15*(1), 124-130. Retrieved from http://onlinelibrary.wiley.com/journal/10.1111/(ISSN)1442-2018

[155] Autor, D., & Duggan, M. (2006). The growth in the social security disability rolls: A fiscal crisis unfolding (Working Paper 12436). Cambridge, MA: National Bureau of Economic Research. Retrieved from http://www.nber.org/papers/w12436.pdf

[156] Kowalski, A. (2012). Disabled Americans shrink size of U.S. labor Force. *Bloomberg Personal Finance.* Retrieved from http://www.bloomberg.com/news/2012-05-03/disabled-americansshrink-size-of-u-s-labor-force.html

[157] Chen, Y., & Feeley, T. (2012). Enacted support and well-being: A test of the mediating role of perceived control. *Communication Studies, 63*(5), 608-625. doi: 10.1080/10510974.2012.674619

[158] Nikitin, J., & Freund, A. M. (2008). The role of social approach and avoidance motives for subjective well-being and the successful transition to adulthood. *Applied Psychology: An International Review, 57*, 90-111. doi:10.1111/j.1464-0597.2008.00356.x

[159] Dunn, E., Aknin, L., & Norton, M. (2008). Spending money on others promotes happiness. *Science 319*(5870), 1687-1688. doi:10.1126/science.1150952

[160] Aknin, L. B., Dunn, E. W., & Norton, M. I. (2012). Happiness runs in a circular motion: Evidence for a positive feedback loop between prosocial spending and happiness. *Journal of Happiness Studies, 13*(2), 347-355. doi:10.1007/s70902-011-9267-5

[161] Fredrickson, B. L., Cohn, M. A., Coffey, K. A., Pek, J., & Finkel, S. M. (2008). Open hearts build lives: Positive emotions, induced through loving-kindness meditation, build consequential personal resources. *Journal of Personality and Social Psychology, 95*(5), 1045-1062. doi:10.1037/a0013262

[162] Piff, P. K., Kraus, M. W., Côté, S., Cheng, B., & Keltner, D. (2010). Having less, giving more: The influence of social class on prosocial behavior. *Journal of Personality and Social Psychology, 99*(5), 771-784. doi:10.1037/a0020092

[163] Fredrickson, B. L. (2001). The role of positive emotions in positive psychology: The broaden-and-build theory of positive emotions. *American Psychologist, 56*(3), 218–226. doi:10.1037/0003-066X.56.3.218

[164] Lyubomirsky, S., King, L., & Diener, E. (2005). The Benefits of Frequent Positive Affect: Does Happiness Lead to Success? *Psychological Bulletin, 131*(6), 803-855. doi:10.1037/0033-2909.131.6.803

[165] Harker, L. (2001). Expressions of positive emotion in women's college yearbook pictures and their relationship to personality and life outcomes across adulthood. *Journal of Personality and Social Psychology, 80*(1), 112-124. doi:10.1037//0022-3514.80.1.112

[166] Sorhagen, N. S. (2013). Early teacher expectations disproportionately affect poor children's high school performance. *Journal of Educational Psychology.* Advance online publication. doi:10.1037/a0031754

[167] Rosenthal, R., & Jacobson, L. (1966). Teachers' expectancies: Determinants of pupils' IQ gains. *Psychological Reports, 19*(1), 115-118. doi:10.2466/pr0.1966.19.1.115

[168] de Boer, H. Bosker, R. J., van der Werf, M. P. C. (2010). Sustainability of teacher expectation bias effects on long-term student performance. *Journal of Educational Psychology, 102*(1), 168-179. doi:10.1037/a0017289

[169] Rosenthal, R., & Fode, K. L. (1963). The effect of experimenter bias on the performance of the albino rat. *Behavioral Science, 8*(3), 183-189. doi:10.1002/bs.3830080302

[170] Ruthig, J. C., Haynes, T. L., Perry, R. P., & Chipperfield, J. G. (2007). Academic optimistic bias: Implications for college student performance and well-being. *Social Psychology of Education, 10*(1), 115-137. doi:10.1007/s11218-006-9002-y

[171] Kluemper, D. H., Little, L. M., & DeGroot, T. (2009). State or trait: Effects of state optimism on job-related outcomes. *Journal of Organizational Behavior, 30*(2), 209-231. doi:10.1002/job.591

[172] Dicke, A. (1998). Optimism and its effect on romantic relationships. *Dissertation Abstracts International: Section B. Sciences and Engineering 58*(10-B), 5697.

[173] Emmons, R. A., & McCullough, M. E. (2003). Counting blessings versus burdens: An experimental investigation of gratitude and subjective well-being in daily life. *Journal of Personality and Social Psychology, 84*(2), 377-389. doi:10.1037/0022-3514.84.2.377

[174] Abend, T. A., & Williamson, G. M. (2002). Feeling attractive in the wake of breast cancer: Optimism matters, and so do interpersonal relationships. *Personality & Social Psychology Bulletin, 28*(4), 427. doi:10.1177/0146167202287001

[175] Rasmussen, H. N., Scheier, M. F., & Greenhouse, J. B. (2009). Optimism and physical health: A meta-analytic review. *Annals of Behavioral Medicine, 37*(3), 239-256. doi:10.1007/s12160-009-9111-x

[176] Culbertson, S. S., Fullagar, C. J., & Mills, M. J. (2010). Feeling good and doing great: The relationship between psychological capital and well-being. *Journal of Occupational Health Psychology, 15*(4), 421-433. doi:10.1037/a0020720

[177] Orenstein, S. W. (1999). Predictors of explanatory style among Holocaust survivors. *Dissertation Abstracts International: Section B. Sciences and Engineering 59*(10-B), 5583.

[178] Augusto-landa, J., Pulido-martos, M., & Lopez-zafra, E. (2011). Does perceived emotional intelligence and Optimism/pessimism predict psychological well-being? *Journal of Happiness Studies, 12*(3), 463-463-474. doi:10.1007/s10902-010-9209-7

[179] Brown, J. D., & Marshall, M. A. (2001). Great expectations: Optimism and pessimism in achievement settings. In E. C. Chang, E. C. Chang (Eds.), *Optimism & pessimism: Implications for theory, research, and practice* (pp. 239-255). Washington, DC: American Psychological Association. doi:10.1037/10385-011.

[180] Seligman, M. E. P. (2002). *Authentic happiness: Using the new positive psychology to realize your potential for lasting fulfillment.* New York, NY: Free Press.

[181] Kim, D. (2006). Employee motivation: "Just ask your employees." *Seoul Journal of Business, 12*(1), 19-35. Retrieved from http://s-space.snu.ac.kr/bitstream/10371/1819/1/sjbv12n1_019.pdf

[182] Fredrickson, B. L., & Losada, M. F. (2005). Positive affect and the complex dynamics of human flourishing. *American Psychologist, 60*(7), 678-686. doi:10.1037/0003-066X.60.7.678.

[183] Gottman, J. M. (1994). *What predicts divorce: The relationship between marital processes and marital outcomes.* New York: Lawrence Erlbaum.

[184] Long, J. J., & Davis, J. O. (2011). Pen and Paper: A Prescription for Adolescents' Emotional and Psychological Well Being? *Journal of Correctional Education, 62*(1), 7-25. Retrieved from http://journals.cambridge.org/action/displayJournal?jid=BCP

[185] U.S. Department of Transportation (2012). Bureau of Transportation Statistics, U.S. Air Carrier Safety Data. Retrieved from http://www.rita.dot.gov/bts/sites/rita.dot.gov.bts/files/publications/national_transportation_statistics/html/table_02_09.html

[186] U.S. Department of Transportation (2012). *Air Travel Consumer Report.* Retrieved from http://www.dot.gov/sites/dot.dev/files/docs/2012NovemberATCR.pdf

[187] Kepler, T. S. (1951). The Christian Life. *Journal of The American Academy of Religion, 19*(4), 234-a. Retrieved from http://jaar.oxfordjournals.org/

[188] Dupuy, J. B., Beaudoin, S. S., Rhéaume, J. J., Ladouceur, R. R., & Dugas, M. J. (2001). Worry: Daily self-report in clinical and non-clinical populations. *Behaviour Research And Therapy, 39*(10), 1249-1255. doi:10.1016/S0005-7967(01)00011-0

[189] Gorman, J. M. (2009). *Anxiety and Panic – The DANA Guide.* Retrieved from The DANA Foundation website: http://www.dana.org/news/brainhealth/detail.aspx?id=9770

[190] Smalbrugge, M., Pot, A., Jongenelis, L., Gundy, C., Beekman, A., & Eefsting, J. (2006). The impact of depression and anxiety on well being, disability and use of health care services in nursing home patients. *International Journal of Geriatric Psychiatry, 21*(4), 325-332.

[191] U.S. Department of Transportation (2012). Bureau of Transportation Statistics, Transportation Safety by the Numbers. Retrieved from http://www.rita.dot.gov/bts/sites/rita.dot.gov.bts/files/publications/by_the_numbers/transportation_safety/index.html

[192] Vlemincx, E., Vigo, D., Vansteenwegen, D., Van den Bergh, O., & Van Diest, I. (2013). Do not worry, be mindful: Effects of induced worry and mindfulness on respiratory variability in a nonanxious population. *International Journal of Psychophysiology: Official Journal of The International Organization of Psychophysiology, 87*(2), 147-151. doi:10.1016/j.ijpsycho.2012.12

[193] Klco, S. E. (2010). *A neuropsychological examination of the effects of mindfulness meditation in elementary school children.* (Masters Thesis). Available from ProQuest Dissertations and Thesis Database. (UMI No. 1484644)

[194] Emmons, R. A. (2006). Spirituality: Recent progress. In M. Csikszentmihalyi & I. S. Csikszentmihalyi (Eds.) *A life worth living: Contributions to positive psychology* (pp. 62-81). New York: Oxford University Press.

[195] Baker, D., & Stauth, C. (2003). *What happy people know: how the new science of happiness can change your life for the better.* Rodale.

[196] Wood, A. M., Joseph, S., & Maltby, J. (2009). Gratitude predicts psychological well-being above the Big Five facets. *Personality and Individual Differences, 46*(4), 443-447. doi:10.1016/j.paid.2008.11.012

[197] Wood, A., Joseph, S., & Linley, A. (2007). Gratitude - Parent of all virtues. *The Psychologist, 20*(1), 18-21. Retrieved from http://personalpages.manchester.ac.uk/staff/alex.wood/gratitude%20psychologist.pdf

[198] Wood, A., Joseph, S., & Maltby, J. (2008). Gratitude uniquely predicts satisfaction with life: Incremental validity above the domains and facets of the five factor model. *Personality and Individual Differences, 45*(1), 49-54. doi:10.1016/j.paid.2008.02.019

[199] Grant, A., & Gino, F. (2010). A little thanks goes a long way: Explaining why gratitude expressions motivate prosocial behavior. *Journal of Personality and Social Psychology, 98*(6), 946-955. doi:10.1037/a0017935

[200] Wood, A., Maltby, J., Gillett, R., Linley, P., & Joseph, S. (2008). The role of gratitude in the development of social support, stress, and depression: Two longitudinal studies. *Journal of Research in Personality, 42*(4), 854-871. doi:10.1016/j.jrp.2007.11.003

[201] Emmons, R. A., & McCullough, M. E. (2003). Counting blessings versus burdens: An experimental investigation of gratitude and subjective well-being in daily life. *Journal of Personality and Social Psychology, 84*(2), 377-389. doi:10.1037/0022-3514.84.2.377

[202] Seligman, M. E. P., Steen, T. T., Park, N., & Peterson, C. (2005). Positive psychology progress: Empirical validation of interventions. *American Psychologist, 60*(5), 410-421. doi:10.1037/0003-066X.60.5.410

[203] Froh, J. J., Sefick, W. J., & Emmons, R. A. (2008). Counting blessings in early adolescents: An experimental study of gratitude and subjective well-being. *Journal of School Psychology, 46*(2), 213-233. doi:org/10.1016/j.jsp.2007.03.005

[204] Otake, K., Shimai, S., Tanaka-matsumi, J., Otsui, K., & Fredrickson, B. L. (2006). Happy people become happier through kindness: A counting kindnesses intervention. *Journal of Happiness Studies, 7*(3), 361-375. doi:10.1007/s10902-005-3650-z

[205] Toepfer, S. M., & Walker, K. (2009). Letters of Gratitude: Improving Well-Being through Expressive Writing. *Journal of Writing Research, 1*(3), 181.

[206] Cohn, M. A., & Fredrickson, B. L. (2010). In search of durable positive psychology interventions: Predictors and consequences of long-term positive behavior change. *The Journal of Positive Psychology, 5*(5), 355-366. doi:10.1080/17439760.2010.508883

[207] Fredrickson, B. L., Cohn, M. A., Coffey, K. A., Pek, J., & Finkel, S. M. (2008). Open hearts build lives: Positive emotions, induced through loving-kindness meditation, build consequential personal resources. *Journal of Personality and Social Psychology, 95*(5), 1045-1062. doi:10.1037/a0013262

[208] Davidson, R. J. (2005). Emotion Regulation, Happiness, and the Neuroplasticity of the Brain. *Advances in Mind-Body Medicine, 21*(3-4), 25-28. Retrieved from http://www.advancesjournal.com/index.cfm?page=back_issues

[209] Lyubomirsky, S. (2008). *The how of happiness: A scientific approach to getting the life you want.* New York, NY: Penguin

[210] Polak, E. L., & McCullough, M. E. (2006). Is gratitude an alternative to materialism? *Journal of Happiness Studies, 7*(3), 343-360. doi:10.1007/s10902-005-3649-5

[211] Dunn, E. W., Gilbert, D. T., & Wilson, T. D. (2011). Research Dialogue: If money doesn't make you happy, then you probably aren't spending it right. *Journal of Consumer Psychology, 21*(2), 115-125. doi:10.1016/j.jcps.2011.02.002

[212] National Science Foundation (2008). *Chore wars: Men, women and housework.* Retrieved from http://www.nsf.gov/discoveries/disc_summ.jsp?cntn_id=111458

[213] Dunn, E., & Norton, M. (2013). *Happy money: The science of smarter spending.* New York, NY: Simon & Shuster.

[214] Aaker, J. L., Rudd, M., & Mogilner, C. (2011). Research Dialogue: If money does not make you happy, consider time. *Journal of Consumer Psychology, 21*(2), 126-130. doi:10.1016/j.jcps.2011.01.004

[215] Chancellor, J., & Lyubomirsky, S. (2011). Research Dialogue: Happiness and thrift: When (spending) less is (hedonically) more. *Journal of Consumer Psychology, 21*(2), 131-138. doi:10.1016/j.jcps.2011.02.004

[216] Krasnova, H., Wenninger, H., Widjaja, T., & Bexmann, P. (2013). *Envy on Facebook: A hidden threat to users' life satisfaction?* Symposium conducted at 11th International Conference on Wirtschaftsinformatik. Retrieved from http://warhol.wiwi.huberlin.de/~hkrasnova/Ongoing_Research_files/WI%202013%20Final%20Submission%20Krasnova.pdf

[217] Fujita, F. (2008). The frequency of social comparison and its relation to subjective well-being. In M. Eid, R. J. Larsen (Eds.), *The science of subjective well-being* (pp. 239-257). New York, NY US: Guilford Press.

[218] Milanovic, Branko (2010). *The haves and the have-nots: A brief and idiosyncratic history of global inequality.* New York, New York: Basic Books.

[219] Schwartz, R., Reynolds, C., Thase, M., Frank, E., Fasiczka, A., & Haaga, D. (2002). Optimal and normal affect balance in psychotherapy of major depression: Evaluation of the balanced states of mind model. *Behavioural and Cognitive Psychotherapy, 30*(4), 439-450. doi:10.1017/S1352465802004058

[220] Schwartz, B. (2004). The tyranny of choice. *Scientific American, 290*(4), 70-75. Retrieved from http://www.swarthmore.edu/SocSci/bschwar1/Sci.Amer.pdf

INDEX

active attention 120, 122, 123
adaptation 48, 54, 140, 173, 215, 249
affirmations 125
akrasia 161
altruistic goals 213
anxiety 231, 234, 236
appreciation 245
appreciative inquiry 38
apprehension 245
archetypes 9
assessing 247
attenuation 36

belief creation process 17
best possible self 44, 45
Big Five personality traits 245
broaden-and-build theory 215

catastrophizing 193, 232, 236
change 22, 31–34, 54–58, 67, 70,
        104, 137, 159–161, 198–203,
        211, 239, 251
cognitive behavior therapy 25, 70
cognitive dissonance 33
communication 213, 216
comparison 250, 251
compassionate goals theory 209, 213
confirmation bias 18
conscious 117
contemporaneous anhedonia 251
contingency plan 150
critical path 162, 164, 165

delayed gratification 150
depression 139–141, 181
diminishing marginal return 162,
        206
discipline 45, 89, 133, 148–151, 154,
        167

distraction 88, 96, 160, 169, 172–176
distractive dilution 170

80:20 rule 162
eco-centric 209
effort-based rewards 140, 141
ego 231
ego-centric 209
emotions 32, 35 68, 70, 71, 94, 215,
        226, 236
end of history illusion 104
enough 87
eudaimonia/eudaimonic 94, 95
evolutionary psychology 54
expectations 19, 26, 219–230
external sense of control 63
extrinsic goals 205

failure 25, 140, 151–154, 231,
        239–241
fear 231–233, 235–241
flow 78
focused attention 37, 39, 46
focused effort 169
framing 43, 221–224

generativity 195
goals 29, 37, 40, 45, 64, 94, 97,
        100–105, 108–117
    extrensic 205
    intrensic 205
    other-centric 212
    setting 108
goal setting theory 110
golden shadows 81–84
Golem effect 220
gratitude 245–249
growth momentum 199

habits 21, 48, 49, 52, 55, 57, 58, 161, 162
happy hermit 210
hedonia/hedonic 94, 95
heuristics 161
hyperbolic discounting 95
hypnosis 116, 126

immediate gratification 103, 104
inattentional blindness 174
incurvatus in se 209
inertia 55, 135, 136, 199
interests and passions 78, 79, 83
internal sense of control 63
intrinsic goals 205

learned helplessness 152
life of leisure 147, 148
life plans 108, 112, 113, 118
life stories 39, 41
limitations 21, 34, 42, 50, 99
limiting reagent 162
loss aversion 54, 55
loving kindness meditation (LKM) 248

magical thinking 251
maximizer 255
maximizing 90, 145
mindfulness 236
mindfulness meditation 50
miserable saint 210
mission-critical path 162
most-valued goal 172, 186
motivation theory 195
multitasking 172–176

narrative identity 41
negative emotion 215
no fault thinking 35

Oak School study 220
optimism 45, 219–221, 229
optimist 221
other-centric goals 208, 212

paradox 34, 35, 72
passion 78, 79, 82, 83, 85, 89, 92
paying it forward 160, 248
perceived control 61, 63, 66, 67
persistence 151–155
persistent incrementalism 153, 159
pessimism 219, 229
pessimist 221–224
planned behavior theory 137
positive emotion 94, 215
positive psychology 38, 39, 70
positivity offset 7
positivity ratio 228
postponement 150, 154
preparation 149, 150
prevention focused 199
proactive 149, 166
procrastination 68, 165–167
projecting 216, 247, 248
promotion focus 199
Pygmalion effect 220

quitter 176, 177
quitting 140, 152, 177

random acts of kindness 248
reactive 68, 70, 149, 166
reasoned action theory 184
reference points 169
regret 126–128, 202
rocking chair exercise 91, 92
rumination 139, 140

satisfaction 94, 104, 141, 147, 202, 209, 213, 241, 246, 247
Satisfaction with Life Scale 7
satisficing 255
Self Actualization Scale 196, 197
self-awareness 50, 58, 237
self construal theory 209
self-determination theory 209
self-efficacy 214, 215
self-fulfilling prophecy 66
sense of control 63, 66, 67, 137
Sense-of-Control Scale 61

sense-of-self 209
serial doer 180
shadow 9, 81
 golden 81–84
sharing 247, 248
shoulding 217
solution-focused therapy 19
Stanford marshmallow experiments
 150
strategic planning 109, 111, 124
strengths and talents 78–82
subconscious 30, 32, 33, 36, 58,
 116–118, 121, 233
subconscious commitments 50–56

temporal discounting 150, 151
the someday trap 252
third law of motion 135
time management 162–167
time quadrants 162

Type-A personalities 181

unconscious self 9

value-based activities 95
values-in-action theory 209
virtuous cycle 165, 204, 220
vision board 120, 121
visualization 120–124, 236
voluntary simplicity 249

well-being 38, 41 61, 68, 70, 89, 111,
 126, 139, 141, 152, 154, 165, 166,
 188, 202, 209, 210, 213, 215, 216,
 220, 234, 245, 250
win writing 120–123
work 145–156
workaholic 147
worry 42, 140, 166, 232–238, 245,
 246, 254

ABOUT THE AUTHOR

Russ Kamis (KAY-miss) is an actualization strategist who specializes in helping people get more out of life. A motivational speaker, lecturer, and personal development author, Russ guides individuals and organizations to resolve challenging issues and navigate pivotal transitions. He encourages people to reach their full potential through personal growth and increased self-awareness. As founder of The Kamis Group, Russ helps people achieve their goals by living life on purpose. He inspires them to think, plan, act, and enjoy, so they can live more meaningful, successful, and happier lives.

Russ brings with him over twenty years of business leadership experience, across both midsize and Fortune 500 companies, spanning numerous industries. A corporate strategy specialist, he spent two decades expanding companies through organic growth and transforming them through acquisitions. At age 35, he was appointed President and CEO of a $100 million life-safety business— a company that, under his leadership, doubled in size over seven years.

A certified, executive-life coach, nationally-accredited facilitator, and seasoned, seminar instructor, Russ has since worked with thousands of executives to reshape their lives and their businesses by identifying and capturing opportunities for growth and transformation. He has partnered with CEOs and their leadership teams to address central issues, make needed changes, and create winning atmospheres ideal for success. Through a mix of advising, leadership development, and strategic counsel, Russ has guided leaders and organizations to bridge the gap from where they are to where they want to be.

Russ earned a Bachelor of Science Degree in chemical engineering with high honors from Case Western Reserve University, and holds twelve U.S. Patents in adhesive chemistry. Graduating top-of-class, Russ also received a Masters in Management from Northwestern University's J.L. Kellogg Graduate School, where he majored in strategy. As an adjunct professor, he has taught business strategy at the State University of New York. More recently, Russ earned a Ph.D. from Northcentral University with a dissertation in positive psychology.

Russ currently resides in the Great Lakes region with his wonderfully supportive wife and three amazing children.

Made in the USA
Lexington, KY
02 June 2015